CONTEMPORARY CRIME IN INDIAN SOCIETY

CONTEMPORARY CRIME IN INDIAN SOCIETY

Editor
Ramesh H. Makwana

GYAN

ISBN : 978-81-212-1243-4

Price : ₹ 1050

First Published, 2015

Published by

Gyan Publishing House
23, Main Ansari Road, Darya Ganj,
New Delhi- 110 002
Ph. : 23282060, 23261060
Fax : 011-23285914
E-mail: books@gyanbooks.com

Laser Typesetting : Sanya Computers, Delhi
Printed in India at Artxel, Noida 201 301

Cataloging in Publication Data—DK

Courtesy: D.K. Agencies (P) Ltd. <docinfo@dkagencies.com>

Contemporary crime in Indian society / editor, Ramesh H. Makwana.

p. cm.
Includes bibliographical references.
ISBN 9788121212434

1. Crime—India--Sociological aspects—Congresses. 2. Deviant behavior—India—Congresses. I. Makwana, Ramesh.

DDC 364.954 23

Contents

सत्यमेव जयते

Dt: 12-03-2014

Blessings from t he Chief Minister, Gujarat State

I am happy to know that Dr. Ramesh H. Makwana (Professor, Post-Graduate Department of Sociology, Sardar Patel University, Vallabh Vidyanagar, Gujarat, India) is bringing out edited book edited *"Contemporary Crime in Indian Society"* based on selected papers presented in RC-18 'Sociology of Crime & Deviance' under Indian Sociological Society.

The energy around us has in natural course two types of influence, like positive and negative. Every human is born with these two traits, but the social upbringing and the strength of instilling virtues from childhood, play a vital role in defining a person as of good of bad traits. The negative psyche lying dormant in everyone becomes uncontrolled in persons who fail to assess and judge. The psycho-sociological research on the subject and intense brain storming will definitely show new ways and means to address and mitigate the negative impact on our society.

I congratulate all these who have worked hard for preparing the research papers and you, for editing and moulding them into the form of a book. I am sure the book will be successful for the explorers of the subject. Wishing you all the best.

(Narendra Modi)

To,
Dr. Rameshbhai H. Makwana, *Professor,*
Department of Sociology,
Sardar Patel University,
Vallabh Vidyanagar-388120,
Dist. Anand.
Email: drrhmakwanaspu@yahoo.com

Narendra Modi
Chief Minister, Gujarat State

Foreword

It has been a proclaimed policy of the Indian Sociological Society to encourage its Research Committees to bring out publications of the selected papers presented in their sessions at the All India Sociological Conferences and/or their mid-term conferences. It is a matter of great pleasure and satisfaction for me that the ISS Research Committee on Sociology of Crime and Deviance (RC 18) is bringing out such a volume. I welcome the publication of *Contemporary Crime in Indian Society* edited by Professor Ramesh H. Makwana, Convener, ISS RC 18. I do hope it would be widely appreciated and warmly received not only by the scholars interested in the sociology of crime and deviance but also by the community of sociologists and criminologists at large.

It can hardly be overemphasized that crime and deviance are not new phenomena or specific only to some places. Crimes have existed universally. They have evolved and are linked with the evolution of human civilization. The phenomenon of crime and deviance has inalienable relationship with the nature and form of social structure at a given time. In spite of the phenomenon of crime being one of the major concerns of all societies since early times, systematic study of crime was initiated only around the year 1775. While scientific explanation of crime emerged under the aegis of the so called classical school (1775), there emerged a number of other schools of criminology subsequently namely, the Cartographic School (1830), the Socialist School (1850), the Italian School (1875), the Psychiatric School (1905), the Psychological School (1905) and finally the Sociological School. The last one had its root in U.S.A. around 1915.

The evolution of Formal Sociological School of Crime in the U.S.A. was the outcome of the inspirations received from the pioneering contributions of European positivists like Emile Durkheim (1858-1917) (and a less known scholar amongst sociologists Enrico Ferri (1856-1929) who in his book on "Criminal Sociology" focused his ideas on the process of criminal behaviour in society). Emile Durkheim's book *Suicide* and his other works relate crime either directly or indirectly to social structure and deviance. It is needless to restate Durkheim's total contribution in this regard but some significant observations of Durkheim are worth quoting, viz., "Crime is a social fact and human act. Crime is both normal and functional. No society could be completely exempt from it Crime is one of the prices we pay for freedom."

The work of these pioneers had a considerable impact on the writings of other scholars who attempted to study crime from a sociological angle. Over a period of time, a number of significant and outstanding concepts like group conflict, culture conflict, cultural lag, differential association and differential identification, imitation, reference-group, neutralisation of anti-criminal norms, insulation against criminal values, anomies, delinquent sub-culture, integration of conventional and deviant values, inter-generational tension, lower class culture, differential opportunity labeling, delinquency, drift, etc., have emerged in the area of sociology of deviance and crime.

The sociological school of crime continues to enjoy a strong patronage in America. However, in spite of many scholars in America taking an active interest in the sociological explanation of crime, the sociology of crime has frequently been isolated from mainstream of sociology. To be sure, the linkage between Criminology and Sociology has been in existence but only partly.

Looking at the Indian scene one finds that not many sociologists have been attracted towards criminological studies. Although the teaching of Deviance and Crime in the departments of sociology in Indian Universities started around 1949, yet till date, studies on sociological dimensions of deviance or crime have not been too many. However, the teaching of Criminology, which of course deals with crimes and deviance is on up-swing and practically all departments of Sociology in the country are now engaged at least in the teaching of one optional paper on this subject, more so, because the processes of urbanisation, industrialisation, globalisation and consequent alienation have given rise to many new forms of crimes.

It is of common knowledge that in spite of the enactment of several laws related to crime, various kinds of crimes viz., violence against women, corruption and black money, gender biased based crimes, female criminality, human trafficking, juvenile delinquency, caste/community based violence such as honour killings, domestic violence, poverty and unemployment related crimes, crimes related to child and elder abuse, drug abuse and youth crimes, cyber crimes are speedily increasing in India. Several of these issues have been taken up and dealt with in this volume. I do hope that the publication of this volume will not only encourage and motivate a good number of scholars to undertake researches in these areas but will also be made use of by professional social workers and policy makers. I also do hope that the publication of this volume will motivate other ISS Research Committees also to bring out their volumes.

Jaipur
21 December 2013

Ishwar Modi
President, Indian Sociological Society

Preface

The Indian Sociological Society (ISS) was established in Bombay with the vision of pioneering Sociologist G.S. Ghurye, professor and Head, Department of Sociology, University of Bombay in 1951 as a founder president followed by eminent sociologists. The Society started a biannual journal Sociological Bulletin in 1952. The tradition of holding All India Sociological Conference every year began in the year 1967. Since then the Indian Sociological Society has progressed a great deal. Its membership has increased manifold. Its Journal is now published annually with three issues since 2004. Its conferences are held every year and are well attended. In addition to the journal the society publishes two issues of ISS News Letter annually. The Society organises its major academic work through 23 Research Committees (RC), which provides a better opportunity for members to participate in meaningful dialogue and exchange of views. RC-18, Sociology of Crime and Deviance is one of them. In this RC every year many Sociologists, Criminologists, Professional Social Workers, Researchers, Academicians and Individual present their research papers on various issues related to Crime and Society under Indian Sociological Society.

In this edited book entitled "Contemporary Crime in Indian Society" based on selected papers presented in RC-18'Sociology of Crime & Deviance' under Indian Sociological Society. The proposed book is likely received a warm welcome and appraisal from the scholars and the NGOs. Findings and policy recommendations are welcomed by many policy makers and scholars. This positive aspect motivates me to convert such valuable research articles/papers into book form so that positive and constructive message will reach at a large scale.

In India there are many laws related to crime even though crime increases very speedy in contemporary Indian Society. Violence against Women, Corruption, Gender Biased, Female Criminality, Human Trafficking, Juvenile Delinquency, Domestic Violence, Urban Poverty, Slums and Crime, Cyber Crime, Youth Crime, White Collar Crimes etc is not individual problems but it affect the society at large. Salient characteristics of contemporary crime in India like;

- A total of 2,44,270 incidents of crime against women(both under IPC and SLL)were reported in the country during the 2012 as compared to 2,28,650 in the year 2011 recording an increase of 6.4% during the year 2012. Thus, the crime rate is increasing in our society. (NCRB report: New Delhi: 2012).
- Cases of hacking reported in 2011 was 157 and reported in 2012 was 435 thereby 74 % variation in increase in cases over 2011 is 17.1%. A total crime reported under IT act was 1,791 in 2011 and crime reported in 2012 are 2,276. Among these 2,876 crimes reported most of the cases of tempering computer source (1,440) (NCRB report: New Delhi: 2012).
- Of the total IPC crimes, about half (50.6%) are committed in five states of Uttar Pradesh (12.7%), Maharashtra (10.4%), Madhya Pradesh (11%), Bihar (9.1%), and Rajasthan (7.4%). About one-fourth (25.6%) crimes are committed in four southern states of Tamil Nadu (8.5%), Karnataka (6.4%), Andhra Pradesh (6%), and Kerala (4.7%). (NCRB report: New Delhi: 2012).
- Crime rate is much higher for males than females. Out of every 100 offenders, 96 are male and four (3.8) are females.
- The ratio of urban offenders is much less than the rural offenders.
- Crime rate is highest (51%) in the age group of 18-30 years. The percentage in other age groups is less than 1 per cent (0.2%) in age group below 16 years, 1 per cent (1.2%) in 16-18 years age group, 41 per cent in 30-50 age group and 7 per cent in 50+ age group.

In presenting these facts and features, the idea is to point out the weakening of motives for conformity to social norms and the disruption of social relationships and social bonds. The crime is increasing almost in all sections of our society. It is, thus, the organization and the functioning of the existing sub-systems and structures in our society that are more responsible for the increase in crime. The Sociologist's role is to understand how this problems crop up in the functioning of different social structures, to study the operation of varied patterns of Interrelationships in the society and how people are affected by them, and observe how social systems need to be reorganized and restructured in dealing with them.

The present book discusses the various aspects of contemporary issues related to crimes and offences prevailing in Indian society. The book gives certain effective and remedial solutions with which a step towards better society may be taken through the formation of more relevant policies related to the prevention of crime. The book is useful also to researchers who are interested in an area of crime, scholars of social sciences, Government bodies, NGOs and a much wider readers.

Prof. Ramesh H. Makwana
Convener
RC-18 Sociology of Crime and Deviance
Indian Sociological Society

Acknowledgments

I deem it a great opportunity to express my heartfelt thanks to many individuals and institutions that have extended their utmost co-operation at various stages of writing the book.

I am highly thankful to Honorable Narendra Modi Sir, Chief Minister, Gujarat for writing Blessings for this book. The value of this book will enhance with his remarks and endorsement.

I take this privilege to put it on record my deep sense of indebtedness to Prof. Ishwar Modi, President, Indian Sociological Society for writing FOREWARD for this book in spite of his pressing engagements. I am also grateful to him for his creative suggestions and comments.

I am thankful to Prof.Iswar Modi, President and Prof. Rajesh Mishra, Secretary of Indian Sociological Society for his full cooperation extended in this regards.

I am particularly thankful to all contributors and members of RC-18, (Sociology of Crime and Deviance, ISS) who have papers/articles writers for this book and providing valuable suggestions and comments in different stages of the completion of the book.

I am heartly very thankful to Dr. R.K.Mandaliya (Associate Professor, Dept.of English, Sardar Patel University, Vallabh Vidyanagar, Gujarat) for checking the proof of this book.

It gives me immense pleasure to express my sincere thanks to all those who directly or indirectly helped me in completing this book.

At the outset, I am happy to express my indebtedness to all whose directions and suggestions stood me in my good stead and filled me with courage and confidence. The views expressed in the papers are those of contributors and not of the editors.

Lastly, I am thankful to Mr.Amit Garg of Gyan Publication, New Delhi for taking meticulous care in printing and for completing the work well in time.

Prof. Ramesh H. Makwana
Convener
RC-18 Sociology of Crime and Deviance
Indian Sociological Society

List of Contributors

1. **Ramesh H. Makwana,** Professor, P.G. Department of Sociology, Sardar Patel University, Vallabh Vidyanagar, Gujarat.
2. **S. Uma Devi,** Head, Department of Sociology, Andhra University, Andhra Pradesh.
3. **Shubhangi Gavhane-Gote.** Professor, Department of Sociology, Dr. Babasaheb Ambedkar Marathwada University, Aurangabad, Maharashtra.
4. **R.K. Mohanty,** OES-I, Reader in Sociology, BPSPA, Bhubaneswar, Odisha.
5. **Jasmine Damle,** Associate Professor, Centre for Development Studies, Tata Institute of Social Sciences, Mumbai.
6. **P.K. Chaoudhary,** Professor in Charge (H.O.D.), P.G. Department of Sociology, Ranchi University, Ranchi, Jharkhand.
7. **Hanu H. Chavda,** Head, Department of Sociology, Bhavnagar University, Bhavnagar, Gujarat.
8. **Bira Kishore Dash,** Principal, Orissa Jail Training School, Berhampur.
9. **Jyoti Upadyay,** Head, Department of Sociology, Vikram University, Ujain, M.P.
10. **Kaushik C. Raval,** Assistant Professor, University School of Law, Gujarat University, Ahmedabad, Gujarat.
11. **Kamini B. Dashora,** Principal (I/c), P.P. Patel College of Social Science, At: Dahemi Dist: Anand, Gujarat.
12. **Sudeshna Mukherjee,** Assistant Professor Centre for Women's Studies, Bangalore University, Bangalore.
13. **Veerendra Kumar N,** Assistant Professor, Department of Sociology, Vijayanagara Sri Krishnadevaraya University, Bellary, Karnataka.

14. **Avanish Bhai Patel,** Research Scholar, Department of Humanities and Social Sciences, Indian Institute of Technology, Roorkee, Uttarakhand.

A.J. Mishra, Assistant Professor, Department of Humanities and Social Sciences, Indian Institute of Technology, Roorkee, Uttarakhand.

15. **Moitrayee Sanyal,** Assistant Professor, Department of Sociology St. Xavier's College (Autonomous), Kolkata.

16. **Jharana Swain,** Faculty of Social Work, Department BJB Autonomous College. Bhubaneswar, Odisha.

1 Violence Against Women in India

Ramesh H. Makwana

Introduction

Women have been the victims of violence through all ages and in all societies. Women have been vulnerable to acts of violence committed in the family and community. Though violence against women is an obstacle in the achievement of equality, development and peace in society; gender violence is a part of the historical process and has been a significant feature of the human society throughout the course of its evolution.

Violence against women is the manifestation of historically unequal power relations between men and women. The latest available statistics compiled by Indian home ministry's National Crime Records Bureau show that between 1953 and 2011, the incidence of rape rose by 873 per cent, or three times faster than all cognisable crimes put together, and three-and-a-half times faster than murder. In India, a woman is raped in every 22 minutes, and a bride is burnt for dowry in every 58 minutes. The police last year registered 42,968 cases of molestation of women-a figure that is about 80 per cent higher than the number of rapes. The number of crimes recorded against women, including sexual harassment, cruelty by the husband or his relatives, kidnapping or abduction, and human trafficking, exceeds 2, 61,000.

Today, violence against women in India has assumed an alarming proportion. According to surveys and research studies, there are about thirty specific forms of violence being committed against women from the pre-natal stage to their death such as sex determination, female foeticide, lack of chidcare, malnutrition, child prostitution, child marriage, domestic violence, wife battering, eve-teasing, female trafficking, abduction, rape, dowry death, lack of care at old age. Not a single moment passes when a woman is not being harassed.

The number of incidents reported in the press regarding the offences against women especially rape, molestation, kidnapping, family violence, dowry harassment, dowry deaths, wife beating, eve-teasing, go on multiplying. There has been a constant increase in the violence against women and hardly a day passes without reports in the newspapers or in magazines.

In this paper, the main objective is to measure the legal framework about violence against women, various forms, causes and remedial measures of violence against women in India.

Meaning of Violence against Women

The semantic meaning of 'crime against women' is direct or indirect physical or mental cruelty to women. Crimes which are 'directed specifically against women' and in which 'only women are victims' are characterised as 'Crime against Women'. It is equally important to clarify the concept of violence against women. Violence is also known as abuse and include any sort of physical aggression or misbehave. When violence is committed at home it becomes domestic violence and involves family members such as children, spouse, parents or servants. Domestic violence may involve different means such as hitting, kicking, biting, shoving, restraining and throwing objects. In broad terms, it includes threats, sexual abuse, emotional abuse, controlling or domineering, intimidation, stalking, passive/covert abuse and economic deprivation, rape, abduction, kidnapping, murder (all cases of criminal violence, dowry death, wife battering, sexual abuse, maltreatment of a widow and for an elderly women (all cases of domestic violence) and eve-teasing, etc (all cases of social violence), are issues which affect a large section of society. The United Nations defined "Violence against Women" in 1993 in Declaration on the Elimination of Violence against women. It defines—any act of gender-based violence that results in, or is likely to result in, physical, sexual or psychological harm or suffering to women, including threats of such acts, coercion or arbitrary deprivation of liberty, whether occurring in public or private life.

Violence against women includes:

- **Psychological Violence:** Encompasses various tactics to undermine a woman's self-confidence such as yelling, insults, mockery, threats, abusive language, humiliation, harassment, contempt and deliberate deprivation of emotional care or isolation.

- **Physical Violence:** The most obvious ranges from pushing and shoving to hitting, beating, physical abuse with a weapon, torture, mutilation and murder.
- **Sexual Violence:** Any form of non-consensual sexual activity (i.e., forced on a person) ranging from harassment, unwanted sexual touching, to rape. This form of violence also includes incest.
- **Financial Violence:** It encompasses various tactics for total or partial control of a couple's finances, inheritance or employment income. It may also include preventing a partner from taking employment outside the home or engaging in other activities that would lead to financial independence.
- **Spiritual Abuse:** Works to destroy an individual's cultural or religious beliefs through ridicule or punishment, forbidding practice of a personal religion or forcing women or children to adhere to religious practices that are not their own, etc.

Theoretical Explanation of Violent Behaviour

The theoretical propositions on violence typically encountered, whether violence is a normal response of provocation, or whether it involves the acting out of some psychopathology, or whether it acts as an instrument to obtaining some end or reward, or whether it is a response consistent with norms supporting its use, are being explained. Our own conceptual framework is based on a holistic approach and is presented as the 'Social Barrier Theory' which explains violent behaviour to a large extent.

The psychiatric or psycho-pathological school focuses on the aggressor's personality characteristics as the chief determinant of criminal violent behaviour. The socio-psychological school assumes that criminal violence can best be understood by analysing the external environmental factors that exercise an impact on the individual aggressor. This model examines the types of everyday interactions (say, stressful situations or family interactional patterns...) which are precursors to violence theories such as the Frustration-Aggression Theory, the Perversion Theory, the Self-attitude Theory, and the Motive Attribution Theory also fall within the purview of socio-psychological level of analysis. The sociological school provides a macro-level analysis of criminal violence. Besides, the Theory of Subculture of Violence, the Learning Theory, the Anomie Theory and the Resource Theory also fall under the socio–cultural analysis.

Review of Literature

Various studies on violence against women conducted in India, thereby creating a serious underestimation of overall prevalence of violence against women in society. The studies have been conducted at global level. Dr Sunita Kishor, senior gender specialist (USA) has done a lot of research and published many articles on violence against women. Sunita Kishor (2005) discusses about the measurement of domestic violence, challenges and data gaps in this area. World Health Organisation (WHO) and other agencies take initiatives to overcome the violence against women throughout the world. Many international organisations regularly conduct meeting and carry out research to overcome the serious problem of violence against women. Many books and articles are written on various issues and methodology of violence against women—Ruchira Tabassum Naved (2003), Mary Ellsberg and Lori Heise (2005), Johnson Holly, Natalia Ollus, Sami Nevela (2008), Renezetti C.M., Edleson J.L. and Bergen R.K. (2011).

A detailed literature review on statistical methodology used in violence against women has been done by Manboli R N and Tarase N G (2009). Many articles on violence against women in India reveal that there is a need to collect more information on different types of violence as most crimes are not reported (Ashok Kumar and Khan M.E. (2010), Bontha V. Babu and Shantanu K Kar (2009), Ghosh D (2007). This shows that there is an urgent need to collect reliable information in all the regions of India regarding violence against women. Only if reliable and complete data on violence against women is available, the government could take effective steps to curtail violence against women in India. Recently, many books on violence against women have been published (Mukerjee D. (2005), Ahuja R. (2009).

Some of the largest milestones on the international level for the prevention of violence against women include:

- The 1979 Convention on the Elimination of all forms of Discrimination against Women (CEDAW), which recognises violence as a part of discrimination against women in recommendations number 12 and 19.

- The 1993 World Conference on Human Rights, which recognised the violence against women as a human rights violation, and which contributed to the following UN declaration.
- The 1993 UN Declaration on the Elimination of Violence against Women was the first international instrument explicitly defining and addressing violence against women. This document specifically refers to the historically forever-present nature of gender inequalities in understanding violence against women (includes current 2nd paragraph here). This Declaration, as well as the World Conference of the same year, is often viewed as a "turning point" at which the violence against women by the international community were taken more seriously, and after which more countries mobilised around this problem.
- The 1994 International Conference on Population and Development, link violence against women to reproductive health and rights, and also provide recommendations to governments on how to prevent and respond to violence against women and girls.
- In 1996, the World Health Assembly (WHA) declared violence as major public health issue, and the sub-types recognised included were intimate partner violence and sexual violence, two kinds of violence which are often perpetrated as violence against women. This was followed by a WHO report in 2002 (see below).
- In 1999, the UN designated November 25, every year as the International Day for the Elimination of Violence against Women.
- In 2002, as a follow-up of the WHA declaration in 1996 of violence as a major public health issue, the World Health Organisation published the first World Report on violence and health, which addressed many types of violence and their impact on public health, including forms of violence affecting women particularly, stronger. The report specifically noted the sharp rise in civil society organisations and activities directed at responding to gender-based violence against women from the 1970s to the 1990s.

- In 2004, the World Health Organisation published its "Multi-country study on Women's Health and Domestic Violence against Women," a study of women's health and domestic violence by surveying over 24,000 women in 10 countries from all regions of the world, which assessed the prevalence and extent of violence against women, particularly violence by intimate partners, and linked this with health outcome to women as well as documenting strategies and services which women use to cope with intimate-partner violence.
- The 2006 UN Secretary-General's "in-depth study on all forms of violence against women," is the first comprehensive international document on the issue.
- The 2011 Council of Europe Convention on preventing and combating violence against women and domestic violence, which is the second regional legally-binding instrument on violence against women and girls.
- In 2013, the United Nations Commission on the Status of Women (CSW) adopted, by consensus, agreed conclusions on the elimination and prevention of all forms of violence against women and girls (formerly, there were no agreed-upon conclusions).

Additionally, on the national level, individual countries have organised efforts (legally, politically, socially) to prevent, reduce and punish violence against women. As a particular case study, here are some constitutional provisions for women.

Constitutional Provisions for Women

- Article 14, confers on men and women equal rights and opportunities in political, economic and social sphere.
- Article 15, prohibits, discrimination against any citizen on grounds of religion, race, caste, sex etc.
- Article 16, provides for equality of opportunities matters relating to employment or appointment to any office under the state.
- Article 39(a) to (d), mentions security policy of state equality for both men and women—the right to a means of livelihood and equal pay for equal work for both men and women.

- Article 42, directs the state to make provision for ensuring just and humane conditions of work and maternity relief.

Legal Provisions for Women

- Factories Act 1948: Under this Act, a woman cannot be forced to work beyond eight hours and prohibits employment of women except between 6 pm and 7 pm.
- Maternity Benefit Act 1961: A woman is entitled to 12 weeks maternity leave with full wages.
- The Dowry Prohibition Act, 1961: Under the provisions of this act, demand of dowry either before marriage, during marriage and or after the marriage is an offence.
- The Equal Remuneration Act of 1976: This act provides equal wages for equal work: It provides for the payment of equal wages to both men and women workers for the same work or work of similar nature. It also prohibits discrimination against women in the matter of recruitment.
- The Child Marriage Restrain Act of 1996: This act raises the age for marriage of a girl to 18 years from 15 years and that of a boy to 21years.
- Indian Penal Code: Section 354 and 509 safeguards the interest of women.
- The Medical Termination of Pregnancy Act of 1971: The Act safeguards women from unnecessary and compulsory abortions.
- Amendments to Criminal Law 1983: It extends a punishment of seven years in ordinary cases and 10 years for custodial rape cases.
- 73rd and 74th Constitutional Amendment Act: It reserved 1/3rd seats in Panchayat and Urban Local Bodies for women.
- The National Commission for Women Act, 1990: The Commission was set up in January, 1992 to review the Constitutional and legal safeguards for women.
- The Protection of Human Right Act, 1993:

- Protection of Women from Domestic Violence Act, 2005: This Act protects women from any act/conduct/ omission/commission that harms, injures or potential to harm is to be considered as domestic violence. It protects the women from physical, sexual, emotional, verbal, psychological, economic abuse.
- Protection of Women against Sexual Harassment at Workplace Bill, 2010: On November 4, 2010, the government introduced protection of women against sexual harassment at work place Bill, 2010, which aims at protecting the women at workplace not only to women employee but also to female clients, customers, students and research scholars in colleges and universities and patients in hospitals. The bill was passed in Lok Sabha on september 03, 2012.

Human Development Index and Gender Inequality Index

- According to the UNDP Human Development Report 2011, India ranks 134 in the Human Development Index.
- India ranks 129 out of 187 countries in the Gender Inequality Index.
- Gender Inequality Index is a composite measure reflecting the inequality in achievements between women and men in three dimensions: reproductive health (Maternal Mortality Ratio and Adolescent Fertility Rate), empowerment (Female and male population with at least secondary education as well as female and male shares of parliamentary seats) and labour market (Female and male labour force participation rates).

Violence against Women in India

Violence against Women (VAW) is not a new phenomenon. Women have to bear the brunt of domestic, public, physical as well as emotional and mental violence, which affects their status in the society at the larger extent. The statistics of increasing crimes against women is shocking, where women are subjected to violence attacks i.e., foeticide, infanticide, medical neglect, child marriages, bride burning, sexual abuse of girl child, forced marriages, rapes, prostitution, sexual harassment at home as well as work places etc. In all the above cases, woman is considered as aggrieved person.

A total of 2, 28,650 incidents of crime against women (both under IPC and SLL) were reported in the country during the year 2011 as compared to 2, 13,585 incidences in the year 2010 recording an increase of 7.1 per cent during the year 2011.

Table 1. Reported Incidents of Crime

Year	*Cases*
2007	1,85,312
2008	1,95,856
2009	2,03,804
2010	2,13,585
2011	2,28,650

West Bengal with 7.5 per cent share of country's population has accounted for nearly 12.7 per cent of total crime against women by reporting 29,133 cases. Andhra Pradesh, accounting for nearly 7.0 per cent of the country's population, has accounted for 12.4 per cent of total crimes against women in the country by reporting 28, 246 cases in the year 2011.

Trend Analysis: The crime head-wise details of reported crimes during the year 2007-11 along with percentage variation are presented in Table 2 below. The crime against women during the year 2011 has increased by 7.1 per cent over the year 2010 and by 23.4 per cent over the year 2007. The IPC component of crimes against women has accounted for 95.8 per cent of total crimes and the rest 4.2 per cent were SLL crimes against women. The proportion of IPC crimes committed against women towards total IPC crimes has increased during last five years from 8.8 per cent in the year 2007 to 9.4 per cent during the year 2011.

Crime against women in cities are reported (All-India... 2, 28,650 cities...33,789): 53 cities having population over 10 lakh have been identified as mega cities as per population census 2011. A total of 33,789 cases of crimes against women were reported from these 53 cities during the year 2011 as compared to 24,335 cases (35 mega cities) in the year 2010. The rate of crime in cities at 21.0 was comparatively higher as compared to the national rate of 18.9.

Among 53 cities, Delhi (4,489 cases) has accounted for 13.3 per cent of total such crimes followed by Benglaru (1,890 cases) (5.6 per cent) Hyderabad (1,860 cases) (5.5 per cent) and Vijaywada (1,797 cases) (5.3 per cent). The crime rate was

Table 2. Crime Head-wise Incidents of Crime against Women during 2007-11 and Percentage of Variation in 2011 over 2010

Sl. No.	Crime Head	Year					Percentage of Variation in 2010 over 2010
		2007	2008	2009	2010	2011	
1.	Rape (Sec. 376 IPC)	20,737	21,467	21,397	22,172	24,206	9.2
2.	Kidnapping and Abduction (Sec. 363 to 373 IPC)	20,416	22,939	25,741	29,795	35,565	19.4
3.	Dowry Death (Sec. 302/304 IPC)	8 093	8,172	8.383	8,391	8,618	2.7
4.	Cruelty Husband and Relatives (Sec. 498-A IPC)	75,930	81,344	89,546	94,041	99,135	5.4
5.	Molestation (Sec. 354 IPC)	38,734	40,413	38,711	40,613	42,968	5.8
6.	Sexual Harassment (Sec. 509 IPC)	10,950	12,214	11,009	9,961	8,570	-14.0
7.	Important of Girls (Sec.366-B-IPC)	61	67	48	36	80	122.2
8.	Suttee Prevention Act, 1987	0	1	0	0	1	100.0
9.	Immoral Traffic (Prevention) Act, 1956	3,568	2,659	2,474	2,499	2,435	-2.6
10.	Indecent Representation of women (prohibition) Act, 1986	1,200	1,025	845	895	453	-49.4
11.	Dowry Prohibition Act, 1961	5,623	5,555	5,650	5,182	6,619	27.7
	Total	1,85,312	1,95,856	2,03,804	2,13,585	2,28,650	7.1

Table 3. Proportion of Crime against Women (IPC) towards Total IPC Crimes

Sr. No.	*Year*	*Total IPC Crimes*	*Crime Against Women (IPC Cases)*	*Percentage of Total IPC Crime*
1.	2007	19,89,673	1,74,921	8.8
2.	2008	20,93,379	1,86,617	8.9
3.	2009	21,21,345	2,03,804	9.2
4.	2010	22,24,831	2,13,585	9.6
5.	2011	23,25,575	2,19,142	9.4

significantly higher in Vijayawads, Kota, Kollam, Jaipur and Asansol at 120.5, 57.5, 54.2, 48.6 and 48.2 respectively as compared to average of mega cities at 21.0.

Delhi city has accounted for 17.6 per cent of rape cases, 31.8 per cent kidnapping and abduction cases, 14.0 per cent of dowry deaths and 10.1 per cent of molestation cases among 53 cities. Hyderabad has reported 12.2 per cent (1, 390) of incidences of cruelty by husband and relatives. Vijayawada has reported 18.0 per cent incident of eve-teasing. Indore and Jabalpur having three cases and two cases respectively, have altogether contributed 83.3 per cent of total cases of 'importation of girls' at all India level.

It is worthwhile to mention that Bangaluru, Hyderabad, Mumbai and Patna have booked more cases under special and local laws among the mega cities. 15.5 per cent (191 out of 1,234) of cases under immortal traffic prevention) Act and 10.1 per cent (553 out of 5501) of cases under molestation was reported in Mumbai alone. Similarly, 56.0 per cent (42) and 34.7 per cent (26) of 75 cases of indecent representation of Women Act was reported in Jaipur and Jodhpur respectively. 70.7 per cent (605) cases under Dowry Prohibition Act during the year 2011 was registered in Bengaluru city.

Rape is a type of sexual assault usually involving sexual intercourse, which is initiated by one or more persons against another person without that person's consent. The act may be carried out by physical force, coercion, abuse of authority or with a person who is incapable of valid consent, such as one who is unconscious, incapacitated, or below the legal age of consent. Internationally, the incidence of rapes recorded by the police during 2008 varied between 0.1 in Egypt per 100,000 people and 91.6 per 100,000 people in Lesotho with 4.9 per 100,000 people in Lithuania as the median. According to the American Medical Association (1995), sexual violence, and rape in particular, is considered the most underreported violent crime. The rate of reporting, prosecution and convictions for rape varies considerably in different jurisdictions. Rape by strangers is usually less common than rape by persons the victim knows. Victims of rape can be severely traumatised and may suffer from post-traumatic stress disorder; in addition to psychological harm resulting from the act, rape may cause physical injury, or have additional effects on the victim, such as acquiring of a sexually transmitted infection or becoming pregnant. Sections 375 and 376 of the Indian Penal Code (IPC) define and provide punishment for the crime of rape. The general principle in Section 375 is that if a man has sexual intercourse with a woman below the age of 16, with or without her consent, he is guilty of rape. But, if the woman is his wife and above 15 years of age, the act is not rape. This means that marital rape is not a crime in India. A nominal punishment is provided, if the wife is between 12 and 15 years of age, or is living separately from him. Rape is an extreme form of sexual abuse; sex is not the main issue here.

Sexual Harassment in the Workplace: Sexual harassment in the workplace is considered a violation of human rights, and an affront to the dignity of the person harassed. It is viewed as a manifestation of violence against women that results in creating an atmosphere of discrimination against her. It is seen as unacceptable conditions of work which have detrimental effects for both female employees and the employer. A survey conducted for the National Commission for Women (NCW) in July 1998, covering over 1,200 women in both the organised and unorganised sectors, found that nearly 50 per cent had experienced gender discrimination or physical and mental harassment at work. Yet, 85 per cent of them had never heard of the existence of any law against sexual harassment. Only 11 per cent of them were aware that they could seek legal redressed in cases of sexual harassment, and that sexual harassment was an offence punishable by law. The NCW survey found women in the unorganised sector more vulnerable to sexual harassment than women in the organised sector. Apart from sexual harassment, 32 per cent of the women covered in the survey also reported discrimination in salaries, leave, promotions, work distribution and working hours.

Domestic Violence: The phenomenon of domestic violence remains one of the most prevalent yet largely 'invisiblised' forms of violence in the public domain. It is a manifestation of inequality within the home. Domestic violence occurs in many forms—physical, emotional, sexual, economic, verbal and others, and a woman may face violence to any one, two or in combination of all of them. A woman may face this cycle of violence as a daughter, a sister, a wife, a mother, a partner, or a single woman in her lifetime. Domestic violence is not always physical. It can involve behaviour that causes psychological harm or attempts to maintain power and control through coercion or intimidation. Name-calling, humiliation, constant criticism, attempts to isolate a woman from her friends or family, extreme jealousy, restrictions on personal freedom, tight control of family finances, and threats of physical harm are all markers of an abusive relationship. Abuse does not have to happen every day or every week for it to be classified as domestic violence. According to a study by the International Centre for Research on Women (ICRW) in 2000: (1) As many as four out of 10 women in India experienced violence in the home. (2) 44 per cent of women interviewed reported at least one incident of physical or psychological violence in their lifetime. Till 2005, there was no single comprehensive law on domestic violence in India. Till then a Section inserted in the IPC in 1983 as 498-A, sufficed for protection from domestic violence. This Section deals with cruelty by a husband or his family towards a married woman.

Murder: Homicide is mainly a masculine crime. Though the all-India figures pertaining to murders and their victims on the basis of sex are not available, it is well known that number of female victims of homicides in comparison to male victims is low. Whereas, in the United States, female victims constitute between 20 per cent and 25 per cent of the total victims of homicides (about 25,000 to 30,000 every year), in India of about 38,000 murders committed every year, women comprise about 10 per cent to 15 per cent of the total victims. Of the total persons arrested every year for committing murders (about 89,000), three per cent are females (Crime in India, 1994: 145).

Dowry-Deaths: Dowry-deaths either by way of suicide by a harassed wife or murder by the greedy husband and in-laws have indeed become the cause of great concern for parents, legislators, police, courts and society as a whole. Not a week passes when one does not read about a girl being harassed, tortured, killed or driven to suicide because of dowry, and yet how many of the accused are punished? Few killers in bride-burning cases are arrested, fewer are prosecuted, and fewest finally sentenced. Though the Dowry prohibition Act, 1961 has banned the practice of dowry but in reality all that the law does is to recognise that the problem exists. It is virtually unheard of for a husband or his family to be sued for insisting on taking a dowry. If anything, the demands for dowry have escalated over the years along with dowry deaths. As a modest estimate, the figure of deaths in India due to non-payment or partial payment of dowry could be placed around 5,000 for one year. The increase in the incidence of dowry offences is evident from the fact that against 1,912 cases of dowry deaths in 1987, there were 4,215 cases in 1989, 4,836 in 1990, 5,157 in 1991, 4,962 in 5,817 in 1993, and 4,935 in 1994 (Crime in India, 1994:212). (Ministry of Home Affairs). Most dowry-deaths occur in the house and with the collusion of the family members. Courts, therefore, admit their inability to convict any one for lack of evidence. Sometimes, the police are so callous in conducting investigation that even the courts question the efficiency and integrity of the police authorities.

Wife-Battering: Violence towards women in the context of marriage becomes more significant when a husband who is supposed to love and protect his wife beats her. For a woman, being battered by whom she trusted most becomes awesome experience. The violence can range from slaps and kicks to broken bones, torture, and attempted murder and even murder. Sometimes, the violence may be related to drunkenness but not always. Bred in Indian culture, a wife rarely thinks in terms of reporting a case of battering to the police. She suffers humiliation in silence and takes it as her destiny. Even if she wants to revolt, she cannot do it because of the fear that her own parents would refuse to keep her in their house permanently after the marital break down.

Outraging the Modesty of a Woman: Any form of sexual violation that does not fall within the narrow ambit of the offence of rape falls under Sections 354 and 509 of the IPC. Even though these sections intend to protect women's 'modesty', the IPC nowhere defines what constitutes 'modesty'. Since the understanding of 'modesty' is moralistically construed, the Section can get subjectively interpreted to apply to only certain kinds of women (chaste, sexually innocent/passive, etc.) who can be said to be the sole possessors of 'modesty'. For example, a woman's mannerism, walk, make-up, mode of dressing, hour of the day when she is out may be deciding factors when she claims the protection of her 'modesty'! So, in 1967, a two-judge division bench of the Supreme Court deliberated on whether a female child of seven-and-a-half years, who was raped, could be said to be possessed of 'modesty', which could be 'outraged'.

Victims of Violence

If we have taken all the cases of violence against women into consideration, we find that the victims of violence are generally those:

- Who feel helpless, depressed, have a poor self-image and suffer from self-devalution, or those who are 'emotionally consumed' by the perpetrators of violence, or who suffer from 'altruistic powerlessness';
- Who live in stressful family situations, or who live in families which, in sociological terms, cannot be called 'normal' families, that is, families which are structurally complete (both parents being alive and living together), economically secure (satisfying basic and subsidiary needs of members, functionally adequate (have rare quarrels and morally conformists);
- Who lack social maturity or social interpersonal skills because of which they face behavioural problems;
- Whose husbands/in-laws have pathological personalities; and
- Whose husbands are alcoholic.

Perpetrators of Violence

Women are generally abused and attacked by men they know. This is proved by one study even in England (University of Warwick: Joanna Liddle), which pointed out that 61 per cent of women are abused by their own family members and only 39 per cent by strangers. In the former category, 72 per cent face violence at the hands of their husbands, by person they know well and that too in places they would consider as safe. In India, the crimes of marital violence reported to police in different states indicate that the marital home is not always a safe place for a woman (which does not mean that a woman is safer outside her home than within). Males argue that today a woman does not adhere to the conventional parameters expected of a wife. Does this reflect that a woman refusing to conform and asking for some freedom and independence needs violence—whether physical, psychological or emotional-to ensure that conformity? Can we accept this type of patriarchal consensus in this age?

Seven types of victimisers of women may be identified. They are:

- Who have depressions, inferiority complex and low self-esteem;
- Who have personality disorders and are psychopaths;
- Who lack resources, skills, and talents and have sociopathic personality;
- Who have possessive, suspicious and dominant nature;
- Who face stressful situations in family life;
- Who are victims of violence in childhood; and
- Who are frequent users of alcohol.

Types of Violence

If we were to develop a typology of violence against women, we may give six types of violence:

- Violence which is money-oriented;
- Violence which seeks power over the weak;
- Violence which aims at pleasure-seeking;
- Violence which is the result of the perpetrator's pathology;
- Violence which is the result of stressful family situations; and
- Violence which is victim-precipitated.

Motivation in Violence

Violence against women may be explained on the basis of three factors: (i) situations which bring about violent behaviour, (ii) characteristics of victims, and (iii) characteristics of victimisers. Four causes may be identified in violence against women: victim's (a) provocation, (b) intoxication, (c) hostility towards women, and (d) situational urge.

National Initiatives to Curb the Gender Violence and National Commission for Women

In January 1992, the government set-up this statutory body with specific mandate to study and monitor matters relating to the constitutional and legal safeguards provided for women, review the existing legislation to suggest amendments wherever necessary.

(i) Reservation for Women in Local Self-Government

The 73rd constitutional Amendment Acts passed in 1992 by Parliament, ensure one-third of the total seats for women in all elected officers in local bodies whether in rural areas or urban areas.

(ii) The National Plan of Action for the Girl Child (1991-2000)

The plan of Action is to ensure survival, protection and development of the girl child with the ultimate objective of building up a better future for the girl child.

(iii) National Policy for the Empowerment of Women, 2001

The department of Women and Child Development in the Ministry of Human Resource Development has prepared a "National Policy for the Empowerment of Women", in the year 2001. The goal of this policy is to bring about the advancement, development and empowerment of women.

(iv) National Mission for Empowerment of Women, 2010

The launch of the National Mission for Empowerment of Women in March, 2010 is an important development that will provide the much required fillip to a co-ordinated assessment of current government interventions and aligning future programmes so as to translate the MPEW prescription into reality. The Mission was operationalised during 2011-12.

Verma Committee Report

A three-member commission, headed by former Chief Justice of India, Justice J.S. Verma which was assigned to review laws for sexual crimes submitted report to the government during January 2013. The commission has recommended comprehensive changes in criminal laws to deal with crimes and atrocities against women which are as under.

Punishment for Rape: The panel has not recommended the death penalty for rapists. It suggests that the punishment for rape should be rigorous imprisonment for seven years of life. It recommends that punishment for causing death or a "persistent vegetative state" should be RI for a term not less than 20 years, but may be for life also, which shall mean the rest of the person's life. Gang-rape, it suggests should entail punishment of not less than 20 years, which may also extend to life and gang-rape followed by death, should be punished with life imprisonment.

Punishment for Other Sexual Offences: The panel recognised the need to curb all forms of sexual offences and recommended-Voyeurism be punished with up to seven years in jail; stalking or attempts to contact a person repeatedly through any means by up to three years. Acid attacks would be punished by up to seven years of imprisonment; trafficking will be punished with RI for seven to ten years.

Registering Complaints and Medical Examination: Every complaint of rape must be registered by the police and the civil society should perform its duty to report any case of rape coming to its knowledge. "Any other person, who fails to register a case of rape reported to him, or attempts to abort its investigation, commits an offence which shall be punishable as prescribed," the report says. The protocols for medical examination of victims of sexual assault have also been suggested. The panel said, "Such protocol based professional medical examination is imperative for uniform practice and implementation."

Marriages to be Registered: As a primary recommendation, all marriages in India (irrespective of the personal laws under which such marriages are solemnised) should mandatorily be registered in the presence of a magistrate. The magistrate will ensure that the marriage has been solemnised without any demand for dowry having been made and that it has taken place with the full and free consent of both partners.

Amendments to the Code of Criminal Procedure: The panel observed, "The manner in which the rights of women can be recognised can only be manifested when they have full access to justice and when the rule of law can be upheld in their favour." The proposed Criminal Law Amendment Act, 2012, should be modified, suggests the panel. "Since the possibility of sexual assault on men, as well as homosexual, transgender and transsexual rape, is a reality, the provisions have to be cognisant of the same," it says. A special procedure for protecting persons with disabilities from rape and requisite procedures for access to justice for such persons, the panel said was an "urgent need."

Bill of Rights for Women: A separate Bill of Rights for women that entitles a woman a life of dignity and security and will ensure that a woman shall have the right to have complete sexual autonomy including with respect to her relationships.

Review of the Armed Forces Special Powers Act: The panel has observed that the "impunity of systematic sexual violence is being legitimised by the armed forces special power act." It has said there is an imminent need to review the continuance of AFSPA (Armed Forces Special Power Act) in areas an soon as possible. It has also recommended posting special commissioners for women's safety in conflict areas.

Police Reforms: To inspire public confidence, the panel said, "police officers with reputation of outstanding ability and character must be placed at the higher levels of the police force." All existing appointments need to be reviewed to ensure that the police force has the requisite moral vision. The panel strongly recommended that "law enforcement agencies do not become tools at the hands of political masters". It said, "Every member of the police force must understand their accountability is only to the law and to none else in the discharge of their duty."

Role of Judiciary: The judiciary has the primary responsibility of enforcing fundamental rights, through constitutional remedies. The judiciary can take *suo-motto* cognisance of such issues being deeply concerned with them both in the Supreme Court and the High Court. An all India strategy to deal with these issues would be advisable. The Chief

Justice of India could be approached to commence appropriate proceedings on the judicial side. He may consider making appropriate orders relating to the issue of missing children to curb the illegal trade of their trafficking.

Political Reforms: The Justice Verma committee observed that reforms are needed to deal with criminalisation of politics. The panel has suggested in the event cognisance has been taken by a magistrate of a criminal offence, the candidate ought to be disqualified from participating in the electoral process. Any candidate who fails to disclose a charge should be disqualified subsequently. It suggested lawmakers facing criminal charges, who have already been elected to Parliament and state legislatures, should voluntarily vacate their seats.

Suggestion and Policy Recommended

It is important to continue to raise awareness about the impact of violence against women so that more groups, communities and leaders priorities this as a programme of work that deserves attention and resources. Awareness helps break down myths and stereotypes that are sometimes used to justify violence, and allows those at risk of violence better understand how they can protect themselves and those around. In addition to empowering women and girls, it is essential to address the sources and perpetrators of violence, whether actual or potential. This requires hands-on engagement with men and boys to help shift attitudes about the use of violence and to empower.

- **Break the silence:** Never condone VAW. Always raise your voice and report it.
- **Know the law:** Gain basic awareness of the laws on VAW so that you are able to recognise when VAW is taking place and know what law to use when.
- **Build solidarity:** With a concerned and committed group of friends and colleagues build an informal solidarity group within your organisation or institution which can extend solidarity to victims of GBV.
- **Connect with women's rights groups:** Get in touch with local women's rights groups if you hear of any VAW-related incident, or if you wish to attend or organise trainings on VAW for your colleagues, friends and peers.

- **Demand to know your rights as a woman:** Within an institution or organisation, you have a right to find out the processes in place to combat VAW. For instance, you have a right to know whether your office or college has set up an anti-sexual harassment cell, and the right to demand that it is set up.
- **Join and mark the 16 Days of Activism against Gender Violence Campaign:** The 16-days of Activism against Gender Violence is an international campaign. Participants chose the dates–November, 25: International Day Against Violence Against Women, and December, 10: International Human Rights Day—in order to symbolically link violence against women and human rights and to emphasise that such violence is a violation of human rights. This 16-day period also highlights other significant dates including November, 29: International Women Human Rights Defenders Day, December, 1: World AIDS Day, and December, 6 that marks the anniversary of the Montreal Massacre. The 16-days campaign has been used as an organising strategy by individuals and groups around the world to call for the elimination of all forms of violence against women by: (a) Raising awareness about gender-based violence as a human rights issue at the local, national, regional and international levels, (b) Strengthening local work around violence against women, (c) Establishing a clear link between local and international work to end violence against women, (d) Providing a forum in which organisers can develop and share new and effective strategies, (e) Demonstrating the solidarity of women around the world organising against violence against women, (f) Creating tools to pressure governments to implement promises made on eliminating violence against women.
- **Working with men:** By and large, men tend to disclaim responsibility for their violent behaviour, often justifying it or simply refusing to admit it. According to Kathy Grogan, project manager with STOP (Start Treating Others Positively), based in Leeds (UK): "For men to stop being violent it is important for them to identify and take responsibility for feelings that are masked by rage. The connection between the prohibition against showing

vulnerable feelings and the tacit societal permission to vent this rage on a woman is a crucial one to be made in programmes with male perpetrators."

- Call the police, if you see or hear evidence of domestic violence.
- Support a friend or family member who may be in an abusive relationship.
- Volunteers at an organisation that helps survivors or works to prevent violence.
- Raise children to respect others.
- Teach children to treat others as they would like to be treated.
- Lead by example.
- Work to create a culture that rejects violence as a way to deal with problems. Speak up against messages that say violence or mistreating women is okay.
- Become an activist.
- Participate in an anti-violence event.
- Volunteer in youth programmes.
- Become a mentor. Get involved in programs that teach young people to solve problems without violence.
- Ask about anti-violence policies and programs at work and educational institutions.
- At work, ask about policies that deal with sexual harassment, for example. On campus, ask about services to escort students to dormitories safely at night and other safety measures.

Action-oriented Research

While the past two or three decades produced many lessons about violence against women, more research and data are needed to better:

- Understand its root causes, magnitude and consequences,
- Identify solutions, and
- Galvanise social, legal and political change.

References

Ahuja, Ram, *Crime against Women*, Rawat Publications, Jaipur, 1987.

Borland, Marie (ed.), *Violence in the Family*, Manchester University Press, Manchester, 1976.Bolton, F.G. and Bolton, S.R., *Working with Violent Families*, Sage Publications, New York, 1987.

Chapman, J.K. and Gates, Margaret (eds.), *The Victimisation of Women*, Sage Publications, Beverly Hills, California, 1976.

Leonard, E.B., *Women, Crime and Society*, Longman, New York, 1982.M.D.A., Freeman, *Violence in the Home*, Saxon House, London, 1979.

Pagelow, M.D., *Family Violence*, Praeger Scientific, New York, 1984.

Renvoire, Jean, *Web of Violence*, Routledge and Kegan Paul, London, 1978.

Steinmetz, S.K. and Straus, M.A. (eds.), *Violence in the Family*, Harper and Row, New York, 1974.

Sood, Sushama, *Violence against Women*, Arihant Publishers, Jaipur, 1990.

Sinha, Niroj, *Women and Violence*, Vikas Publishing House, Delhi, 1989.

2 Combating Corruption: The Role of Whistle-blowers and the Need to Protect Them

S. Uma Devi

Introduction

Corruption is the cancer of public life today corroding the vitals of Indian polity, along with the erosion of traditional value system and the spread of violence. It is a complex problem having its roots and ramifications in society as a whole. There is a growing recognition that corruption is anti-economic development, anti-poor and anti-national. A *Times of India* poll (2002) showed that corruption is perceived to be the biggest problem facing the country—'the number one problem'. N. Vittal, former CVC who boldly crusaded against corruption called it by "far the biggest challenge to the growth of our society and nation". Even financial institutions like the World Bank and International Monetary Fund have stated that corruption has been a serious bottleneck to investment and growth.

Santharam Committee Report 1964 defines corruption as "improper or selfish exercise of power and influence attached to a public office or to a special position one occupies in public life". Corruption in one form or other has always existed in India. Contrary to popular perception, corruption was quite rampant even in pre-independence India when the controls and shortages caused by Second World War resulted in huge illegal profits for bureaucrats and forced the colonial government to pass the Prevention of Corruption Act in 1947. "The scope for bribery and corruption of public servants has been enormously by war conditions and though the war is over now, opportunities for corrupt practices will remain for considerable time to come", said the government, justifying the passing of the new Act.

Over the years, the tentacles of corruption have spread to the system of government–civil, political and military. The planned model of development pursued since the 1950s which vested discretionary powers in bureaucrats and created the 'license permit raj' further aggravated the corruption problem; to move files even at the lowest levels of bureaucracy required speed money. In an economy, where licenses were required for producing virtually anything, shortages became the order of the day and this created even more opportunities to demand and receive bribes. The most disquieting aspect of the widespread corruption in India is the fact that it is anymore not confined to politicians or the government machinery alone as in the colonial era. It is prevalent amongst almost every section of the society and is also encountered at all levels public/private/cooperative sector enterprises, corporate governance, financial institutions, NGOs etc. The most unfortunate thing is that people seem to accept corruption and the lack of accountability as an inescapable part of modern life. Thus, the traditional definition– "Corruption is the abuse of public office for private gain"—is now understood to be unbalanced, unhelpful and is largely discredited. Different organisations engaged in combating corruption have therefore tended to focus on different forms of corruption. The main forms of corruption are bribery, embezzlement, fraud and extortion. Even when these concepts, some of basic characteristics of corruption can identified through these concepts.

As corruption flourished, successive government took various measures to try and stem the problem. The Anti-Corruption Laws (Amendment) Act 1964 was enacted with a view to make the anti-corruption laws more effective and to ensure speedy trial of cases. The Central Vigilance Commission (CVC) came into being in 1964. Conduct Rules of Public servants were reviewed and loopholes plugged. A Prevention of Corruption Act was enacted in 1988 incorporating various corruption-related provisions of the Indian Penal Code. Lok Ayuktas were set up in different states to address the corruption problems at the state level. Despite these measures and substantial economic reforms to eliminate the license permit raj, India remains one of the most corrupt countries in the world. Thus, Transparency International, a Berlin-based NGO has projected India as the 87th most corrupt country of the 178 nation surveyed in 2010. As rightly pointed out by N. Vittal, 'corruption in India is a low-risk and high-profit activity. With the resources of anti-corruption agencies so thinly spread on the ground, there is only a slender chance of getting caught and hence the fear of law is felt very little. Apart from the defective and cumbersome laws and proceedings in investigation, and the increasing tolerance towards corruption and corrupt practices in the society, the low-level of awareness on the part of the average citizen also promoted corruption.

During the last two decades, several cases of corruption and scandals have come to the public notice due to vigilant press, efforts of public spirited individuals and a proactive judiciary. The Bofors, HDW Submarine Deal, Air Bus Deal, ABB Loco Deal, Jain Hawala Racket, Sugar Scam, Security Scam, Urea Scam, Fodder Scam in Bihar, Tehelka tapes and the latest 2G scam etc., are a few instances. These scams, which surfaced were only the tip of the iceberg. Majority of these scams are related to 'public expenditure' by the Central and State Governments. The numerous public bodies that are mandated to carry out various programmes and spend public funds perform poorly. Public audits carried out by bodies such as the office of the Comptroller and Auditor General (CAG) routinely point out glaring examples of wastage of public funds and corruption. Yet, no action follows and laws that are among the finest in the world are often not enforced. Equally alarming are the cases of corruption in the collection of public revenue and arrears thereof. The corrupt practices in the levy and recovery of direct and indirect taxes, non-recovery of loans from industrialists, money-laundering in the banking sector etc., have resulted in the loss of thousands of crore to the national exchequer.

Broadly, corruption can be categorised as routine and specific. Routine corruption is what is indulged in by a person in authority for doing what is required and is paid to do so. It is a form of double taxation, the citizen paying again for a service for which he has already paid through taxes or fees. Specific corruption would be accepting bribes to take decisions in a specific manner in matters in which discretionary power is vested in any person in authority. Specific corruption often goes unnoticed as neither the benefactor nor the beneficiary would talk about. However, it leads to wrong and biased decisions which adversely affect the lives of people and pose a threat to national security as well. Thus, it causes more lasting damage to the society than routine corruption. According to Public Services International Research Unit Report (2003), corruption is an activity that involves two parties: the bribe-maker and the bribe-taker, who driven by the prospect of making significant economic gains, engage in a win-win situation. But in this collusive act between the bribe-giver and bribe-taker, the victim ultimately is the society as a whole. As regards to bribery and corruption, there are two types of informers, one who is implicated or has participated in the giving or receiving of a bribe; a collaborator and the innocent third party who has witnessed some part of the corrupt act or sees evidence to suggest as a whistle-blower. Whilst globally the authorities welcome and protect collaborators through witness protection and plea bargaining, whistle-blowers receive the same level of help or protection.

The Role of Whistle-Blowers in Exposing Corruption

In principle, whistle-blowers provide potentially powerful mechanisms to deter bribery and corruption, whistle-blowers are those who expose misconduct or malpractice in public life (known as wicks Committee); whistle-blowing is defined as "raising concern about malpractice with an organisation or through an independent structure associated with it". However, others hold the view that there is no universally accepted definition of whistle-blowing, but agree with the Australian Senate Select Committee's view that "what is important is not the definition of the term, but the definition of the circumstances and conditions under which the employees who disclose wrong–doing should be entitled to protection from retaliation".

Whistle-blowers referred to as 'bell-ringers' in the Netherlands and 'light-house keepers' in the USA, act as guardians in the interest of the public. The potential value of employees coming forward and raising concern over work place malpractice with a view to defending the wider public interest, is largely self evident. Investigations into a host of disasters that have taken place around the world in both the public and private sectors have revealed that employees were either aware of the problem and too worried about damaging their jobs and careers to raise their concerns or that employees had raised concerns but these had been ignored. The cost of this silence to human life, the environment, public health, livelihood, employment, financial security and the public purse—is devastatingly high.

Whistle-blowing is relevant to all organisations, not just those few who are corrupt or criminal. This is because every business and every public body faces the risk of things going wrong or of unknowingly harbouring a corrupt individual. Where such risk arises, usually the first person to realise or suspect the wrong doing will be those who work in or with the organisation. Yet, these people, who are best placed to sound the alarm or blow the whistle have also the most to lose if they do. Today, whistle-blowers face a harsh reality; those who are courageous enough to blow the whistle often do so at considerable personal cost. The findings of a study of whistle-blowers in the USA illustrate the extent of emotional stress suffered by them and underline society's dominant perception of whistle–blowers as trouble makers. It reveals that all the whistle-blowers suffered damage to their career. Whistle- blowers normally face a lot of problems in their career. By exposing corruption among their superiors, they face the possibility of direct or indirect punishment. This could be in the form of lack of advancement and promotions, ultimately leading to their failing career. But a more important issue is the risk whistle-blowers face in terms of physical harm. There are many instances where they are murdered. Hence, the need of the hour is to protect those who risk their lives by exposing corruption.

Need for Protecting Whistle-blower: Bribery and corruption are most likely to flourish where the likelihood of getting caught is low and the sanctions applied to those who are caught are insufficient. Protecting whistle-blowers, and thus encouraging people to speak out, clearly increases the chance of detection. So long as sanctions are sufficiently severe, extending protection for whistle-blowers should provide an effective deterrent. The protection of whistle-blowers is an issue that has traditionally been extremely important to trade unions who are concerned with the protection and well being of workers. However, in recent years, encouraging and therefore protecting, whistle-blowers has become increasingly important to national and international policy makers engaged in designing anti-corruption policy solutions.

In India, some systematic efforts were made to tackle the issue of corruption. Among them, the passing of the Right to Information Act in 2005 is hailed as major step to empowering civil society and making the government more accountable. Besides, with aims to protect whistle-blowers, the government of India drafted a Public Interest Disclosure (Protection of Informers) Bill, 2002. While the Bill under examination by the Parliament, the murder of Satyendra Dubey, a young engineer working for the National Highways Authority of India, on November 29, 2003, after he complained confidentially against the corrupt practices in the execution of the Golden Quadrilateral road project in Bihar, came as a stark reminder of the absence of such law. There was an unrelenting public outrage over the murder of Dubey and cutting across political lines, leading members of the ruling coalition as well as the Opposition came out in support of legislation that would protect the identity of whistle-blowers in future so that more people can come out against corruption without risking lives. The Supreme Court which heard the public interest litigation on the Dubey murder case prompted the government to draft a resolution seeking to protect whistle-blowers saying that "A condition that can encourage corruption is the absence of mechanism by which instances of fraud and malpractice can be brought to light by a public-spirited person, without risking his or her interest or safety. Such person needs institutional protection against victimisation by the target of his or her action. Ensuring the anonymity of the whistle-blower therefore is essential for any such mechanism to be meaningful."

Consequently, in order to assure meaningful protection of informers and to encourage disclosures of corruption and fraud until the entry into force of the whistle-blower protection Bill, the Central Government of India, Ministry of Personnel, Public Grievances and Pensions, has enacted Resolution No. 89 on April 21, 2004. This resolution grants a protection mechanism similar to the one foreseen by the Public Interest Disclosure (Protection of Informers) Bill, 2002. The Central Vigilance Commission has been designated to handle complaints submitted under the Resolution (Office Order No.33/5/2004). The resolution is an improvement on the draft Bill to the extent it guarantees confidentiality to the whistle-blowers, whereas the Bill seeks to empower the designated agency to determine whether the whistle-blower's identity needs to be kept secret. The Right to Information Act and the whistle-blower act work best in tandem. In the Right to Information Act, the users would have to specify what they want to know but when there is no reason to suspect that something is amiss no one may bother to ask, whereas whistle-blowers would pre-empt disasters.

Besides, passing legislation, what is equally important is promoting a pro-whistle blowing culture in organisations, whereas in the silent majority who think it as not in their interests to blow the whistle on corruption or serious wrongdoing will be encouraged to see internal whistle-blowing as viable, safe and accepted option. Because, without whistle-blowers, we may not get to learn about problems until it is time to mourn the consequncences with the passing of the resolution, India has joined the select band of four democracies protecting whistle-blowers: the USA, the U.K., the Australia and the New Zealand. As and when the Parliament enacts the law to replace the resolution, it will get an opportunity to debate problems afresh arising out of the perceived deficiencies in the draft Bill and the Resolution and hopefully set them right by learning from the experience of the countries that have similar laws.

References

Ades, Alberto and Rafael di Tetla, "*The Causes and Consequences of Corruption: A Review of Recent Empirical Contributions*", IDS Bulletin 27, No. 2, 1996.

Bardhan, Pranab, "*Corruption and Development: A Review of Issues*", Journal of Economic Literature, 1997.

Girling, John. *Corruption, Capitalism and Democracy,* London: Routledge, 1997.

Gurgur, Tugrul and Anwar Shah, 2002, *"Localisation and Corruption: Panacea or Pandora's Box?* In Ehtisham Ahmad and Vito Tanzi, eds., *Managing Fiscal Decentralisation*, London and New York: Routledge Press, pp. 46-67.

Huther, Jeff, and Anwar Shah, 2000, *"Anti-corruption Policies and Programmes: A Framework for Evaluation*", Policy Research Working Paper 2501, Washington: World Bank. India. *Shah Commission of Enquiry Report,* Delhi: Controller of Publications,1978.

Kashyap, Subhash C. (Ed), *Crime and Corruption to Good Governance.* New Delhi: Uppal, 1997.

Pavarale, Vinod, *Interpreting Corruption: Elite Perspectives in India,* New Delhi: Sage, 1996.

Shah, Anwar, 2006. *Corruption and Decentralised Public Governance,* Policy Research Working paper series no. 3824, World Bank, Washington, D.C. Shah, Anwar, Theresa Thompson, and Heng-fu Zou, 2004, "*The Impact of Decentralisation on Service Delivery, Corruption, Fiscal Management and Growth in Developing and Emerging.*

World Bank, 2004, *Mainstreaming Anti-Corruption Activities in World*

Bank Assistance—A Review of Progress Since 1997, Washington: World Bank.

http://articles.economictimes.indiatimes.com/2010-1210/news/27614571_1_*corrupt-country-transparency-international-petty corruption.*

http://business.rediff.com/slide-show/2010/oct/26/slide-show-1-*worlds-most-corrupt-nations*.htm.

Final Draft, *Anti-Corruption strategy by CentralVigilance Commission,* http://cvc.nic.in/NationalAnti CorruptionStrategydr...

This fact has also been recognised by the Law Commission of India in its 166th Report.

3 Crime in India: Trends and Tribulations

Shubhangi Gavhane-Gote

Introduction

Crime is considered as an inevitable and inbuilt phenomenon in every society. Absolute abolition or eradication of crime from any society is not possible. As long as human beings are there, as long as existence of society and human action, reaction and interaction is there, incidence of crime is bound to occur. The views of great sociologist, Emile Durkheim support this actuality. "Crime is present not only in the majority of societies of one particular species but in all societies of all types. There is no society that is not confronted with problem of criminality".[1] (Durkheim Emile: 1979) Thus there cannot be any disagreement about the everlasting nature of crime in any given society. As incidence of crime is harmful to any given society, it ultimately designates the crime as a social problem. Like natural calamities as cyclone, drought and earthquake, crime is a societal calamity. It is a man-made calamity. Therefore, crime and crime control becomes a problem of serious concern, with aim to understand causes of crime and ways to control crime in any form of society.

As the very nature of criminological studies is inter-disciplinary and multi-disciplinary, it needs different kinds of approach to understand the true nature of criminality. That's why, criminology has attracted number of scientists from different disciplines such as sociology, law, psychology, political science, social work, medicine and others. In effect, more and more studies are being conducted, giving newer and newer dimensions to criminological studies in result, all over the world.

Study of Crime in Post-Independence India

After freedom and adopting the democratic system of governance, from 1950's to 2010's, India has changed remarkably. The progress achieved during last six decades in very field of society, has transformed conventional, underdeveloped India into a modern and developed India. This process of progress and development was responsible not only for growth but also for new patterns of conflicts and crimes. This paper attempts to find out nature and characteristics of crime in India, during post-independence period: 1950's to 2010's.

The population of India is growing, so is its crime. The criminality is growing in numbers as well as in terms of seriousness of crime and brutality.

Table 1. Crime in India: 1953 to 2012.

(Cognisable offences under I.P.C.)

Sr. No.	*Year*	*Cognisable Crime under I.P.C.*	*Other Offences under I.P.C.*
1.	1953	6,01,984	1,48,440
2.	1962	6,74,466	1,99,194
3.	1972	9,84,773	3,18,886
4.	1982	13,53,904	6,12,586
5.	1992	16,89,341	9,07,071
6.	2002	17,80,330	7,30,297
7.	2012	23,87,188	9,66,244

I.P.C.: Indian Penal Code.

(*Source:* Crime in India Compendium, National Crime Records Bureau, Ministry of Home Affairs, Government of India, 2012.)

Table. 1 shows that, during past six decades, the cognisable crimes under Indian Penal Code (I.P.C.) have increased nearly four times from six lakh one thousand and 984 to 23 lakh, 87 thousand and 188. Even the other offences under I.P.C. have also increased nearly six times during past six decades of 1953 to 2012. The number of cognisable offence is seen being doubled after every three decades i.e., 1953 to 1982 and 1982 to 2012. On the other hand, the number of other crimes under I.P.C. have seen doubled in first two decades (1953 to 1972) from 1,48,440 crimes in 1953 to 3,18,886 in the year 1972. These other I.P.C. crimes have noticed to be tripled during four decades of recent past (1972 -2012), from 3,18,886 in 1972 to 9,66,244 in 2012.[2] It is also observed that, the number of cognisable offences under I.P.C. is at too high, when compared to other offences of I.P.C.. This statistics indicates the crime numbers and its proportions are on increase with high rate and have reached to a very serious state. This also shows our attempts to control crime rate have also failed.

Table. 2. State of Serious Crimes in India: Some Trends (1953-2012)

Sr. No.	*Type of Crime*	*Year*	*Incidence of Crime*	*Per cent change in 2012 over 1953*
1.	Murder	19532012	9,80234,434	251.3 per cent
2.	Rape	19712012	2,48724,923	902.1 per cent
3.	Kidnapping and Abduction	19532012	5,26147,592	804.6 per cent
4.	Riots	19532012	20,52974,633	263.5 per cent

(*Source*: Crime in India Compendium, National Crime Records Bureau, Ministry of Home Affairs, Govt. of India, (p. 12).[3]

Table. 2 states that, the trends about some serious crimes in India, observed during 1953 to 2012, such as murder, rape, kidnapping and abduction as well as that of riots. The journey of crime in India, during past six decades (1953-2012) in respect of serious kind of crimes, reflects on the illness of our society. Incidence of heinous crime like murder has increased by 251.3 per cent from 9,802 murders in 1953 to 34,434 numbers in 2012. Crimes against persons are increasing; as in Indian society—personal enmity, inter-personal conflicts are growing with growing intolerance and an expression of uncontrolled anger. Most disturbing trend is about the crime of rape, one of the cruel crimes against women and which is not only a physical assault but for victim it also causes mental depression. This crime generates a feeling of insecurity in the minds of other women. Presently, Indian women are facing this social abnormality of fear complex in a big way. During past four decades (From 1971 to 2012), the crime of rape has increased by 902 per cent, this is the highest increase among all crimes in India. In 1971, there were just 2,484 cases of rape and in 2012, the number was as high as 24,923.[4] As India is marching towards gender equality by empowerment of women in India, the victimisation of women is also seen increasing unexpectedly. One can raise the question, "Is this a backlash against women, who are fighting for their just rights and gaining some of them?"

The crime of kidnapping and abduction, which is mainly related with women and child, is also a serious trend of crime. It has increased by 804.6 per cent during 1953 to 2013. After rape, this is the other crime, where women and children are mostly victims. This analysis proves, women and children are day by day becoming more vulnerable in Indian society. Riot is a crime, number which has increased from 20,529 in 1953 to 74,633 in 2012. The increase in the incidence of riot crime is 263.5 per cent. As India is progressing steadily, the caste and communal conflicts are growing and some of them being politically motivated riots. This amply proves the Indian society as a conflicting society, which is losing its tolerance, mutual understanding and peaceful co-existence. This is enough evidence of social sickness of contemporary Indian society.

Cognisable Crimes under I.P.C. and S.L.L.

To understand the overall trends of crime in India, one has to study the incidence of cognisable crimes registered under Indian Penal Code (I.P.C.) and Special and Local Laws (S.L.L.) put together. The analysis of 2008-12 figures of I.P.C. and S.L.L. cognisable crime indicates the status of overall crimes in India. Table 3 gives the statistics about crimes in India from 2008-12. In 2008, I.P.C. and S.L.L. crimes were in all 53, 38,104 and in 2012, the number reached to 60, 41,559.5 However, the figures of total cognisable (IPC + SLL) crimes show, there is fluctuation in incidence of such crimes.

Table 3. India Cognisable Crimes Registered during 2008-12

Year	*Number of Offences*		*Total Offences (IPC+SLL)*	*Crime Rate per 1,00,000 Population*
	I.P.C.	*S.L.L.*		
2008	20,93,379	38,44,725	59,38,104	515.0
2009	21,21,345	45,53,872	66,75,217	570.8
2010	22,24,831	45,25,917	67,50,748	569.3
2011	23,25,575	39,27,154	62,52,729	516.7
2012	23,87,188	36,54,371	60,41,559	497.9

(*Source:* Crime in India 2012, Compendium, National Crime Record Bureau, Ministry of Home Affairs, Govt. of India, New Delhi (p. 23).[6]

Table 4. India: Violent Crimes Reported during 2008-12

No.	*Crimes*	*2008*	*2009*	*2010*	*2011*	*2012*
1.	Total Violent Crimes	2,28,663	2,41,986	2,41,986	2,56,329	2,75,165
1.1	Affecting Life Share in Total Violent Crimes	1,03,660 (45.3 per cent)	1,07,580 (46.7 per cent)	1,13,369 (46.8 per cent)	1,22,679 (47.9 per cent)	1,29,017 (46.9 per cent)
1.2	Affecting Property Share in Total Violent Crimes	28,269 (12.4 per cent)	29,845 (12.9 per cent)	30,366 (12.5 per cent)	31,880 (12.4 per cent)	34,756 (12.6 per cent)
1.3	Affecting Public Safety Share in Total Violent crimes.	75,267 (32.9 per cent)	71,678 (31.1 per cent)	76,079 (31.4 per cent)	77,564 (30.3 per cent)	86,469 (31.4 per cent)
1.4	Affecting women Share in total Violent crimes.	21,467 (9.4 per cent)	21,397 (9.3 per cent)	22,172 (9.2 per cent)	24,206 (9.4 per cent)	24,206 (9.1 per cent)

(*Source:* Crime in India 2012, Compendium, National Crime Record Bureau, Ministry of Home Affairs, Govt. of India, New Delhi (p. 51).[7]

Table 4 states the statistics about incidence of violent crimes reported during 2008-12. Among violent crimes, majority of crimes come under category of crimes against person or affecting life and they are 45 per cent to 48 per cent. The other major category of violent crimes is that of crime 'affecting public safety' and their share is seen in between 30 per cent to 33 per cent. The 'crimes against property' amounts to 12 per cent to 13 per cent and 'crimes affecting women' are about nine per cent to 9.5 per cent.[8] This analysis proves that crimes against persons are almost half of the violent crimes. Even crimes affecting women are also crimes affecting life of women, hence we can say that, such crimes are nearly 55 per cent to 60 per cent of all violent crimes. As in Indian society, inter-personal conflicts within and outside family are growing, as a result of that crimes affecting life are seen growing and taking major share of violent crimes.

Variations in Crime Rates of States

The crime rate is an indicator of proportion of increase in crimes. It is measured as the crimes per one lakh population. As different states are having variation and big differences in their population, thus measuring only number of crimes is not enough to compare the crime's increase or decrease. Therefore, the crime rate is considered as the better measuring tool of crime's growth or fall. The crime rates of different states show the realistic crime situation of states.

Table 5 states the state-wise crime rate of I.P.C. crimes during year 2012. These are the states/union territories which have higher crime rate than the national I.P.C. crime rate average of 196.7. It is surprising to note that the state of South India are among the 15 high I.P.C. crime rate states. Kerala is with highest I.P.C. crime rate 455.8 and other southern states such as Tamil Nadu, Pondicherry, Andhra Pradesh and Karnataka are with higher I.P.C. crime rate than Indian average. Normally, general perception among public is that the crime rate is high in northern states such as U.P. and Bihar, which is not a fact. Madhya Pradesh, Rajasthan, Haryana, Chhattisgarh are the Hindi-speaking states having higher crime rates than national average. Delhi is among top five high crime rate states. From eastern part, Assam and Western part Gujrat are the states in the list of top 15 high crime rates states. Jammu and Kashmir, Kerala and Goa are the three states, which are very important

Table 5. India: State-wise IPC Crime Rate: 2012.

(Top 15 States /Union Territories of India)

S. No.	*States and Union Territories*	*Crime Rate (Crimes per 100,000 Population)*
1.	Kerala	455.8
2.	Madhya Pradesh	298.8
3.	Tamil Nadu	294.8
4.	Pondicherry	291
5.	Delhi	283.3
6.	Assam	250
7.	Rajasthan	246.9
8.	Haryana	240.4
9.	Chandigarh	235.4
10.	Andhra Pradesh	224.5
11.	Karnataka	222.5
12.	Chhattisgarh	221.1
13.	Gujrat	216.6
14.	Jammu & Kashmir	206.5
15.	Goa	196.7
16.	All India Average	196.7

IPC: Indian Penal Code

(*Source:* Crime in India 2012, Compendium, National Crime Record Bureau, Ministry of Home Affairs, Govt. of India, New Delhi (p. 53).[9]

tourist destinations with high rate of crime. On the other hand, the crime rate of states like Uttar Pradesh and Bihar much known and discussed for their criminality are having I.P.C. crime rate lower than the national average of 196.7. The I.P.C. crime rate of Bihar is 147.4 and that of U.P. (Uttar Pradesh) is just 96.4. The state of U.P. actually comes under ten states with lowest I.P.C. crime rate, along with Meghalaya, Uttarakhand, Sikkim, Nagaland. However, in terms of state-wise violent crime rate of 2012, it is noticed that, the state of Bihar with violent crime rate of 30, ranks sixth among top violent crime rate states. At the same time, it is surprising that the Uttar Pradesh even in terms of violent crime rate is well below the national average of 22.7 with violent crime rate of just 16.5. The highest violent crime rate in India is that of Assam state and it is 54.2.[10]

The state-wise I.P.C. crime rate and violent crime rate give us the undercurrents of criminality in India and these crime rates also break the popular misconceptions about states with so-called higher criminality such as Bihar and Uttar Pradesh. The 2012 crime in India report reveals the state like Kerala is with highest I.P.C. crime rate of 455.8 and even ranks third in violent crime rate with 42.7.

Crime against Women

In the year 2011, 2012 and 2013, India as a country was shaken by brutal atrocities on women from case of Nirbhaya to many more untold and unreported cases of violence against women. Violence against women is defined as the "any act of gender-based violence that result in, or is likely to result in, physical, sexual or psychological harm or suffering to women, including threats of such acts, coercion or arbitrary deprivation of liberty, whether occurring in public or in private life"[11] [Jaising Indira 2007]. This is the definition universally accepted and defined by 'the UN declaration on Elimination of violence against Women 1993'. Violence against women make multi-dimensional negative effects on mind, body and lives of Women'.it appears that violence keeps women economically dependent and super -exploited, while economic dependence and exploitation render them unable to combat violence'.[12] [Omvedt Gail 2000]

The resolution of Nari Mukti Sangharsh Sammelan, Patna held on February 8th, 1988 also implicitly states harms of violence against women. 'Women face specific forms of violence: rape and other forms of sexual abuse, female foeticide, witch-killing, Suttee, dowry murders, wife-beating. Such violence and the continued sense of insecurity that is installed in women as a result keeps them bound to the home, economically exploited and socially suppressed'.[13] [Omvedt Gail]

On this background of dangerous after—effects of violence against women, it is necessary to study the trends in such crimes in India during recent past, 'the principles of gender equality is enshrined in the Indian Constitution in its preamble, fundamental rights, fundamental duties and Directive Principles. The constitution not only grants equality to women, but also empowers the state to adopt measures of positive discrimination in favour of women for neutralising the cumulative socio-economic, education and political disadvantages faced by them.'[14] (Reference Note, Loksabha Secretariat, 2013)

The atrocities on women are increasing year by year and these acts are also becoming more and more brutal and heinous. Despite constitutional provisions and stringent laws passed in recent past, disturbing reality is that the crimes against women are growing.

Table 6. India: Crime against Women 2007 to 2012

Under I.P.C. (Indian Penal Code) and S.L.L. (Special and Local Laws)

Year	*Incidence of Crime against Women*
2007	1,85,312
2008	1,95,856
2009	2,03,804
2010	2,13,585
2011	2,28,650
2012	2,44,270

(*Source*: Crime Against Women, Loksabha Secretariat, Reference Note, 2013, p. 9 and Crime in India 2012, National Crime Records Bureau, Ministry of Home Affairs, Govt. of India, p. 87).[15]

Table 7. India: Incidence of Crime Against Women: Percentage of Change from 2002 to 2012

Year	*2004*	*2007*	*2010*	*2012*
Percentage of change over 2002 (Base year 2002)	7.9 per cent	29.6 per cent	49.3 per cent	70.8 per cent

(*Source:* Crime in India 2012 Compendium, NCRB, Ministry of Home Affairs, Govt. of India, p. 86).

The table 6 and 7 present the quantum of crime against women in India increased during recent past 2007 to 2012 and increase in percentage from 2002 to 2012. The incidence of crime against women was 1,85,312 in 2007 and that has increased inteciably to 2,44,270 in the year 2012.[16] This means that crime against women are consistently increasing over the years under study. Therefore, there is growing concern in public at large about atrocities on women in India. Women in general and young women in particular are feeling themselves insecure and psychologically their free movements are self-controlled by the fear. This in a way is restricting their freedom and free movements. Even if we see the increase of incidence of crime against women from year 2002, it is seen that, it is growing with higher and higher rate. In 2004, the increase was 7.9 per cent and in 2007 it went up to 29.6 per cent, in 2010, it reached to 49.3 per cent increase and in 2012 it has increased as high as 70.8 per cent in comparison with year 2002. This proves that, in the decade of 2002-12, growth of incidence of crime was more than 70 per cent. If the crime increases with such high percentage, there is possibility that, it may double with increase of 100 per cent over next decade. During last four/five decades, women are entering more and more in public life by undertaking multiple roles through their empowerment in various sectors of public life by protective discrimination, they are victimised more and more against masculine attitude of Indian Society. Among the crimes against women during 2012, the classification of crime types show that, 43.6 per cent crime against women are of cruelty by husband or his relatives, 7.1 per cent amount to crimes under Dowry prohibition Act and Dowry Deaths. This means that more than 50.7 per cent crime against women are conducted by their family members. These crimes and atrocities took place within four walls of their own house. Indian family system is failing to protect women of their own family. This indicates that Indian family system is becoming sick and unhealthy.

Among other crime against women, the share of heinous crime such as rape is 10.2 per cent that of kidnapping and abduction is 15.7 per cent. The share of assault on women with intention to outrage her modesty is 18.6 per cent and that of insult to the modesty of women is 3.8 per cent. This again means that, insult and assault on modesty constitute 22.4 per cent crime against women. This proves that, women are not treated well in Indian society and their security outside home is also a big question. Atrocities against women in India and their patterns is an evidence, showing that Indian women are insecure within their private as well as public life.

Crime against S.C./S.Ts

The other important weaker sections of Indian society are the Scheduled Caste (S.C.) and the Scheduled Tribes (S.T.)

communities, which are weaker, poor and deprived for centuries because of socio-cultural reasons.

Table 8. India: Crime against S.C./S.Ts (2008 to 2012)

Sr. No.	*Weaker Section*	*Year 2008 Incidence of Crime*	*Year 2010 Incidence of Crime*	*Year 2012 Incidence of Crime*
1.	Scheduled Castes (S.C.)	33,615	32,712	33,655
2.	Scheduled Tribes (S.C.T.)	5,582	5,885	5,922

(*Source:* Reformulated from Crime in India 2012, National Crime Record Bureau, Ministry of Home Affairs, Govt. of India, New Delhi, pp. 110 and 116).

The crimes against S.C. communities have remained between 32,500 to 33,700 during five years of 2008 to 2012. There is not much increase or decrease found in the incidence of crime against S.C. communities. However, after studying state-wise share of crime against S.C. communities it is observed that as much as 57.7 per cent crime against S.C. communities in India took place in only four states namely Uttar Pradesh, Rajasthan, Bihar and Madhya Pradesh states.[17] These are states of Hindi speaking areas, where caste conflicts are more often noticed and deprivation and exploitation of communities is also high in comparison with other states.

In respect of the Scheduled Tribes (S.T.) communities, it is observed that, majority atrocities have taken place in Rajasthan (22.8 per cent), Madhya Pradesh (20.6 per cent), Odisha (11.6 per cent) and Andhra Pradesh (11.2 per cent). The share of all these four states combinely is 66.2 per cent of crime against S.Ts in India. Overall in India, the crime against S.T. have remained in between 5,500 to 6,000 during five years period of 2008 to 2012.[18] One can say that, it's a blot on Indian society that even after six decades of independence, the crime against weaker sections because of actions still rampant caste-system in India. If concerned state government takes stringent against culprits and extend protective surveillance support to under-privileged sections of society, it is possible to control these crimes, which are a shame to any civilised society.

Criminal Justice System: Questionable Efficiency

The Criminal Justice System of any civilised nation plays

an important role in providing justice and punishment to the guilty or criminals. The deterrent role of criminal justice system is, therefore makes impact on crime control. Here, the role of police in investigating any case and filing chargesheet is equally important in giving timely and rightful justice. Public apathy towards police is also due to the fact that quite a large number of cases prosecuted by the police result into the acquittal of accused due to some or other procedural or technical flaws, defects or omission on the part of police officials in dealing with the suspects or offenders. '... Unfortunately, the relationship between the police and Magistracy in India lacks mutual trust and confidence. In quite a large number of cases, police evidence is not considered sufficient and honesty of the police is doubted by the judicial officers'[19] (Paranjape N.V.:175)

The end result of this weaknesses result into low conviction rate. The judicial system is also not efficient and sufficient enough for speedy disposal of cases. The inadequate number of courts and judicial officials result in high amount of pendency of cases and delay injustice.

Hence, the conviction rate indicates how efficient and productive is the criminal justice system.

Table 9. India: Disposal of I.P.C. Crime Cases by Court and Conviction Rate (1972 to 2012).

Sr. No.	*Year*	*Total No. of Cases for Trial (Including pending Cases*	*No. of Case Tried*	*Convicted*	*Conviction Rate*
1.	1972	10,11,699	3,12,744	1,96,089	62.7
2.	1982	23,04,389	5,52,054	2,86,690	51.9
3.	1992	42,74,361	7,33,191	3,40,058	46.3
4.	2002	64,64,748	9,81,393	3,98,830	40.6
5.	2012	93,28,085	12,52,138	4,82,260	38.5

(*Source*: Reformulated Crime in India 2012, NCRB, Ministry Home Affairs, Govt. of India New Delhi, p. 73).[20]

Table 9 gives us the information about the pending cases, tried cases, convicted cases and conviction rate of the disposal by the Courts in India from 1972 to 2012. The statistics and its analysis exhibits that over the years, percentage of cases tried by courts is going down every decade since 1972 to 2012. What is more serious is the conviction rate has lowered down from 62.7 per cent of 1972 to just 38.5 per cent of 2012.[21] This downfall in the conviction rate raises question about the efficiency and performance of judicial system in India. Pendency of more than 80 lakh cases, delay in judicial disposal and lowering of conviction rate shows the inadequate and inefficient judicial infrastructure in India. This needs to be addressed by way of judicial and police reforms and that too of drastic nature. Otherwise, growing crimes, poor investigation, inadequate police force with poor efficiency and constant downfall of conviction rate and low rate of disposal taking the whole criminal justice system towards utter failure. Futile exercise of criminal justice system without adequate success ratio will not give result of crime control. Indian criminal justice system needs breakthrough basic reforms in terms of reengineering the whole structure with more modern, fast, transparent and efficient functioning. The present structure is sick and weak and the time has come to restructure.

References

Durkheim Emile, 1979. The Normal and The Pathological in Kolly H. Dole's (ed). *'Deviant Behaviour-Readings in the Sociological Deviance':* Newyork. St. Martin Press: p. 51.

Crime in India compendium. 2012. National Crime Bureau, Ministry of Home Affairs, Govt. of India: New Delhi: pp. 7-10.

Ibid., 12.

Ibid., 12.

Ibid., 23.

Ibid., 23.

Ibid., 51.

Ibid., 51.

Ibid., 53.

Ibid., 53.

Jaising, Indira, 2007. *'Constitutional Law and The Protection of Women Preventing Violence against Women, in 'Gender Equality and The India Republic'*: Mumbai, Women Development Cell-Mumbai University, Editor Jejurkar Kranti: pp. 25-26.

Omvedt Gail, 2000. *'Violence against Women: New Movements and New Theories in India'*. New Delhi, Kali for Women, p. 5.

Ibid., 1.

Crime against Women Reference Note.2013. Loksabha Secretariat, No. 2/RN/Ref./2013:2.

Ibid., 9.

Crime in India 2012. NCRB. Ministry of Home Affairs, Govt. of India:86.

Ibid., 110.

Ibid., 116.

Paranjape N.V., 1991. *'Criminology and Penology'*, Central Law Agency: Allahabad, Seventh Edition, p. 175.

Crime in India. 2012. *Ibid.*, 73.

Ibid., 73.

4 Is Domestic Violence a Private Dispute or Public Disquiet?

(A Contextual Analysis of the State of the Art on Structural Dualism)

R.K. Mohanty

Introduction

There are a couple of current heuristic concerns about domestic violence in India, nay the world over. What is the content of current public discourse in relation to domestic violence? Is Domestic violence a private family dispute or open public crime against women? Can domestic violence be understood only in terms of violence perpetrated by intimate male against the female partner? Do men/women experience violence in the same way? Does the government or law enforcement agency have a say in something that happens in the home? Several terms are used to denote domestic violence (DV) such as domestic abuse, spousal abuse, battering, intimate partner violence and family violence. It is broadly defined as a type of abusive behaviour by one against other partners in an intimate relationship such as marriage, dating, family, or cohabitation. It is inflicted against the will of the person with the purpose being to humiliate, intimidate, coerce and control the victim, and the victim very often is left without recourse to any remedies: the police and law enforcement mechanisms are often gender-insensitive, hostile or indifferent.

Domestic violence includes forms of violence that perpetuate and exploit the dichotomy between women and men in order to assure the subordination and inferiority of women and everything associated with the feminine. Domestic violence, not only includes physical aggression or assault or threats thereof; but also sexual abuse; psychological abuse; controlling or domineering; intimidation; stalking; passive/covert abuse and economic deprivation. Economic violence can both be a means to make the victim more vulnerable to other forms of violence, but can also be the reason why other forms of violence are inflicted.

World economic figures show that (Ferree, 2004) women generally more economically vulnerable than men. Most typical forms of socio-economic violence include taking away the earnings of the victim, not allowing them to have a separate income ('housewife' status, working in the family business without remuneration), or making her or him unfit for work through targeted physical abuse. This paper through extensive survey of literature attempts to capture the issues accordingly under the following heads—(1) the concepts, (2) world scenario on domestic violence, (3) dualism in domestic violence: private or public, (4) a feminist revision of the public/private, (5) nature of violence perpetrated against men, (6) degree of victimisation of women and men. The paper concludes with an overview of the state of the art.

Several terms are used to denote domestic violence (DV) such as domestic abuse, spousal abuse, battering, and family violence. It is broadly defined as a type of abusive behaviours by one against other partners in an intimate relationship such as marriage, dating, family, or cohabitation. It is inflicted against the will of the person with the purpose being to humiliate, intimidate, coerce and control the victim, and very often the victim is left without recourse to any remedies: the police and law enforcement mechanisms are often gender-insensitive, hostile or indifferent (Copelon, 1994). Domestic violence includes forms of violence that perpetuate and exploit the dichotomy between women and men in order to assure the subordination and inferiority of women and everything associated with the feminine. Domestic violence, not only includes physical aggression or assault or threats thereof; but also sexual abuse; psychological abuse; controlling or domineering; intimidation; stalking; passive/covert abuse and economic deprivation (Shipway, 2004). Economic violence can both be a means to make the victim more vulnerable to other forms of violence, but can also be the reason why other forms of violence are inflicted. World economic figures show that (Ferree, 2004) women generally more economically vulnerable than men. Most typical forms of socio-economic violence include taking away the earnings of the victim, not allowing them to have a separate income ('housewife' status, working in the family business without remuneration), or making her or him unfit for work through targeted physical abuse.

DV and IPV

The term “Intimate Partner Violence” (IPV) is often used synonymously with domestic abuse/domestic violence. Domestic violence is a broader concept, often used to include child abuse, elder abuse, and other violent acts between family members (Wallace, 2004). Wife abuse, wife beating, and battering are descriptive terms that have lost popularity recently for at least two reasons: (1) many victims are not actually married to the abuser, but rather cohabiting or in other arrangements (Waits, 1985) and (2) males as well as females are victims of domestic violence (Johnson, 2005).

The U. S. Office on Violence against Women (OVW) defines domestic violence as a “pattern of abusive behaviour in any relationship that is used by one partner to gain or maintain power and control over another intimate partner”. The definition adds that domestic violence “can happen to anyone regardless of race, age, sexual orientation, religion, or gender”, and can take many forms, including physical abuse, sexual abuse, emotional, economic, and psychological abuse.

The Children and Family Court Advisory and Support Service in the United Kingdom in its “Domestic Violence Policy” reads domestic violence to refer to a range of violent and abusive behaviours, defining it as patterns of behaviour characterised by the misuse of power and control by one person over another who are or have been in an intimate relationship. It can occur in mixed gender relationships and same gender relationships and has profound consequences for the lives of children, individuals and service providers in the families. Distinctions are made among the types of violence, motives of perpetrators, and the social and cultural context based upon patterns across numerous incidents and motives of the perpetrator.

In 1983, domestic violence was recognised as a specific criminal offence by the introduction of section 498-A into the Indian Penal Code. This section deals with cruelty by a husband or his family towards a married woman. The recognition of domestic violence as a crime has resulted in broadening the understanding of what domestic violence is, who may seek protection under the Domestic Violence Act, 2005, and what type of protection may be sought (Mohanty and Mohanty, 2012). Laws in India to deal with domestic violence do exist and they include Section 113(a) of the Indian Evidence Act, Section 498(a) and 304(b) of the Indian Penal Code and the Dowry Prohibition Act, 1961 as amended in the year 1986.

Johnson (1995, 2000, 2006 and 2006) argues for three major types and one rare type of intimate partner violence. Types of violence (IPV) identified by Johnson are: (1) Common Couple Violence (CCV) is not connected to general control behaviour, but arises in a single argument where one or both partners physically lash out at the other, (2) Intimate Terrorism (IT) may also involve emotional and psychological abuse. Intimate terrorism is one element in a general pattern of control by one partner over the other. Intimate terrorism is less common than common couple violence, more likely to escalate over time, not as likely to be mutual, and more likely to involve serious injury. IT batterers include two types: "generally-violent-antisocial" and "dysphoric-borderline". The first type includes men with general psychopathic and violent tendencies. The second type is men who are emotionally dependent on the relationship. Support for this typology has been found in subsequent evaluations (Hamberger, et.al, 1996), (3) Violent Resistance (VR), sometimes thought of as "self-defence", is violence perpetrated by victims against their abusive partners, (4) Mutual Violent Control (MVC) is rare type of intimate partner violence occurs when both partners act in a violent manner, battling for control (Johnson and Ferraro, 2000; Saunders, 1988). Types of male batterers identified by Holtzworth-Munroe and Stuart (1994) include "family-only", which primarily fall into the CCV type, who are generally less violent and less likely to perpetrate psychological and sexual abuse.

According to the Duluth Model (2008), women and children are vulnerable to violence because of their unequal social, economic, and political status in society. The Duluth Model suggests that "violence is patriarchal". The model focuses solely on the men's use of violence in abusive relationships, rather than on the behaviour of all parties concerned. This helps the men to focus on changing their personal behaviour in order to be nonviolent in any relationship. The model relates to a "Power and Control Wheel" to illustrate this: it has power and control at the centre, surrounded by spokes (techniques used), the titles of which include: coercion and threats, intimidation, emotional abuse, isolation, minimising, denying and blaming, using

Table 1. Use of Power and Control in Domestic Violence

Sr. No.	*Use of Power and Control*	*Type of Violence*
1.	Using Male Privilege:	Treating her like a servant; making all the big decisions; acting like the "master of the castle" ; being the one to define men's and women's roles
2.	Using Economic Abuse:	Preventing her from getting or keeping a job; making her ask for money; giving her an allowance; taking her money; not letting her know about or have access to family income
3.	Using Coercion and Threats:	Making and/or carrying out threats to do something to hurt her; threatening to leave her; threatening to report her to welfare; making her drop legal charges; making her do illegal things
4.	Using Intimidation:	Making her afraid by using looks, actions, gestures; yelling; throwing furniture; smashing things; destroying her property; abusing pets; displaying weapons
5.	Using Emotional Abuse:	Putting her down; making her feel bad about herself; calling her names; making her think she's crazy; playing mind games; humiliating her; making her feel guilty
6.	Using Isolation:	Controlling what she does; who she sees and talks to; what she reads; where she goes; limiting her outside involvement; using jealousy to justify actions
7.	Minimizing, Denying and Blaming:	Making light of the abuse and not taking her concerns about it seriously; saying the abuse didn't happen; shifting responsibility for abusive behaviour; saying she caused it
8.	Using Children:	Making her feel guilty about the children; using the children to relay messages; using visitation to harass her; threatening to take the children away

Source: The Domestic Abuse Intervention Project in Duluth, University of Minnesota 2008 (Compiled).

children, economic abuse, male privilege. The model attempts to address abuse by challenging the misuse of power by the perpetrator. The power wheel model is not intended to assign personal responsibility, enhance respect for mutual purpose or assist victims and perpetrators in resolving their differences. It is an informational tool designed to help individuals understand the dynamics of power operating in abusive situations and identify various methods of abuse.

World Scenario on Domestic Violence

Domestic violence is one of the few phenomena which cut across all the cultural, socio-economic, educational, ethnic and religious barriers. Violence against wives has a very long history: laws authorising husbands to chastise their wives date back to 753 B.C., when Romulus ruled in Rome (Kelly, 2002; Okun, 1986:2). Domestic violence occurs across the world in various cultures, (Watts and Zimmerman, 2002) and affects people of all economic statuses (Waits, 1985). Modern attention to domestic violence began in the women's movement of the 1970s, particularly within feminism and women's rights, as concern about wives being beaten by their husbands gained attention. The first known use of the expression "domestic violence" in a modern context, meaning "spouse abuse, violence in the home" was in an address to the Parliament of the United Kingdom in 1973. Then the world's first domestic violence services federation (Women's Aid) was set up in 1974, providing practical and emotional support as part of a range of services to women and children experiencing violence in England. With the rise of the men's movement of the 1990s, the problem of domestic violence against men has also gained significant attention. Harvard Psychology Professor Steven Pinker argues that feminism has reduced domestic violence, especially against men as their likelihood of being killed by a female intimate partner has decreased six-fold (Pinker, 2011). According to one study, the percentages of women who have reported being physically abused by an intimate partner vary from 69 per cent to 10 per cent depending on the country (Heise et.al., 1999). Evidence that wife abuse was common can be found not only in legal codes, but also in religious documents, personal testimonies from victims, court records, newspaper accounts, and published discussions by authors such as—Cobbe (1878), "Wife Torture in England," and John Stuart Mill, The Subjection of Women, ed. Wendell Robert Carr (1989).

In the United States, according to the Bureau of Justice Statistics in 1995, women reported a six times greater rate of intimate partner violence than men (Bachman and Saltzman, 1995). The National Crime Victimisation Survey (NCVS) indicates that in 1998 about 876,340 violent crimes were committed in the U.S. against women by their current or former spouses, or boy-friends. According to the Centres for Disease Control, in the United States 4.8 million women suffer intimate partner related physical assaults and rapes and 2.9 million men are victims of physical assault from their partners. However, studies have found that men are much less likely to report victimisation in these situations. According to some studies, less than one per cent of domestic violence cases are reported to the police (Roberts and Springer, 2007). In the United States 10–35 per cent of the population will be physically aggressive towards a partner at some point in their lives (Archer, 2000; Fiebert, 2011). As abuse becomes more severe women become increasingly overrepresented as victims (Straus, 1999).

Violence by intimate family members is one of South Asia's darkest legacies. In a survey on violence against women in India, 94 per cent of the cases involved an offender who was a member of the family (*Ibid.*). Freedom not only from violence but also from the threat of violence is the first indicator of rise in women's capacity for survival and empowerment (Seth, 2010). The United Nations Declaration on the Elimination of Violence against Women states in its preamble that violence against women is a product of the "unequal power relations" that characterise gender relations in all parts of the world. Violence against women is a universal reality but at the same time it is invisible. The UNDP's gender development index ranks India 108 among 174 countries in terms of gender equity.

In the North-Eastern states, women related violence is highest among the *Khasi* society in Meghalaya which is a matriarchal society where the status of women is higher than that of men. Women inherit all family properties and who brings her husband into her home. However, the other issue which deserves further investigation is whether hyper-masculinity or hyper-femininity inbreeds more violence against women. Next to Meghalaya comes Mizoram which is a patriarchal society. The MHIP (Mizo Hmeichhe Inzawmkhawm Pawl), the most active woman organisation in the state has been trying to eradicate the commercialisation of bride-price, the dowry system, sexual exploitation of women of any kind and inequality between man and woman. However, in spite of this movement launched by the MHIP, violence against woman is still higher leaving a great concern (Coomaraswamy, 2005).

Fighting the prevalence of domestic violence in Kashmir has brought Hindu and Muslim activists together in 2009. Additionally, aspects of Islamic law have been criticised for promoting domestic violence (Constable Pamela, 2007). One study found that half of Palestinian women have been the victims of domestic violence (Alexander, 2000). 80 per cent of women surveyed in rural Egypt said that beatings were common and often justified, particularly if the woman refused to have sex with her husband. The Human Rights Watch found that up to 90 per cent of women in Pakistan were subject to some form of maltreatment within their own homes. Unofficial statistics estimate that 97 per cent of Indian women experience violence at some point in their lives. Up to two-thirds of women in certain communities in Nigeria's Lagos State say they are victims to domestic violence. Statistics published in 2004 show that the rate of domestic violence—victimisation for Indigenous women in Australia may be 40 times the rate for non-Indigenous women. In Turkey, 42 per cent of women over 15 have suffered physical or sexual violence (Tahir, 2011).

Dualism in Domestic Violence: Private or Public

Abuse and violence is a widespread problem which lies hidden within communities irrespective of class and race. It occurs behind closed doors and the most common victims are women, often because standards set by society restrict them from speaking out or seeking help. Women may fear the stigma to their families or humiliation and loss of reputation in society. The dualism between public and private spheres of action has been identiûed as a key feature of Western, liberal thought. Dualism is the desire to see our world in term of opposites, such as good and bad, success and failure, heaven and hell, daughter and son, left and right, light and dark, past and future and so on. One of the greatest challenges facing the domestic violence movement is the widespread perception that spousal abuse is a "private matter." There is a felt need in order to move a private matter into the sphere of public concern and to translate that public concern into a widespread social consensus for action (Ghez and Marin, 2002). It seems that out of this thinking a lot of our assumptions, concepts and expectations materialise. Sometimes this leads to stress, disappointment and unhappiness.

According to Carole Pateman (1989), the feminist critique of the dualism between public and private "is central to almost two centuries of feminist writing and political struggle; it is, ultimately what the feminist movement is about". Although the terms public and private are used quite differently in feminist debates, there are two assumptions that can be considered as common grounds. On one hand, the dichotomy is criticised, as it implies a hierarchical, sexualised and gendered binary order. On the other hand, the assumption of a clear distinction between two spheres is called into question. The representation of the public world as superior to the private, and the traditional location of women within the latter renders them largely invisible in public life.

For a long time in history, the inferior position of women or certain ethnic or racial minorities was considered natural. Therefore, acts that are now considered human rights violation were not widely condemned because the victims of these violation were not acknowledged by those in power in society to have those rights. Civil and political rights (the so-called first-generation rights) (Titley, 2007), for example, are mainly concerned with violence in the public sphere and with limiting the state and its representatives in perpetrating violence as a means to abuse power. This has meant that specific forms of violence against women have gone unnoticed, or have only been gradually addressed. The very terms 'husband' and 'wife' embody gendered relationship, based on male dominance and female submission. The meaning of 'wife' is embodied in traditional culture as 'gendered property'. There has been long debate about the privacy of the family (Pagelow, 1984). There are those who support the sanctity of the privacy of the family, and resist the intrusion of outside forces, viewing intrusion as anti-family. Correlated with this attitude is support for traditional gender relations within the family. The opposing argument is that the distinction between private and public is artificial and serves the interests of those with power. The family is often not a haven of happiness and safety, and may require outside forces to assist and protect less powerful family members.

The context in which men abuse their partners is complex

because intimate relationships are sites of highly charged emotions involving a multitude of tangled, subtle meaning, many supported by cultural prescription. The emotional nature of intimate relationships and their location in the private/domestic sphere makes it difficult, if not impossible, to develop a simple single solution to the problem. What may be effective in assisting one victim/survivor may be rejected by another. What may be effective in stopping one abuser may backfire with another. Assault and violence in the private/domestic context is at least as criminal as violence in a public context and must be dealt with by the criminal justice system. Abuse and violence in intimate relationships is not the result of normal conflict between two equals.

According to Pagelow, (1984:13) "some of the insistence on maintaining family privacy is based on the historical establishment of patriarchal marriage and common law rights and privileges". Marriage under the common law of England (a heritage adopted in USA and Australia) was the merger of husband and wife into a single legal identity—that of the husband. Until recently, wives relatively had no right to sell, sue or contract without their husband's approval. This notion of a single legal identity has provided immunity from testifying against or suing a spouse and maintained the fiction that there is no such thing as spousal rape.

"Today, domestic assault is illegal in every state. However, confusion about whether this is a public or a private problem has not disappeared. On the one hand, the criminalisation of domestic violence transforms into a problem warranting intervention and even sanction. On the other hand, very low reporting levels, police and judicial indifference, and a pattern of blaming the victim all suggest that many people, including some victims, continue to see domestic violence as a private matter" (Kelly, 2003:2). Kelly argues that our misguided notion of privacy, derived from Locke, undergirds this confusion. Drawing upon feminist theory and interviews with professionals who work with battered women, she theorises a more nuanced version of privacy that would permit or perhaps even require public responses to domestic violence. Notably, these "public responses" go beyond legal intervention to include community forces and organisations.

Kelly discusses Locke's distinction of public and private. A closer examination of Locke's theory reveals two different models of public and private. The first separates the family from politics; the second separates the individual and the state. The first model is premised on his exhaustive discussion of the difference between political and paternal power. Here he creates a picture of social relations in which the domestic realm is defined as paradigmatically private and the political realm of state power is defined as public. The second model arises from Locke's efforts to explain how individuals, who supposedly are born into a state of freedom and equality, are able to consent to a government without relinquishing the natural freedom that is theirs by God's intention. Locke solves this dilemma by reducing the government's involvement in citizens' lives to that of a referee in cases of direct conflict between individuals. Within this second model, the family plays a crucial role. Locke depicts it as a relatively peaceful association that in contrast to civil society does not require the continuous presence of a neutral arbitrator with the power over life and death to maintain order. Thus, the domestic realm provides Locke with the conceptual and the physical space for individuals to realise their potential as rational free beings even after they have consented to partial rule by government.

An important thread to this argument is that Locke presents two models of public and private that we conflate—one operating to separate the family from political life, and one operating to separate the individual from the state (*Ibid.* 20). From the first model we conceive of family life as a private matter, and from the second we conceive of privacy as being left alone. Kelly argues that a family of liberal individuals, who seek to develop themselves, in part through connection to others in this primary and private unit, poses a problem. All is well when we assume a harmony of interests among family members, but Locke's models of privacy are inadequate for helping us to conceive of responses to the pervasive reality of family violence.

In contexts where rigid gender roles are more determining, the batterer has more freedom to deny responsibility. The set of gender roles that we are taught belong to—as women and men contain many contradictions, or demands that cannot be fulfilled. At the same time, part of the hegemonic male gender role is to oversee women and children in fulfilling their roles, and if necessary, discipline them. These two conditions combine to create a common justification for those who are abusive in relationship because they can easily find something or another to (a) blame the woman for the violence committed against her, and (b) to claim the right to inflict it (Titley, 2007).

The ideology of patriarchy has viewed the family in 'ideal' terms as a place of private succour (particularly for men who experience the vicissitudes of the 'public' arena). Writers such as Lasch (1977) and Donzelot (1979) have eulogised the family as a 'haven in a heartless world' and rallied against what they saw as intrusions by the state into this 'private' domain. In so doing, they endorsed the 'rule of the father' as the legitimate 'head of the household' with the authority and responsibility to have power and control over women and children. The dominant religions of Christianity, Islam, Hinduism and Judaism have long supported patriarchy. The ideology of possessive individualism and self-reliance also supported the notion of the home being the realm of the 'private'. The development of suburban living with individual, self-contained, nuclear households has meant that 'privacy' is even more possible – and culturally seen as desirable. Thus, there are three key notions that permit wife abuse to occur with little or no 'interference' from outside. First is the 'idealised' notion of the home as a haven from the outside world, a place of security, happiness and contentment with stereotypical male and female gender roles. Second is the notion that occurs in the home as 'private' and is not the province of outsiders, particularly agencies of the state and third is notion of the individual who is self-determining and unconnected to society (Gardiner,1996: 23).

The reasons behind women staying in a violent relationship (Titley, 2007) include financial dependence on the abuser, social constraints, and a lack of alternatives such as shelters for abuse victims. Domestic violence often involves isolation of the victim from the family and friends, deprivation of personal possession, manipulation of children, threats of reprisals against her and her children or other family members. Furthermore, common social pressures regarding the nature of the family–'some kind of father is better than no father for your children'—makes getting out of an abusive relationship not only difficult but also extremely dangerous.

The residual area of domestic jurisdiction has been greatly

reduced by human rights law which itself adds another layer of public/private opposition through its traditional applicability only to the relations between the state and individuals, through the acts of public officials. Human rights discourse thus largely excludes abuses committed by private actors. The idea is to delineate the reserved area from international intrusion. Feminist writers argue that the liberal opposition between public life, the domain of business, economics, politics and law, and private life, the domestic sphere of the family, has both supported and obscured the structural subordination of women. The separation of public and private spheres has traditionally been supported by the state. This parallels the traditional distinction between male and female roles in our society. The private or domestic sphere has been associated with women's 'expressive' roles while the public sphere has been popularly understood as men's 'instrumental' sphere of activity and influence (Parsons and Bales, 1955). Domestic violence, or intimate partnership violence is very different from violent incidents that occur among strangers. Consideration of domestic violence as a private, domestic issue has significantly hampered recognition of the phenomenon as a human rights violation. The invisibility of the phenomenon was exacerbated by the fact that traditionally, international human rights law was believed to be applicable to relations between individual and the state and human rights organisations focused only on politically motivated violations (such as torture or the inhumane treatment of prisoners). However, it has gradually become recognised that state responsibility under international law can arise not only from state action, but also from state inaction where the state fails to protect its citizens from violent crimes.

A Feminist Revision of the Public/Private

Kelly (2003) divides feminist theories into three camps, all of which criticise liberal theory's public/private dichotomy. In this ideological division, women are typically relegated to the private realm, thereby denying them opportunities for development as citizens, removing women's voice from public policy decisions, and aiding the characterisation of domestic violence as a private affair (pp. 33-34). Dividing these feminist camps is their responses to the public and private dichotomy. Radical feminists such as MacKinnon (1984) propose the elimination of the public/private distinction, on the grounds that the dichotomy will always lead to women's subordination. Conservative feminists such as Elshtain (1981) criticises the radical feminists for undercutting the family. Elshtain (1981:38-41) holds the family to be necessary; happily, it is also a possible site for women, through their mothering, to transform the public realm through the development of values such as compassion and sensitivity. While liberal feminists also reject the radical feminist project of obliterating the public/private dichotomy, they tend to focus on reducing barriers to equal participation in the public realm by women. The trouble with all three camps, according to Kelly is that they are essentialist, treating all women alike: "The differences among feminist theorists concerning the public/private split can be traced to a fundamental disagreement among them regarding the aspect of women's lives most in need of liberation. Is it women as mothers, women as individuals, or women as sex objects?" (*Ibid.* 49). Kelly's own position then emerges from the complexity of and tension between women's multiple identities and roles.

As mentioned above, it is possible to identify some common ground between those feminist positions which, despite being critical of the public/private dichotomy, still think of it as a useful framework. After all, the definition of what is private and what is public is decisive for the allocation of power and resources (Fraser, 1997). In this context, public/private is often considered as an analytical concept, rejecting the "mechanistic separation of the two spheres" (Bargetz, 2009), while not denying the real consequences following from the dichotomy. Bargetz, Brigitte (2009) analyses three criticisms on public/private distinction. Firstly, the public/private distinction has been criticised to reproduce a dichotomous thinking that it was meant to overcome in the first place (Chris and Squires, 2002:161). As critics point out, dichotomies like public/private, mind/body, reason/emotion, etc. are not neutral and innocent but imply powerful and exclusionary hierarchies. Starting from a critique of the opposition reason/emotion, Prokhovnik, seeks to elaborate an alternative to dichotomous thinking by exploring the potential of a relational theory. Dichotomous thinking, she posits, inevitably entails an opposition between two identities that are hierarchically ordered. Subsequently, she identifies four specific problematic aspects: Because dichotomous thinking is gendered and sexualised, it "leads specifically to the denigration of women" (Prokhovnik, 1999:37) An additional conceptual problem occurs when the dichotomy is accepted as dominant cultural metaphor and thus powerfully determines further ways of thinking and acting. A third problem arises with dichotomy when it is applied to the conception of truth, which presupposes "that only one party can be right" whereas "the other must be wrong" (*Ibid.* 33). Finally, Prokhovnik argues, thinking within a dichotomous frame leads to constituting two and just two parts of a whole, and therefore rejects a "prospect of heterogeneity" (*Ibid.* 31-38).

Whereas Prokhovnik's critic of Eurocentric dichotomous thinking relates to its epistemological and philosophical foundations, Chris and Squires (*Ibid.*) question the empirical-analytical value of the dichotomy. They doubt that the public/private distinction may be an adequate instrument for keeping up "with the current means by which sexual inequalities are perpetuated" (*Ibid.*). Conceiving the distinction rather as empirically irrelevant and politically ineffective, they share Diana Coole's (2000:347) suggestion that the categories of public and private should be discarded and replaced by "new maps".

The usefulness of the public/private frame has been criticised by Black feminists as a liberal and white concept. Pointing out that public/private does not mean the same thing for different women, these critics reveal the concept's Eurocentric bias. Collins (1991), for example, argues that for African-American communities, public and private may not be useful categories, since they rely on the "archetypal white, middle-class nuclear family". Since racial oppression has impoverished many Black families, Black women and other women of colour seldom fit this model. Poor families, she argues, do not have the same distinction, equating private with home and public with work, as Black women's paid labour is often domestic labour. Therefore, black women's labour has also often been neglected by feminist discourses.

The dominant feminist critique of the liberal public/private distinction focuses on the patriarchal oppression of women in the realm as well as through the existence of the separated realm of the private. However, some feminists question this conception because of its devaluation of the private. While acknowledging the private as a place of deprivation and violence-historically as well as at present—they enhance a more ambivalent vision of the private by emphasising its empowering potentials. Thus, Bell Hooks (1990:42) points out that home can constitute a site of resistance and of "self-conscious constructed identity". "Historically," she concedes, "African American people believed that the construction of a home place, however, fragile and tenuous (the slave hut, the wooden shack), had a radical political dimension". That the gendered and sexualised distinction of "public man and private woman" cannot be maintained empirically has been strongly disputed by feminists pointing for example to the active participation of women in public in different historical contexts, to current movements of girl power, or to the feminisation of the workforce. Emphasing the "critical liberating potential" (Young, 1997:134) and therefore a more positive vision of the home, both Hooks and Young, reject a public/private opposition that mainly focuses on the private as the sphere of deprivation, and instead bring forward a more ambivalent conception of the private.

Feminists argue that people are often reluctant to use the power of the state in cases of domestic violence. To them, many victims are reluctant to report abuse, and many law enforcement and court personnel are reluctant to use their discretion and resources to pursue these matters they conceive of as private. The criminalisation of domestic violence and the sensitising of criminal justice agents should by no means be abandoned (Ghez and Marin, 2002). Nancy Fraser (1990:56-80) points out that "there are no naturally given, *a priori* boundaries" between matters that are generally conceived as private i.e. of "individual concern", and ones we typically label as public (*i.e.* of "common concern"). As an example, she refers to the historic shift in the general conception of domestic violence, from previously being a matter of primarily private concern, to now generally being accepted as a common one: "Eventually, after sustained discursive contestation we succeeded in making it a common concern". Domestic violence and communal violence are acquiring disturbing dimensions—one within the private sphere of the household and the other in the public domain of civil society (Shabana Azmi, 2003). She says, "In fact, all other freedoms lose their shine and become meaningless unless all individuals are ensured a life without fear' (*Ibid.*).

Studies suggest that the most common causes for women stalking and battering include dissatisfaction with the dowry and exploiting women for more of it, arguing with the partner, refusing to have sex with him, neglecting children, going out of home without telling the partner, not cooking properly or on time, indulging in extra-marital affairs, not looking after in-laws etc. In some cases, infertility in females also leads to their assault by the family members. The greed for dowry, desire for a male child and alcoholism of the spouse are major factors of domestic violence against women in rural areas. There have been gruesome reports of young bride being burnt alive or subjected to continuous harassment for not bringing home the amount of demanded dowry. Women in India also admit to hitting or beating because of their suspicion about the husband's sexual involvement with other women. The *Tandoor Murder Case* of Naina Sahni in New Delhi in the year 1995 is one such dreadful incident of a woman being killed and then burnt in a *tandoor* by his husband. This incidence was an outcome of suspicion of extra-marital affairs of Naina Sahni which led to marital discord and domestic violence against her (Seth, 2010).

Violence against Men: Is it an Issue?

Awareness, perception, definition and documentation of domestic violence differ widely from country to country, and from era to era. Findings of studies regarding the prevalence of domestic violence vary significantly, depending on specific wording of survey questions, how the survey is conducted, the definition of abuse or domestic violence used, the willingness or unwillingness of victims to admit that they have been abused and other factors. Straus (2005) conducted a study which estimated that the rate of minor assaults by women in the United States was 78 per 1,000 couples, compared with a rate for men of 72 per 1,000 and the severe assault rate was 46 per 1,000 couples for assaults by women and 50 per 1,000 for assaults by men. Neither difference is statistically significant. He claimed that since these rates were based exclusively on information provided by women respondents, the near-equality in assault rates could not be attributed to a gender bias in reporting (*ibid.*).

There is no question that domestic violence directed against women is a serious and bigger problem, but domestic violence against men is also increasing gradually in India. The supremacy of men in the society makes one believe that they are not vulnerable to domestic violence. Battering of men by their spouse and family members has become a latest issue and is another form of domestic violence under purview of judiciary. In India, compared to violence against women, violence against men is less frequent but it has already taken a deadly shape in many of the western countries by now (Martin, 1999:418). Males have reported incidences of assault against them like pushing, shoving, slapping, grabbing, hitting which are intended to harm them and also take their lives on many occasions. Recently, hundreds of husbands gathered in Chandigarh and Shimla to voice their opinion for men's rights and protection against domestic violence subjected to them by their wives and other family members. It reflects the need for a special law for curbing domestic violence against men in present times (*Ibid.*).

Studies reveal some of the possible causes such as not abiding by the instructions of the wives', inadequate earning of men, infidelity towards wives, not helping the partner in household activities, not taking a proper care of children, abusing the spouse's family, infertility of men, spying the activities of partner, doubting the partner all the time and not trusting her, revolt by the wife when asked to look after in-laws etc. On many occasions, the spat between men and women becomes public thereby influencing the society around especially in the villages. In urban areas, such forms of violence may go unreported because of greater privacy. The families also find their reputation at stake in urban areas.

One analysis found that "women are as physically aggressive or more aggressive than men in their relationship with their spouses or male partners". However, studies have shown that women are more likely to be injured. Archer's meta-analysis (Archer, 2000) found that women in the United States suffer 65 per cent of domestic violence injuries. A Canadian study showed that seven per cent of women and six per cent of men were abused by their current or former partners, but female victims of spousal violence were more than twice as likely to be injured as male victims, three times more likely to fear for their life, twice as likely to be stalked, and twice as likely to experience more than ten incidents of violence (Time Magazine, 1995). However, Straus notes that Canadian studies on domestic violence have simply excluded questions that ask men about being victimised by their wives (Straus, 2005).

Determining how many instances of domestic violence actually involve male victims is difficult. Male domestic violence victims may be reluctant to get help for a number of reasons. Another study has demonstrated a high degree of acceptance by women of aggression against men (Straus, 2006). Problems in conducting studies that seek to describe violence in terms of gender is the amount of silence, fear and shame that results from abuse within families and relationships. Another is that abusive patterns can tend to seem normal to those who have lived in them for a length of time. Similarly, subtle forms of abuse can be quite transparent even as they set the stage for further abuse seeming normal. Finally, inconsistent definition of what constitutes domestic violence makes definite conclusions difficult to reach when compiling the available studies. Theories that women are as violent as men have been dubbed "gender symmetry" theories (Archer, 2000; O'Leary, 2000; Frieze, 2000; White et.al, 2000 and Johnson, 2005).

Straus and Gelles (1990) found that in couples reporting spousal violence, 27 per cent of the time the man struck the first blow; in 24 per cent of cases, the woman initiated the violence. The rest of the time, the violence was mutual, with both partners brawling. The results were the same even when the most severe episodes of violence were analysed. In order to counteract claims that the reporting data was skewed, female-only surveys were conducted, asking females to self-report, and the data was the same. The simple tally of physical acts is typically found to be similar in those studies that examine both directions, but some studies show that male violence may be more serious. Male violence may do more damage than female violence. Women are more likely to be injured and/or hospitalised. Wives are more likely to be killed by their husbands than the reverse (59 per cent to 41per cent, Department of Justice study), and women in general are more likely to be killed by their spouses than by all other types of assailants combined (Angela and Kirk, 1989).A 1997 report says significantly more men than women do not disclose the identity of their attacker (Rand and Strom, 1997). One researcher, however, says that there is no evidence that male victims are more likely to under-report than female victims. In fact, men tend to over-estimate their partner's violence and under-estimate their own, while women do the reverse (Kimmel, 2001). A 2009 study showed that there was greater acceptance for abuse perpetrated by females than by males (Robertson and Tamar, 2009). Several studies have confirmed that women's physical violence towards intimate male partners is often in self-defence (Swan and Snow, 2002; Muelleman and Burgess, 1998).

Degree of Victimisation of Women and Men

Domestic violence is a significant problem. Measures of the incidence of violence in intimate relationship can differ markedly in their finding depending on the measures used. Survey approaches tend to show parity in the use of violence by both men and women against partners than do approaches using data from reports of domestic violence that tends to show women experiencing violence from male partners as the majority of cases (over 80 per cent). Research based on reported domestic violence or on police records show men to be responsible for the majority of domestic violence and the high frequency of women as victims. The problem of under-reporting is believed to be substantial.

There are a number of reasons (Gardiner, 1996: 28) for the lack of reporting or recording: (a) victim/survivors feel shame and humiliation at revealing that the person who society expects to love them, actually despises them enough to hurt them; (b) The privacy in which the abuse occurs means there are no supporting witnesses, except perhaps children; (c) Cultural attitudes that condone 'wife' abuse; (d) Denial that what is occurring is abuse or is a serious problem; (e) Economic dependence on the abuser; (f) Lack of access to information and services; (g) The perception that nothing can be done to stop the abuse; (h) Belief that the victim/survivor may have deserved it or the husband had the right to be violent; (i) Emotional attachment to the abuser, particularly if he is the children's father.

Although reliable, gender-sensitive statistics are still rare, there is evidence to suggest that women and men experience violence in different ways (Titley, 2007). The World Health Organisation's World Report on Violence and Health notes that whereas men '...are much more likely to be attacked by a stranger or an acquaintance than by someone within their close circle of relationships...one of the most common forms of violence against women is that performed by a husband or male partner' (*Ibid.*). In other words, women experience more violence in the private sphere, whereas for men it is more likely to occur in the public sphere.

Erin Pizzey (1982), the founder of an early women's shelter in Chiswick, London, expressed an unpopular view in her book, *Prone to Violence*, that some women in the refuge system had a predisposition to seek abusive relationship. She also expressed the view that domestic violence can occur against any vulnerable intimates, regardless of sex. In the same book, Erin Pizzey stated that, of the first 100 women to enter the refuge, 62 were as violent, or more violent, than the men they were, allegedly, running away from.

The statistics cited by *Women's Aid* and *Ahimsa* are that violence by women against men is a tiny proportion of all domestic violence is rejected by advocates for male victims of domestic violence. They claim that this finding is based on the situation that many studies report only male-on-female violence because that is all they ask about, those studies that do examine prevalence in both directions overwhelmingly find little difference by gender. Martin S. Fiebert of the Department of Psychology at California State University, Long Beach, has provided an analysis (2011) of 195 scholarly investigations: 152 empirical studies and 43 analyses, which he believes demonstrate women are as physically aggressive, or more aggressive, than men. The aggregate sample size exceeds 175,700.

The U.S. National Family Violence Survey has consistently indicated, in repeated surveys over more than 30 years, that women are more than twice as likely as men to initiate domestic assault, and more than twice as likely to use weapons. Other studies have demonstrated a high degree of acceptance by women of aggression against men. The available data (BBC Survey on 16.06. 2006 indicates that million men experience "minor" abuse (such as "pushing, grabbing, shoving, slapping, and hitting") per year. In the United States, approximately 800,000 men per year (3.2 per cent) are raped or physically assaulted by their partner. At least 371,000 men are stalked annually. Three per cent of nonfatal violence against men stems from domestic violence. In 2002, men comprised 24 per cent of domestic violence homicide victims. Over 20 years, the instances of homicide from domestic violence against men decreased by approximately 67 per cent. Approximately 22 per cent of men have experienced physical, sexual, or psychological intimate partner violence during their life (Centre for Disease Control and Prevention, Intimate Partner Violence: Fact Sheet, Atlanta Georgia, 2006). There are many reasons why there is not more information about domestic abuse and violence against men. A major reason is the reluctance of men to report incidents to the police, unless there are substantial injuries. Data indicate that although mutual violent behaviour is quite common in intimate relationships, men are rarely harmed seriously.

The Australian Bureau of Statistics Personal Safety Survey (2006), show that overall, more males than females are victims of physical assault (10.8 per cent *vs* 5.8 per cent). However, women are most at risk of assault in the home and from men they know, while men are most at risk of assault in public spaces and from men they don't know. Among the large numbers of men physically assaulted each year, close to 70 per cent were assaulted by strangers. Less than five per cent were assaulted by a female partner or ex-partner. In contrast, among the female victims of physical assault, 31 per cent were assaulted by a male partner or ex-partner. Thirty per cent of people who had experienced violence by a current partner since the age of 15 were male, while 70 per cent were female. In the European Union (EU), one in five women suffers some form of domestic violence. Ninety-five per cent of this violence occurs in the home. According to Respecting Accuracy in Domestic Abuse Reporting (RADAR) report in USA, women are just as likely as men to engage in partner aggression. Men experience over one-third of domestic violence-related injuries (Archer, 2000). Men are far less likely to report domestic violence incidents than women (Stets and Straus, 1990). The myths about domestic violence are numerous (Gelles, 1997). Many of these myths are based on domestic violence studies that use biased survey methods (Arriaga and Oskamp, 1999).

According to a report produced by Southern Connecticut State University: In 95 per cent of family violence cases the victims are women beaten by male partners. In one per cent of the cases the reverse is true. There are an estimated 28 million battered women in the U.S., more than half of all married women in the country. In the U.S., one woman is beaten by her husband or partner every 9 seconds. Battering is the single major cause of injury to women between the ages of 15 and 44 in the U.S.; more than car accidents, muggings, and rapes combined. 70 per cent of the assault victims seen in the emergency room of Boston City Hospital are women who have been attacked in their own homes. Research published in the Journal of Family Psychology says that contrary to media and public opinion women commit more acts of violence than men in eleven categories: Throw something, push, grab, shove, slap, kick, bite, hit or threaten a partner with a knife or gun (Capaldi, D.M., et.al., 2004). A study reported in Washington Times (12.06.2006), which is based on interviews with 1,615 married or cohabiting couples and extrapolated nationally using census data, found that 21 per cent of couples reported domestic violence.

An Overview

When violence occurs within the context of these competing goals, a wide range of troublesome questions result. For instance, should a victim's primary concern be to protect her by leaving, or should she stay to work things out so that the family is not torn apart? How far should the external agencies go to protect victims or potential victims from violence? What is the role of neighbours, the church, and/or the community more generally in addressing instances of domestic violence? If a victim does not want to leave or prosecute her abuser (even in extreme cases), should she be allowed to stay in a situation even if it means subjecting herself and her children to continued abuse?

Most speculation has focused on the individual recipients of abuse. The emphasis is not surprising, for the victim most clearly embodies and expresses the associated tensions. The battered woman who protects her abuser by denying the abuse (sometimes in the presence of the police) embodies the contradictions that occur when an individual seeks simultaneously to protect herself and her family. The apparent dilemma/trauma in such behaviour rivets the heuristic attention on why she responds in the manner that she does. Many people simply are not able to get past such questions as "Why does she stay?" and "What did she do to cause a person who loves her to commit such violent acts?" Unfortunately, the widespread lack of awareness about the nature and depth of the (frequently irresolvable) tensions that are inherent in domestic violence has made it easier to blame the victim than to acknowledge our lack of clarity on situational dynamics about what is happening.

Blaming the victim can take a number of forms, including holding her directly responsible for causing the violence or distancing ourselves from the situation with thoughts like "I would never allow it to happen to me." Another common reaction is to explain domestic violence as the product of external factors such as unemployment or alcohol and/or drug abuse. Although external factors may contribute to particular instances of domestic violence, such explanations are fundamentally incomplete. These accounts fail to appreciate the tensions as embedded within the origins of the liberal construction of the family as a private institution. The development of a working knowledge of the derivation and operation of these tensions is crucial to contemporary efforts to address domestic violence. When we replace idealisations of the family that presume familial peace that recur in Locke's theory with an understanding that the domestic sphere is a site of significant conflict and/or repetitive acts of violence, we recognise the need for an understanding of the relationship between public and private that is capable of accommodating the paradoxes and contradictions that arise in instances of familial conflict. Failure to fully engage these tensions results too easily in a pattern whereby the interests of some individuals are systematically subordinated in order to achieve a level of clarity that simply may not be possible.

Jean Elshtain argues that traditional liberal models such as Locke's fail to provide women with a vocabulary to articulate their position in the family. According to Elshtain (1981), women were left with only two choices; to identify themselves with the rationalistic self-interest of the public sphere or the sentimentality of the private sphere. This observation helps to explain the double bind that is created for so many victims of domestic violence. If a woman's role in the family is identified with the rational sphere, then failure to leave an abusive husband is likely to be portrayed as irrational. Furthermore, according to this standard, it becomes much easier to blame women for getting into the situation in the first place because they "should have known better." If, on the other hand, a woman's role in the family is viewed through the sentimental lens, we are likely to assume that as the moral beacon of the domestic sphere she should put family above all else. According to this interpretation, if she leaves she is a failed wife and if she stays she can be blamed for endangering her children. The feminist critique of the public/private dichotomy has been an important contribution to feminist research. Exposing the gendered and sexualised dimensions and the inherent hierarchies, feminists have revealed the public/private distinction as an influential liberal power mechanism of modernity. In particular, in view of some Eurocentric biases, it is suggested that taking into account the concept of everyday life makes it possible to overcome some of the public/private framework's analytical shortcomings.

Coming to Indian scenario, while the Domestic Violence Act, 2005 is an important first step in terms of the concepts it introduces into the Indian legal system, the viability of its implementation may be contested on certain grounds. Many laws are gender neutral, however, their application is gender biased. The effects of this public/private divide in the international law are more evident in domestic violence, which literally happens in the private. Moreover, the economic and social context of its (laws) application has not been considered seriously by both the governmental and at the same time non-governmental organisations, all over the world. Opposition to the introduction of this Act has also been expressed on the grounds of its interference with the private sphere—that of the home and family. Interference into domestic privacy; has traditionally been seen as a greater evil than actual violence inflicted upon a wife. However further step came in understanding domestic violence as a violation of human rights itself and attempts were made to dissolve the same. However, any purported intrusion enabled by the Act is necessary for the increased recognition of domestic violence as a valid social concern. And it is a reading of the provisions of the Domestic Violence Act in this light that will enable it to play a significant role.

References

Alexander, Doug (2000), "*Addressing Violence Against Palestinian Women*", International Development Research Centre, Ottawa, Ontario.

Angela B and K R. Williams (1989), "*Exploring the Effect of Resource Availability and the Likelihood of Female-perpetrated Homicides*", Law and Society Review 23 (1): pp. 75-94.

Archer J (2000), "*Sex Differences in Aggression between Heterosexual Partners: A Meta-Analytic Review*", Psychol Bull 126 (5): pp. 651-80.

Arnot, ML. and U, Cornelie (2003), *Gender and crime in modern Europe, London*: Routledge. p. 123.

Arriaga, XB and S Oskamp (1999), *Violence in intimate relationships*, Sage Publishers.

Bachman, RT and L E. Saltzman (1995), *Violence against Women: Estimates from the Redesigned Survey*, Bureau of Justice Statistics, US.

Bargetz, Brigitte (2009), *The Politics of the Everyday: A Feminist Revision of the Public/Private Frame. In: Reconciling the Irreconcilable*, ed. I. Papkova, Institute of Human Sciences, Osterreich, Austria.

Bell Hooks (1990), "*Homeplace: A Site of Resistance*", in: *ibid. Yearning: Race, Gender and Cultural Politics*, Boston (South End Press), p. 42.

Capaldi, D.M., Kim, H.K., and Shortt, J.W. (2004), *Women's involvement in aggression in young adult romantic relationships.* In K.L. Putallaz and K.L. Bierman (Eds.), *Aggression, antisocial behaviour, and violence among girls* (pp. 223-241). New York: Guilford.

Carole Pateman (1989), "*Feminist Critiques of the Public/Private Dichotomy*", in: *ibid., The Disorder of Women. Democracy, Feminism and Political Theory*, Cambridge (Polity Press), p. 118.

Chris Armstrong and Judith Squires (2002), "*Beyond the Public/Private Dichotomy: Relational Space and Sexual Inequalities*", in: Political Theory, No. 1, p. 261.

Cobbe Francis Power, (1878), "*Wife Torture in England,*" Contemporary Review Vol. 32.

Collins, Patricia Hill (1991), "*Work, Family, and Black Women's Oppression*", in Black Feminist Thought: Knowledge, Consciousness, and the Politics of Empowerment, London, Routledge, p. 46.

Constable, Pamela. "*For Some Muslim Wives, Abuse Knows No Borders.*" Washington Post, May 8, 2007.

Coole, Diana (2000), "*Cartographic Convulsions: Public and Private Reconsidered*", in: Political Theory, Vol. 28, No. 3, p. 347.

Coomaraswamy, Radhika (2005), *'Human Security and Gender Violence'*, EPW, Oct 29, pp. 4729-36.

Copelon, R., (1994), *'Understanding Domestic Violence as Torture'* in Cook, R. (Ed.). *Human Rights of Women. National and International Perspectives.* University of Pennsylvania Press. pp.116-152.

Donzelot, J. (1979), *The Policing of Families*. New York, PAN.

Elshtain, Jean (1981), *Public Man: Private Woman*, Princeton: Princeton University Press.

Erin Pizzey (1982), *Prone to Violence*, Jeff Shapiro: Books.

Ferree, M.M., (2004), *'Assessing the Science: Key Issues for Research on Violence against Women'*. Paper presented at the Conference Everyday violence and human rights in Osnabrück, Germany.

Fiebert, Martin (2011), *"References Examining Assaults by Women on Their Spouses or Male Partners: An Annotated Bibliography"*, California State University.

Fraser, Nancy (1997), *Justice Interruptus: Critical Reflections on the "Postsocialist" Condition*, London/New York, Routledge.

Frieze IH (2000), *"Violence in Close Relationships—Development of a Research Area: Comment on Archer"*, Psychol Bull 126 (5) pp. 681-4.

Gardiner, G. (1996), *From Private to Public: Creating a Domestic Violence Community Intervention Project*, School of Social Work, Curtin University, Australia.

Gelles Richard J. (1997), *Intimate Violence in Families*, Sage publications.

Ghez M and L Marin, (2002), *"Domestic Violence"* Encyclopedia of Public Health. Ed. Lester Breslow, Vol. 2. Gale Cengage.

Hamberger, L.K., *et.al* (1996), *"A Large Sample Empirical Typology of Male Spouse Abusers and its Relationship to Dimensions of Abuse"*. Violence and Victims 11 (4): 277-92.

Heise, Lori; et.al. (1999), *"Ending Violence against Women."* Population Reports, Series L. No. 11.

Holtzworth-Munroe, A., and G.L. Stuart, (1994). *"Typologies of Male Batterers: Three Subtypes and the Differences among Them"*, Psychological Bulletin 116 (3): pp. 476-97.

John Locke (1988), *Two Treatises of Government*, ed. Peter Laslett, Cambridge University Press.

Johnson MP (1995), *"Patriarchal Terrorism and Common Couple Violence: Two Forms of Violence against Women"*. Journal of Marriage and the Family (National Council on Family Relations) 57 (2) pp. 283-94.

Johnson MP (2000), *"Conflict and Control: Images of Symmetry and Asymmetry in Domestic Violence"* In Booth, A., A.C. Crouter, and M. Clements Couples in Conflict, Erlbaum.

Johnson MP (2005), *"Domestic Violence: It's Not About Gender—or Is It?"* Journal of Marriage and Family 67 (5) pp. 1126-30.

Johnson MP (2006). *"Conflict and control: gender symmetry and asymmetry in domestic violence"* Violence against women 12 (11) pp. 1003-18.

Johnson M.P. (2006), *Violence and abuse in personal relationships: Conflict, terror, and resistance in intimate partnerships*, in A.L. Vangelisti and D. Perlman (Eds.), Cambridge handbook of personal relationships (pp. 557-576) Cambridge University Press.

Johnson M.P. and K.J. Ferraro (2000), "*Research on Domestic Violence in the 1990s: Making Distinctions*", Journal of Marriage and the Family 62 (4) pp. 948-63.

Kelly K.A, (2002), *Private family, private individual: John Locke's distinction between paternal and political power, Social Theory and Practice*, Vol. 28 No. 03.

Kelly, K.A. (2003), *Domestic Violence and the Politics of Privacy*, Ithaca: Cornell University Press, 2003.

Kimmel, M.S. (2001), "*Male victims of domestic violence: A substantive and methodological review*". Report to the Equality Committee of the Dept. of Education and Science, Ireland, pp. 10-11.

Lasch, C. (1977), *Haven in a Heartless World: The Family Beseiged*, New York, Basic Books.

MacKinnon, Catharine, (1984), *Feminism Unmodified: Discourses on Life and Law*. Cambridge: Harvard University Press.

Martin L.S. et al. (1999), *Domestic Violence in Northern India*, American Journal of Epidemiology,150 (4) pp. 417-426.

Mill, John Stuart (1989), *The Subjection of Women*, ed. Wendell Robert Carr, Boston: MIT Press.

Mohanty R.K. and S. Mohanty (2012), *Criminology Penology and Victimology*, Mumbai, Himalay Publication.

Muelleman, R.L.; Burgess, P. (1998), "*Male Victims of Domestic Violence and Their History of Perpetrating Violence*".Academic Emergency Medicine pp. 5-9.

O'Leary, K. Daniel (2000), "*Are Women Really More Aggressive than Men in Intimate Relationships*? Comment on Archer". Psychological Bulletin 126 (5): pp. 681-684.

Pagelow, M.D. (1984), *Family Violence*, New York, Praeger.

Pinker, Steven (2011), *Women's Economic Power Decreases Domestic Violence against Both Genders*, Forbes, December 5, 2011.

Prokhovnik, Raia (1999), *Rational Woman. A feminist Critique of the Dichotomy*, London/New York, Routledge, p. 37.

Rand M., Strom K., *Violence-Related Injuries Treated in Hospital Emergency Departments*, Washington (DC), Bureau of Justice Statistics, U.S. Department of Justice, 1997.

Roberts, Albert R.; Springer, David W., eds. (2007), *Social Work in Juvenile and Criminal Justice Settings* (3rd ed.). Springfield, Illinois, Charles C Thomas. p. 270.

Robertson, K. and M., Tamar (2009), *"Attitudes and Attributions Associated with Female and Male Partner Violence"*. Journal of Applied Social Psychology 39 (7) p. 1481.

Saunders D.G. (1988), *"Wife Abuse, Husband Abuse, or Mutual Combat?A Feminist Perspective on the Empirical Findings"*, In Bograd ML, Yllö K. Feminist perspectives on wife abuse. Thousand Oaks, Sage Publications. pp. 90-113.

Sen, S. and A., Sanhita (2006), *The Domestic Violence Act,* 2005: *a new direction,* Advocacy Internet, 8(5): pp. 3-8.

Seth Sunmit (2010), *Domestic Violence as a Human Rights Issue, Legal Services India,* November, 3.

Shabana Azmi (2003), *Domestic Violence is Not So Private,* Deccan Herald (India), 13th August.

Shipway, Lynn (2004), *Domestic Violence: A Handbook for Health Professionals,* New York, Routledge.

Stets, J.E. and M.A. Straus, (1990), *Gender Differences in Reporting Marital Violence and its Medical and Psychological Consequences.* In Straus and Gelles (editors): Physical violence in American families, NJ: Transaction publishers.

Straus, M.A. (1999), *The Controversy over Domestic Violence by Women: A Methodological, Theoretical, and Sociology of Science Analysis.* In X.B. Arriaga and S. Oskamp (Eds.), Violence in Intimate Relationships (pp. 17-44). Thousand Oaks, CA: Sage.

Straus, M.A. (2006), "Paper presented at conference on Trends in Intimate Violence Intervention". New York University.

Straus, M.A., and Gelles, R.J. (1990), *Physical Violence in American Families,* Somerset, NJ: Transaction.

Strauss M.A. (2005), "*Women's Violence toward Men is a Serious Social Problem.*" pp. 55-77 in Current controversies on family violence, Ed by R.J. Gelles and D R Loseke, Newbury Park: Sage.

Swan, S.C.; Snow, D.L. (2002), *"A Typology of Women's use of Violence in Intimate Relationships"*. Violence against Women 8: pp. 286-319.

Tahir, Fahrettin (2011), *"Behind the Veil"*. The Economist, 12th May.

Time (1995), "*Women: Killed by Agreed and Oppression,*" TIME Magazine, Sept 11, Vol. 146, No. 11.

Titley Gavan (Ed) (2007), *Gender Matters*, Council of Europe, Publication Division, Hungery, Budapest.

Waits, Kathleen (1985), "*The Criminal Justice System's Response to Battering: Understanding the Problem, Forging the Solutions*", Washington Law Review 60: pp. 267.330.

Wallace, Harvey (2004), *Family Violence: Legal, Medical, and Social Perspectives.* Allyn and Bacon. p. 2

Watts C and Zimmerman C (2002), "*Violence against Women: Global Scope and Magnitude*". Lancet 359: pp. 1232-7.

White JW, et.al (2000), "*Intimate Partner Aggression—what have we Learned? Comment on Archer* (2000)", Psychol Bull 126 (5): pp. 690-6.

Young, Iris Marion (1997), "*House and Home. Feminist Variations on a Theme*", in: *ibid.*, Intersecting Voices, Dilemmas of gender, political philosophy, and policy, Princeton University Press, p. 160.

5 Urban Poverty, Slums and Crime with Specific Reference to the Underworld Crime in Mumbai

Jasmine Damle

Introduction

The paper attempts to look at the close relationship between urban poverty slums and crime. To put it briefly, urban poverty acts as a contributor to the growth of slums and thereby crime. Along with a rise in urban poverty and subsequently the slums, crime is also on the rise especially in a mega city like Mumbai, where every other day the print and television media has lot of crime reporting-daily news-murders, rapes, terrorist attacks economic crime and what not! The paper also discusses about the genesis of Mumbai's underworld with a sociological explanation. In order to establish the link between urban poverty and slums and slums and crime, I would like to borrow the concept of 'axiomatic ordering' propounded by Hans Zetterberg (1954) as well as that of J. S. Mill (1843) 'Cannons of Agreement' and Raymond Boudon (1974). 'The Sociological Explanation' for a social phenomenon to exist, certain conditions become necessary and at the same time must be sufficient. In this case for crime to exist, the necessary condition as well as sufficient condition would be urban poverty. Therefore due to the rise in urban poverty, it would result in the growth of slums thereby contributing to deprivation, anomie. The unchecked flow of migrants from villages, etc., further accentuates density of population, thereby heterogeneity of the population thus leading to anonymity. Thereby the conducive condition of both necessary and sufficient conditions for crime to exist and flourish. Often the motivating factor to commit crime is poverty, deprivation, family disorganisation, bad companionship (environmental factors).

Slums thus provide all the necessary as well as sufficient conditions for crime. Thus urban poverty acts as a cause as for slums and slums become the cause of crime, which is the effect.

To carry the argument further, I would like to borrow John Stuart Mills' (1843) Cannon's of Agreement (Methods of Agreement and Differences). If urban poverty exists, (insufficient/necessary) it gives rise to slums and thus contribute to crime. However in the absence of urban poverty, the growth of slums and crime would be adversely affected. The hidden cause of urban poverty is the unchecked flow of migrants into cities. Raymond Boudon (1974) had stated that we cannot generalise the classical logic of J. S. Mill or that of deductions stated in the Aristotle's lean logic, but instead it would be: If A is (urban poverty), then more frequently B (slums) C would follow (crime) rather than if A then B, popularly known as if and then. However, Hans Zetterberg (1954) has given the concept of 'axiomatic ordering' format: Thus, if urban poverty were to increase, it would subsequently lead to the rise in the growth of slums, and if slums were to increase so would the heterogeneity (due to unchecked migration) density of population, thereby anonymity, resulting in the incidence of crime. If slums were to increase phenomenally so would the crime and the *vice versa.* Zetterbergian Axiomatic ordering format would be: If urban poverty increases then slums increase and if slums were to increase so would crime. The crucial parametre valuable here is that of urban poverty which becomes the crucial connecting link between the growth of slums as well as it acts as a facilitator of crime.

Rapid urbanisation has posed many challenges to all but the developing countries are the ones which are finding it increasingly difficult to respond to these challenges. An alarming feature of urban population growth is the substantially high proportion of people living in poverty. Thus the growth in urbanisation also leads to the urbanisation of poverty. It is seen as a spill over of rural poverty. As stated by Guggler (1988), 'Population in the urban areas expand due to the following three factors: (1) Natural growth of population, (2) Rural to urban migration and (3) The reclassification of rural areas as urban in course of time. Around two-fifth of the total urban growth in the 'Third World' is accounted by the rural to urban migration. The process can be identified as 'over-urbanisation' as long as (a) rural-urban migration leads to a misallocation of labour between rural and urban sectors, in the sense that it raises urban unemployment, under-employment and poverty, and (b) rural-urban migration increases the social cost for providing for a country's growing population. Thus this rapid rate of urbanisation in developing countries has been premised upon two major hypothesis. (1) Unusually rapid rates of population growth pressing on limited farm acreage and thus pushing landless labourers into cities (2) migrants being pulled into cities by the economic forces such as domestic terms of trade squeezing agriculture, the diffusion of technology from the developed world favouring modern large scale urban industries, foreign capital flows into urban infrastructure, housing, power, transportation and large scale manufacturing.

Thus due to the increasing pressure of population on farmland in densely populated agrarian economies, thereby contributing to the problem of rural unemployment and underemployment which leads to rural to urban migration. However, this problem gets further compounded due to limited demand for labour in the formal sector and especially lack of requisite skills push rural migrants into the informal sector. The low rate of growth of industrial employment and the high rate of rural to urban migration contribute to an explosive urban unemployment and underemployment. Therefore the process of transformation of rural poverty into urban poverty, the phenomenon is also described as 'urbanisation of poverty' (see Williamson J. G. 1988). Thus due to rural-urban migration the excess labour within the informal sector leads to reduction in earning thereby contributing to urban poverty thereby paving way for the slums.

It is migration the push and pulls factors (Everett Lee) which contribute substantially to urban poverty. Slums have become worldwide phenomena in urban areas and 31.6 per cent the world urban population lives in slums. According to the census of India 2001, 27.8 per cent population of India is living in urban areas where as 15 per cent of total urban population lives in slums.

Slums are dilapidated housing structure/squatters/ temporary housing structures without basic infrastructural facilities such as water supply, drainage toilets. As mentioned due to the exodus of rural population migrating into cities in search of employment, many find refuge in such slums/ squatters. Slums become a 'safe haven for such migrants. The classic example of Asia's largest growing slum is that of Dharavi in Mumbai. In Maharashtra 11.2 million people live in slums.

In Mumbai (Gr. Mumbai) 35 per cent of the urban population lives in slums, and 5.82 per cent live in slums, whereas total of 6.09 per cent of population of Maharashtra lives in slums. According to Registrar General Government of India Report, 2001 in Mumbai (Gr.) 5.82 per cent of the population lives in slums and 60 per cent of the population lives in non-slums out of a total urban population of 11.91 million.

A characteristic feature of slums is anonymity, thus the migrants along with the local inhabitants who live there do not know each other personally at all. Along with unemployment, underemployment as well as temporary employment is the crucial factor of urban poverty. Thus slums constitute that element of population in urban areas not required or digested nor respected by the society. Slums unfortunately constitute a typical case of social pathology i.e., it provides a safe haven/ breeding ground for alcoholics, drug peddlers, gamblers and prostitutes and criminals to live. The approach road itself is very difficult to enter dingy, poor or at times practically no street lights, garbage flies, rodents littered all over the place and stray dogs open gutters barking around wild pigs etc. Thus along with social pathology, absence of hygienic, fresh air ventilation sunlight give rise to a number of diseases such as T. B., malaria, chickengunia etc. Urban poverty acts both as a facilitator between slums and crime. Thus to put it, if and then methodologically if urban poverty exists then slums develop and often crime follows. Therefore, urban poverty becomes the crucial connecting link between slums and crime. Thus the heterogeneity, density, anonymity of the population residing in the slums provide the much needed support structure for crime to flourish along with the factors of companionship reference group behaviour.

Defining Slum?

Whenever action is required, it is necessary to identify the target population. So what is a slum?

Today, the noun 'slum' is employed in popular usage to describe 'bad' shelter. It is used as varying scales: anything from a house to a large settlement—can be classified as a slum providing that it is perceived to be substandard and is occupied by the poor. The Oxford Encyclopedic Dictionary (OED) provides two definitions: 'an overcrowded and squalid back street, district, etc., usually in a city and inhabited by very poor people; and a house or building unfit for human habitation' (Hawkins and Allen, 1991: 1369).

In practice, every city in the world tends to define slums differently, even though efforts have been made for years to establish objective measures with which to demarcate the major problem areas. Even in Victorian cities: 'An essential backdrop to all nineteenth century slum campaigning was the development of the science of statistics'; a tendency 'epitomised by the research of Charles Booth' (Prunty, 1998: 5-6).

Recently, the Cities Alliance attempted to define what they meant by a slum (World Bank/UNCHS, 2000: 1):

Slums do not have:

- Basic municipal services—water, sanitation, waste collection, storm drainage, street;
- Lighting, paved footpaths, roads for emergency access;
- Schools and clinics within easy reach, safe areas for children to play and
- Places for the community to meet and socialise.

Later deliberation refined that definition:

The operational definition of a slum that has recently been recommended [by a UN Expert Group Meeting] ... defines a slum as an area that combines, to various extents, the following characteristics (restricted to the physical and legal characteristics of the settlement and excluding the more difficult social dimensions): inadequate access to safe water, inadequate access to sanitation and other infrastructure, poor structural quality of housing, overcrowding, and insecure residential status' (UN-Habitat, 2003a: 12).

The Negative Associations

As previous authors have pointed out the word 'slum' has nearly always been used pejoratively or ideologically, often both at the same time. Yelling (1986: 1) observes that the word 'slum' carries a condemnation of existing conditions and, implicitly at least, a call for action'. Marris (1979: 419) points out that: 'The word "slum" is like the word "dirt": evocative, disapproving, and indefinable except in the context of our expectations of what should be'. More recently, Flood (2002:3) has recognised that:

> 'Slum' has become an unfashionable term in the West, being strictly perjorative and associated with all forms of negative social outcomes and squalor expressed in a spatial or housing sense. It is a term very much in the spirit of Christian reformism and later Western capitalism, which has sought to define it as counterfactual, both conceptually and in the physical sense, to modernist ideals of social and physical order, morality, health, spaciousness and urban quality.

The very origins of the word 'slum' are cloaked in negativity. In so far as we know when or where the word was first used, it seems initially that it did not apply to housing at all. The first written appearance of the term was apparently in 1812, when it appeared in Vaux's Vocabulary of the Flash Language (Davis, 2004: 12; Oxford Economic Dictionary Online, no date: 216), when a slum was inauspiciously labelled as being 'synonymous with "racket" or "criminal trade" (Prunty, 1998:2).

But slums were also identified, and stigmatised, because they were seen to be centres of crime. In the 'earliest recorded definition' the 'slum' describes 'any particular branch of depredation practiced by thieves, and a "lodging slum" [is] defined as "the practice of hiring ready furnished lodgings and stripping them of the plate, linen and other valuables" (Prunty, 1998:2). Is it by chance that Dickens (1846) housed Fagin and the Artful Dodger in a slum? In most cities around the world, the association between slums, ill-health and crime still resonates in most people's minds.

Has the heterogeneity of low-income settlement been recognised in the recent rediscovery of slums? Yes and no. The World Bank/UNCHS (2000:1) recognises squatter settlements without legal recognition or rights, sprawling at the edges of cities. But, more worryingly, 'slums are neglected parts of cities where housing and living conditions are appallingly poor slums have various names... yet share the same miserable living conditions.

Unchecked flow of migrants into Mumbai city for better opportunities to earn their livelihood, from rural small towns and underdeveloped states of India for example BIMARU states. The availability of space itself possesses a serious problem. The vital question of having a roof overhead is solved by slums (dilapidated housing squatters), having no access to water, sanitation etc. Along with squalor, grime, social problems like alcoholism, drugs and gambling are prevalent in slums due to lack of jobs, poverty etc. Hence, the paucity of living space itself poses a serious problem regarding quality of life of its residents. The population density in 2001 (census) for Mumbai was 27,000 people per km. The 'C' ward is most populous 114,001 people per sq km.In Mumbai 60 per cent population lives in slums.

***Crime:* Content Analysis of Newspaper Articles (Major Features of Urban Crime)**

1. The crime rate in urban centres in Maharashtra has increased by 6.83 per cent in the year 2005 as compared to 2004.
2. Mumbai tops the list with 42.57 per cent criminals cases as compared to the nine commissionerates followed by Pune city (16.01 per cent) whereas in Navi Mumbai (New), Thane, Amravati and Solapur saw a decline in crime rate as compared to Pune, Mumbai, Aurangabad, Nagpur and Nashik.
3. The latest statistical report 'Crime in Maharashtra 2005' a total 73,830 cognisable offences under Indian Penal Code (IPC) as compared to 69,108 cases in 2004. Hence an increase in crime rate has occurred by 6.08 as compared to 2004.

A very interesting phenomenon regarding the type of crime has occurred i.e., murder cases were 730 in 2004, as compared to 685 in 2005, whereas in the case of dowry deaths are also on the decline i.e., 29 in 2005 as compared to 43 in 2004, hence we find a decline. At the same time, there has been a steady increase in crimes like attempt to murder has increased by 4.69 per cent and rape (17.06 per cent).

Kidnapping and abduction 13.45 per cent robbery 7.46 per cent, theft (4.48 per cent) and riots (9.25 per cent). Thus, today murder is not merely an act of personal vendetta but today the ugly elements of kidnapping, abduction, extortion has increased manifold –due to the entry of underworld gangsterism which is synonymous with D-company. Very often newspaper headlines carry the news items like Prominent Builders, business men's son kidnapped ransom demanded Rs 41 crore. The vicious circle of kidnapping, extortion, murder is prevalent. Sexual crime/ hate crime/rape is on the rise. The recent brutal murder of children in Noida and rape of girls is an eye opener. Another aspect is eve teasing (or passing vulgar lewd commentary at girls/women, bottom pinching, touching, and rubbing against private parts in local trains. In Mumbai alone 99 cases as compared to 95 in Pune are noticed. Cases of eve teasing shot up by 1.18 per cent in 2005. Mumbai recorded highest number of cases of molestation (385) followed by Thane (110).

Corruption: Punjab tops the chart with 449 cases being registered under the Prevention Corruption Act. Maharashtra with 437 cases at second place, Delhi 2,273 and Mumbai 1,664.

Maharashtra state topped the chart in terms of reporting serious major frauds i.e., 39 cases in 2005 followed by Gujarat (32) and Nagaland (12). Thus a peculiar trend is observed relating to crime especially in Mumbai—with respect to economic crimes, it tops the list in counterfeiting of currency and valuable securities and was seen in terms of cybercrime after Hyderabad. The overall picture of Maharashtra state was that it had topped the chart in terms of reporting serious/major frauds. During 2005, it was 39 cases followed by Gujarat (32) and Nagaland (12). Thus crime in Mumbai today, has become more internationalised, underworld gangsterism, smuggling, narcotics, counterfeiting, frauds, sexual offence crimes and economic crimes and last but not the lease i.e., corruption.

Drug/Substance abuse is also on the rise. Mumbai reported 941 cases out of total of 1,100 cases in Maharashtra. Thus factors associated with it could be breakdown of family, bad companionship, failure at examination/love being jilted, peer group pressure (emulating them), urban crime was 81 per cent in the state of Maharashtra in the year 2005.

Another major aspect of crime has been economic offences or white collar crime. Economic crime includes cheating, counterfeiting of currency and valuable securities and criminal breach of trust. An interesting phenomenon is that in 2005 according to National Crime Records Bureau (NCRB), India reported 69,580 cases of economic crimes. Hyderabad topped the list (3,029), Delhi (2,808) and Mumbai (2,369). After the major 1990s Harshad Mehta scam, Mumbai the capital of the country has cooled down. However, in cases related to counterfeiting of currency notes and valuable securities. Mumbai had 169 cases followed by Bangalore (90), Lucknow 45. With respect to cases of cheating, Hyderabad recorded highest number of cases, 2,830.

The Perpetrators of Crime

Why crime exists; the growing incidence of crime, its sophistication, terrorism, internationalisation, globalisation of crime, criminalisation of politics and politicisation of crime makes one ponder over the factors contributing to crime. Ignorance and incapacity on the part of police force, pose as major factors towards perpetrating crime. The police force who are supposed to be well informed, especially through their key informants or '*Khabris*', in spite of all this their intricate networks, a lot of criminals hang around free and commit crime. The police machinery is incapable of dealing with crime due to lack of adequate number of vehicles sophisticated ultra tech machinery such as bomb detection and diffusion devices, less number of sniffer dogs and most importantly trained manpower. The legal machinery/system too is ill equipped to deal with present day crime, as the laws CPC and IPC made by the British have become obsolete how to deal with new types of crimes for, e.g., Cybercrime. Along with the laws having become obsolete lack of adequate training, motivation on the part of the police officers, overload of work stress, overburden on few officers pose a serious problem. The legal machinery (laws) also have several loopholes in them, hence very often one hears of a hardened criminal getting anticipatory bail. Closely associated with it, is the connivance on the part of the police officers to let the accused off the hook or not report crime at all. Very often no FIR is lodged or a complaint is registered at the police *chowky*, cases are closed, often hushed up. At times if honest/sincere police officer tries to reopen the case he is transferred to some remote area or asked to go on compulsory leave of absence or (CRS). The over interference by the home ministry with regard to police investigations, transfers, favourism, demotions, promotions getting medals e.g., *Rashtrapati Padak* on 26th January, 15th August is all controlled by the ministers/secretaries. Often the police force is controlled as per the whims of ministers that very often police officers say' *Hamare Haat bandhe hai or Bada Saab ne Manaa Kiya hai.*

The classic example of 1980s, Govind Nihlani's film '*Ardha Satya*' depicts the case of helpless police officer Mr Velankar, actor Om Shivpuri who then resorts to mercilessly flogging locked up criminals partly due to impotency on the part of effective functioning. The nexus between politicians, criminals/goons and now the underworld is too conspicuous to be ignored. Along with it is corruption, taking/accepting bribes thereby perpetrating crime. Max Weber Gerth and Mills (1958), had stated while explaining bureaucracy–legal-rational authority; that there are some people (honest) who live for politics whereas some live off politics. Unfortunately today we find more police officers of the second category – taking bribes, *haftas*, not only to supplement their meagre incomes. A police sub-inspector is paid Rs. 5-8-10,000 per month. Hence very often indulge in luxury at the expense of others to let off criminals. Lawyers too have a close nexus with corruption. Many criminal lawyers specialise in letting off criminals, or granting anticipating bail before a non-bailable warrant is issued against a hardened criminal, destruction of evidence, threatening and kidnapping, bribing are the most common ways resorted to, that today such lawyers are in great demand. I would like to coin a term '*bhai lawyer*'. For example during the trial of the convicted 1993 Bomb Blasts cases, Srikrishna Commission Report many a times the prime accused sits at home or Dubai and lawyers try to settle it for them for a hefty fee. Thus, we find today more and more news pouring in about the 1993 Bomb Blast case verdict Srikrishna Commission report that most of the hardened underworld dons mastermind criminals are living outside and the cases against them are dropped. The phenomenon of bridging in between the moral and immoral order is persistent. Today, it has become very difficult to find an honest police officer or lawyer; it is literally like hunting for a needle in a haystack.

The third crucial valuable or what is methodologically known as the effect of crime.

What is Crime?

Crime is behaviour that violates laws. The laws that prohibit such behaviour and that mandate punishment for committing it. Crime is a short term and circumscribed behaviour in which an individual uses fraud or force to commit deviant behaviour. Robert Mier (1984) has distinguished nine types of crime.

1. It is homicide and assault whereby perpetrator uses lethal weapon/violence on victim.
2. Forcible rape-sexual assault act performed on women without her consent.

3. Occasional property crime where one party illegally transfers or damages property of another person.
4. Crime against public/moral order-prostitution, drugs, gambling these requires the participation of a customer who purchases the opportunity to engage in that behaviour.
5. Political crime resistance (dissent evasion, disobedience or violence) by members of the society in power.
6. White collar crime/corporate crime which is an economic crime offence (anti-trust offences bribery, bank frauds, embezzlement) committed by means of fraud, deception or collusion.
7. Gang delinquency, in which a group of individuals numbering from a few to several thousand, engage in criminal activity as a part of group norms.
8. Organised crime–wherein a syndicate of individual criminals organise to promote their criminal activity and protect themselves from legal authorities for e.g., mafias.
9. Professional theft refers to individuals who make a likelihood or occupation of crime, much like any legal professions or job e.g., pick-pocketing, burglary, shoplifting, forgery, extortion and confidence swindling. There are two other forms of crime.
10. Kidnapping
11. Abduction–consists of crime where in a person is illegally seized and detained for purpose of ransom or illicit sex or in order to regain a child lost in a custody action.
12. Hate crimes –they are against persons of a particular race, religion, ethnic orientation or sexual orientation for e.g., Maniacs such as Jack the Ripper, Boston Strangler.

While studying crime, its ecological environmental aspect is of crucial importance. Clinard Marshal and Meir Robert (1975) have stated that often slum areas have been taken equivalent to delinquent areas, evil strange low income, low class neighbourhood, squalid and criminal population. In nearly all the countries, there is strong evidence that slum neighbourhood provides the milieu for delinquency and crime, it is here that stolen goods are sold (e.g., Mumbai's Chor or Junna Bazzar) and attitudes of antagonism towards the police and outside authorities are developed. In developing countries the criminalising effect of slums is potentially strongest, as a young person who migrates to areas with high crime rate, becomes at the same time emancipated from their village and home towns. Criminal homicide, rape, assault in many of United States of American cities is concentrated in slums. With the rapid growth of urbanisation cities of developing countries, too, are beginning to face similar problems. Mumbai where ordinary crime and not white collar crime or business and political corruption erupt almost entirely from slum areas and often there offences are committed against other slum dwellers. In short, slums offer a breeding ground for all types of crime ranging from murder, rape, robbery, cheating, hate, crime, riots, gang and wars etc. In Mumbai especially the area of Kamathipura has been branded, labelled as 'a red light area' which is infested with prostitutes, drug peddlers, and more than 10-12 people live in old dilapidated buildings. Very often two-three generations stay together. Sociologically speaking, 'greater generation depth. Often the streets are narrow and a Muslim ghetto (Louis Wirth 1927), where no 'amenities/facilities for like water drainage, garbage disposal is available.

A major aspect associated with the phenomenon of slum is the crowding or (over-crowding) theory, Refer to Herbert (1982). It links population and residential densities with a wide range of deviant behaviour. High density and a sense of crowding create strains tensions, which can lead to aggression, withdrawal mental or physical illness—e.g. tuberculosis. The initial link between crowding and stress is attributed by many to an innate sense of territoriality.

Emile Durkheim, in his noted work Division of Labour (1893), has not only explained the concept but has also prognosticated that with overcrowding in i.e., with increase in material density the moral density decreases and people's interaction with each other is reduced, the factor of anonymity sets in. He was preoccupied with moral social disintegration of modern society.

What Simmel had stated about a European city

unfortunately holds true, in the case of a metropolis called "Mumbai'. Today a sense of detachment, lack of emotional involvement in social relationship often leads to a dehumanising effect which sharply affects the mental health of many—unstable, maniacs, psychotics' personality and perverse mentalities can contribute effectively to an increase in criminal tendency, anti-social element. In fact, it is Darwian concept of survival of the fittest (smartest–calculative or in terms Paretoan term's instinct for combinations. Louis Wirth (1938) in a very poignant way in his work 'Urbanism as a way of life', has stated that it is a characteristic of modern urban society. He has mentioned three important characteristics of urbanism.

1. Size—The greater the size of a given population the greater the likelihood that different kinds (races, statuses) of people make it up. There is often a spatial segregation of people, the social relations are instrumental in and different neighbourhoods are formed based on race class, ethnicity e.g., ghettos, slums, social relationship are fragmentary in nature (secondary contractual).
2. Density—The increasing concentration of people in a limited space also prompts a number of consequence not only environmental but mental health social as well due to economic disparities and due to close proximity with each other the constant competition conflict 'survival of the fittest, mutual exploitation friction irritation often leading to nervous disorders at very similar to, Simmel's idea of mental life.
3. Heterogeneity—Due to the expanding division of labour, the city is characterised by a largely heterogenous population. Due to increased specialisation of skills, the urban class structure becomes more complicated and opaque. Hence the individual no longer knows his place, contributing to a sense of 'rootlessness' and in security. In short, a mass society (Kornhauser) emerges. People are left socially uprooted and politically powerless. Hence today's Mumbai (Bombay) has gradually started becoming a faceless mass society.

Crime in Mumbai (with Specific Reference to Gangsters and the Underworld)

Today, unfortunately the world 'crime' has become

synonymous with the city of Mumbai, which is the financial capital of our country. Every other day one finds news about murders, blasts, riots and what not. Especially this has emerged as a more or less daily/monthly/yearly phenomenon for the past 10-15 years or so. As a sociologist and now inhabitant of Mumbai, I pondered over it and tried to understand the genesis/crux of the issue at large. The paper attempts on sociological analysis of the phenomenon of 'crime'. But in order to do so one has to often glean through the past as well as study the present in order to understand the future. In the words of noted historian Schlesinger, 'The long arm of past is not behind us, but it is within us'.

The deterioration of labour movement has been responsible for crime in Mumbai. Hence in order to understand the phenomenon of crime, a brief look at its past is pivotal. Mumbai (Bombay) is essentially an industrial and financial 'island' city. The city had a lot of textile mills and places such as 'Parel' was identified with several mills in the vicinity, most of the textile labour in Mumbai came from nearly the Konkan, Western Maharashtra and Southern India. Hence, there was phenomena migration. Hence a sizeable proportion of migrants (textile labourers) migrated to Mumbai and started settling down here for generations together ever since pre-independence period. Sociologically speaking it was indeed transcendence from a family of orientation to a family of procreation and thus started constituting the backbone of the labour force in Mumbai, along with dockyard and labour employed in factories, industries. However, there was a sudden jolt to it; a (The concept of Relative Deprivation–Robert K. Merton (1959), Runciman and Goldthorpe's and David Lockwood concept of embourgeiosement (1969)—as a result of affluence Runciman). A major strike occurred in the textile mills in Mumbai in 1982-83 led by antipathy towards communist Dr Datta Samant (prominent labour leader) crippled the workforce and workers for a wage rise and rights, it led to workers losing their jobs as the then state government sided with the employers. Hence the number of mill workers in cities, declined to 1, 23,000 from 2, 50,000 in 1983. By mid 1990s only 80,000 workers worked in mills. The resulting unemployment and socio-economic vulnerability provided a rich recruitment ground for gangsterism and certain millionaires entered into lucrative deals with gangs to secure profits from land deals, extortion and murders. See (Ex-textile

Mill Workers in Central Mumbai, Sharit Bhowmick and Shekhar EPW December 29th, 2001 pp. 4822-4827).

Dreaded gangster now MLA Mr Arun Gawli, earlier worked at Khatau Mills. Amar Naik (another dreaded gangster) was the son of a former textile mill worker killed Suneet Khatau (son of owner of Khatau Mills) in 1994. Thus the nexus between ex-textile mill worker now turned criminals and "under world", started growing. The socio-economic vulnerability organisational conflicts high rate of unemployment and communal turmoil resulted in an increase in crime in 1980s to mid 1990s. IPC in Mumbai recorded cases rose from 33,374 in 1975 to 35,977 in 1985 and 40,512 in 1995 but have thereafter declined to 25,686 in 2003 (*Source:* Crime in India Year 1975, 1985, 1995, 2003).

The 1982-83 textile strike in Mumbai had a very devastating effect on the life of the textile workers, their dependents and families. It was indeed a classic case of anomie. (Refer to Emile Durkheim 1893, 1964) and (1897, 1952). "Anomie" according to him was the condition of normalness, where old norms become obsolete and new ones are to be formulated. A case of chaos, normalness, powerlessness, from the co-worker, his family and community.

The concept of 'anomie' suicide whereby the sudden change in the socio-economic condition can lead to a condition of chaos, powerlessness, dejection, helplessness and frustration–it is a sense of isolation meaninglessness of life and work. A condition of economic depression; Durkheim was deeply concerned with the adverse effect of industrial society, loss of morality and a loss of social integration.

Due to loss of jobs and depletion of economic condition, the families of textile workers started disintegrating especially the children, teenagers and young adults. Many of these families lived in old *chawls* or were forced to stay in slums dilapidated housing structure with lack of infrastructural facilities-sanitation water a typical case of social pathology.

Howard Becker (1961) Boys in white and (1963) Outsiders, his famous theory of labelling or social branding is in fact a societal reaction 'theory of deviance'. An individual or groups are defined as a deviant 'labelled' and very often areas where such deviants live are also labelled. Hence deviance is not the act itself but the response of other to the act Labelling procedure amplifies deviance. (refer to S.S. Srivastava (1963) Juvenile delinquents in Kanpur and Lucknow.) In the case of Mumbai, very often certain areas are labelled as a haven of deviance/ deviants e.g., Mumbra, J.J.Road, Bhendi Bazar, etc. Many youngsters get drawn into deviant suburban or bad companionship factor (Juvenile Delinquency. Many of the now dreaded gangsters Amar Naik etc., used to mix around with antisocial elements for e.g., on Temkar Street where most of them grew up often played cricket and it is here that the seeds of deviancy criminal behaviour were sown. It has been stated that in the late 1950's Dawood (Dreaded Don) Chota Shakeel and Haji Mastaan used to play and thereby gradually s street gang type (William Whyte Street corner society started emerging– a deviant sub-culture.

Many of these young deviants have now matured into mentors big gangsters, dons and what not. Many of them had been apprenticed under mentor Karim Lala. Haaji Mastan and Bada Rajan (Rajan Nair) Vardharajan (Varda) just to name a few. Robert K. Merton (1957) elaborated upon the 'concept of anomie; he has defined anomie as the disjunction between cultural goals and the socially prescribed institutionalised means of achieving these goals. He had tried to improve and elaborate upon Durkheim's concept of anomie. A social structure society having a strain towards anomie, an individual tries to adapt to it.

Table 1 Modes of Adaptation

Modes of Adaptation	*Cultural Goals*	*Institutionalised Means*
1. Conformity	+	+
2. Innovation	+	-
3. Ritualism	-	+
4. Retreatism	-	-
5. Rebellion	- +	- +

While attempting to understand crime in Mumbai I have attempted to explain it with the help of a few of these modes of adaptation.

1. Innovation: A great cultural emphasis upon the success-goal occurs but often effective means of attaining it (institutionalised means). An individual has assimilated the cultural emphasis upon the goal without equally internalising the institutional norms governing ways and means for its attainment. Thus deviant behaviour is generated in society. The broad social category of robbers, smugglers and deviants into these categories for e.g., Mario Puzzo's Godfather (Italian Mafia) is a classic case not only of anomie but that of innovation. The crucial variables of poverty (deprivation) often lead people to commit crime. The concept of 'From Rags to riches i.e., in this using unethical/immoral means of attaining success e.g., smuggling—Hazi Mastaan, Manu Narang (all ace smugglers). A symbol of wealth and thereby power (sociologically speaking naked power, use of force coercion and not social legitimation (Max Weber). There is a complete rejection of legitimate means in favour of deviant ones. Sociologically it is 'rationalisation of deviant behaviour/criminal.

2. Retreatism: A response to the strain or anomie is to drop out of the society altogether *i.e.*, rejecting both the means and ends. The social categories of psychotics, outcastes, vagrants, chronic drunkards, drug addicts, such people are often labelled as 'a social'. They all have relinquished culturally prescribed goals and their behaviour does not accord with institutional norms—'a recluse'. Here is a classic dilemma between abandoning legitimate means and inability to use illegitimate means. Hence a near complete abandoning of the means is done and an escape route is sought.

2. Rebellion: It presupposes alienation from reigning goals and standards and the possibility of the pursuit of new ones, first by means of countervailing myths, second, once new myths exist by organised political action.

The very concept of resentment; refer to Max Scheler who tried to sociologically develop the concept drawing the inspiration from Nietzsche. It comprises three interlocking elements. (1) First diffuse feelings of hate, envy and hostility (2) a sense of being powerless to express these feelings actively against the person or social stratums evoking them and then a continual re-experiencing of this impotent hostility. Merton (1949) concept of prejudice and discrimination where he has explained the types of crime by using 'hate crime' which reacts of violence towards degradation of others prompted by extreme prejudice against them because of their race, gender, sexual orientation for e.g.,

Jack the Ripper, Boston Strangler or religion for e.g., in India in Mumbai after 1992 demolition of Babri Masjid, Ayodhya, the communal hate crime riots on January 6th, 1993 and 12th and 13th March, 1993. The retaliation of Shiv Sainiks *vs.* Muslims and the mass genocides at J.J. Hospital, etc. The horrible communal riots bomb blasts that rocked the city of Mumbai is testimony to the extreme of rebellion, hate, crime and thereby retaliation.

Under the backdrop of Mumbai and its ever increasing crime rate and its sociological analysis with the help of major sociological theories dealing with anomie deviance, it is extremely important to understand the concept of crime. Crime may be considered as deviant behaviour against which society has passed laws.

Mumbai's Crime Situation

Mumbai city is characterised by huge tall buildings, skyscrapers and slums/hutments nearby. The life thus in Mumbai itself presents a paradox. Mumbai is the financial capital of India, and has also served as a playground for several criminal activities. The city unfortunately has emerged as hub of gang, inter-warfare gang and nowadays has been a safe ... for organised criminal gangs or a more westernised concept of 'mafiadom' with all its nefarious activities. Today, unfortunately crime has been internationalised, globalised and terrorism has taken a heavy toll on the lives of the 'Mumbaikars'. In the words of well known journalist Suketu Mehta, Mumbai is indeed a Maximum city (2005) where one finds religion, trade, sex, death on the pavements. On the one hand, we find corporate, economic crime scams dominating southern parts of Mumbai, such as Colaba and Malabar Hill, etc. The Harshad Mehta Share Stock scam, which rocked Mumbai in the early nineteen nineties. In fact Harshad Mehta was popularly known as 'The Big Bull'. Thus white collar crime predominates here.

As discussed earlier, urban poverty, slums area are the chief facilitators of crime, the textile mills strike of 1982 led by Dr Datta Samant literally crippled the backbone of the textile industry as well as that of its workers. Thus, the classic case of Durkheim anomie coupled with Mertonian anomie prevailed in places such as Parel, where earlier textile mill workers used to live, as of now these old *chawls* have become slums and as Durkheim (1893) had stated that when the density of population increases, the moral density goes down. In short as had been stated by S. Herbert (1982). Thus due to the phenomenon of slum, overcrowding and high population density, it can result in aggressive behaviour, deviance. Thus due to the phenomenon of slum, overcrowding and high population density it can result in aggressive behaviour, deviance. Thus a classic example of what happened to the textile mill workers teenaged children– coupled with companionship factor (bad company factor– resulted into the formation of micro mini gangs of deviant boys who finally found their way into gangs for e.g., Amar Naik, Arun Gawli (Big Daddy of Dagdi Chawl). Along with the slums crime in Mumbai has assumed a communal overtone, especially after 1992 Babri Masjid Demolition and the 1993 Riots, that followed. The involvement of the notorious 'D' Dawood factor i.e., Dubai to Mumbai connection bombings, mass killings that rocked the island city and still continues to rock, the latest being 11th July, 2006 Borivali Train Blasts. In Mumbai areas such as J. J. Hospital Marg, Bhendi Bazar, Nagpada, Agripada, Shivajinagar, Mankhurd, Mahim creek where Muslim population is almost in majority. If one were to travel by train in Mumbai especially near Deonar near Katal Khana (Butcher home), Chembur (East), Govandi (Harbour Line) the ...... slums, *chawls* on both sides of the rail track, the squalor, despair, deprivation, unemployment, poverty, illiteracy, malnourishment along with social pathology exists. Mumbai being an island city has several beaches such as Juhu, Madh Island, where a lot of smuggling takes place, it houses several night clubs, shady hotels, bars etc., where human trafficking is common along with smuggling of intoxicants drugs is on the rise. The night life of Mumbai, nocturnal life marked by proliferation of dance bars, pubs, casinos and thereby Veblen (1925) Conspicuous Consumption for e.g., in many Hindi films such as 'Don' 'Deewar' "Satya", Munnabhai MBBS, 'Vastaav' such nocturnal life has been depicted aptly. The sleazy bars and sizzling dance bar girls, 'barbalayein' are too flashy/cheap to be ignored. In the 1970's-80's the notion of vamp as exemplified by noted actress Nadira-1950, Helen-1960, Bindu-1960s-70s, Aruna Irani-1970s-80s. The perennial eternal vamp of the Hindi Bollywood have somehow managed to epitomise the Indian filmy vamp—the sultry pussycat flame seductress of yesterdays–India's reply to Hollywood Actress Bridgetle Bardou.

Mumbai's Underworld (Organised Crime)

Organised Crime: The menace of organised crime has been on the increase and as there was no effective law in Maharashtra against organised crime except the Maharashtra Control of Organised Crime Act 1999. Maharashtra Act no. 30, 1999 was formulated. Mumbai being the economic capital of India, it is a targeted centre of criminals who hoard money through illegal means. In the recent years, criminal activities like murders of tycoons related to film industry, as well as by builders, extortion of money from businessman, abductments, show that criminal gangs are active in the state. To cope with it, such as unlawful elements spreading terrorism in the society, need to be controlled to a great extent and also minimising the feeling of fear spread in the society; organised crime has been for quite some time emerged as a serious threat to our society. It knows no national boundaries and is fuelled by illegal wealth generated by contract killing, extortion smuggling in contrabands illegal trade in narcotic, kidnappings for ransom, collection of protection money and money laundering. The illegal black wealth money generated by organised crime being very huge, it has a serious effect on our economy. The organised criminal syndicates made a common cause with terrorist gang and foster narco terrorism which extends beyond the national bondage. Organised criminals have also been making extensive use of wire electronic and oral computer modules communicating in their criminal activities. Hence the existing laws were found to be ineffective to deal with it; hence a new law has been formulated.

Organised crime refers to (1) Crime done by a single person or done in a paved way with the help of others in an organised way. It presupposes that the criminal, before committing the crime has obtained complete information regarding the economics as well as social status of the person against whom the crime is committed. Organised crime syndicate means a group of two or more persons who are acting singly or collectively as a syndicate of gang in the activities of organised crime.

Organised crime or criminal organisations are groups or operations run by criminals, most commonly for the purpose of generating a monetary profit. Such criminal organisations keep illegal actions secret and members communicate by word of mouth, therefore police would never be able to trace the phone calls/letter. Most of these organised criminals have licensed gambling, building construction, or which operate in parallel with and provide a cover for drug trafficking, money laundering, prostitution, extortion, murder for hire (*supari* in Mumbai underworld terminology) hijacking, fraud other criminal activities include human trafficking, political corruption, black marketing, political violence racist/religiously motivated *e.g.,*1993 Bombay blast violence, terrorism, abduction, prison break and crimes against humanity. However, for the criminal organisation to prosper, support from the society is essential, hence it is achieved by bribing, blackmailing honest members of the society. A symbiotic relationship is established with legitimate business judicial and police officers/legislators (MLAs MPS ministers) are targeted for control by organised crime via bribes. Thus corruption, connivance on the part of judiciary/ police officials and collusion of interests sets in. Due to globalisation, criminal gangs/organisations can easily cross between countries e.g., human trafficking. However, today organised crime in Mumbai took a new route via cyber/Internet/ which makes it harder for the police to track down criminals. The common methods are identifying theft (identity impersonation) online extortion, threats and pornography.

Organised crime in Mumbai can be divided into the following broad phases:

1. 1960s—late 1970s:–A phase where smuggling/ contraband was very popular/common.
2. Late 1970s—80s: A period of turbulent trade unionism prevailed.
3. Late 1980s: The collapse of the textile mills in Mumbai.
4. 1990s: The phase of economic liberalisation, removal of Monopolies Trade Restrictive Act of late 1960s-70s and onset of globalisation.
5. 1992—Hindu nationalism– demolition of Babri Masjid– Communal Riots in1993 and commercialisation of crime.

The genesis of Mumbai's underworld can be traced to gambling, bootlegging, hooch arrac stocks, liquor dens set up by Pathan Karim Lala in the 1940. He was literally like a Godfather (Mano Puzzo, 1976) and Indian equivalent to the Italian Mafia, who was referred to as 'Mumbaia Mafia', is an organised body of criminals (syndicates). Thus he operated several gambling dens at Nagpada. Sociologically speaking, it was a case of Mertonian (1957) mode of adaptation' i.e. innovation. Anomie (Merton 1957) refers to a clear disjunction between cultural goals and the legitimate institutional means. Thus, in this case illegitimate means were used to achieve success. Many of the present dons such as Dawood were trained by him. After him in the late 1950s and early 1960s Varadarajan Mudaliar migrated from Tamil Nadu and worked as a porter at the railway station Matunga, which had literally become ghetto (Louis Worth, 1927) of the South Indian migrants to Mumbai (A mini South India). He too was involved in gambling, smuggling and other related anti-social activities. Mr Varde a senior Mumbai Police officer in his diary about Crime in Mumbai has described in great detail as to how Vardarajan had become a hero, a modern day Robinhood and a galli dada for the slum dwellers. The poor people used to literally worship him and for example if a baby boy was born they would literally put the baby at the feet of Varda to seek his blessings. Matunga had a big Ganapati set up by Varda which was over 20 feet. He was killed in a police encounter in the mid 1980s. Haaji Mastaan Mirza was Mumbai dockyard worker who got the first taste of crime, when was asked to deliver a small parcel (which contained gold biscuits). He accidentally out of curiosity opened and there began his infamous sojourn into the dark world of smuggling. Thus he was initiated into crime and transformed into becoming an ace smuggler.

Haji Mastaan had a strong political connection with the then ruling party and often mingled with several police officers, ministers and MLAs. Thus it was the benchmark for politisation of criminals and subsequently the criminals of politics, his infamous taste of Bollywood actresses becoming his mistresses. He used to throw lavish *Iftehar Eid* parties and invite ministers, get photographed with prominent political leaders, members of the Wagf Board Haj Pilgrimage committee, lawyers, film stars etc. He often even rubbed shoulders with prominent social workers. In a very candid interview in a leading Mumbai magazine, he had blatantly stated that 'Even if you arrest me at daytime, most of your political friends come to my house at night to collect money (*chanda*). He became a social worker and built several hospitals for the needy/poor early in 1990s. Thus social work got transformed into Bhai style social work. In the words of Munnabhai (MBBS), underworld social work refers to *kissi ko tapkana* (threaten to kill) *mandavali* (compromise money), *vasuli* (take back lent money), game *baja dena* (killing). Thus 'underworld social work is robbing the rich and helping the needy.

Another crucial factor responsible is the textile strike 1982-82 led by late Dr Datta Samant, a trade/leader which literally crippled the backbone of the textile mills and most importantly the textile mill workers who were rendered jobless thereby poverty set in, their teenage children loitered in the streets, mixed with similar street corner school dropout boys indulging in petty deviance. Thus the seeds of crime were sown for *e,g.* Amar Naik, Arun Gawli and even Dawood used to meet on Temkar Street (Nagapada) play cricket and gradually learnt the tricks of the trade, in fact Dawood fell into bad company and then became an apprentice of Karim Lala. Thus a Mumbai street corner gang was formed. (Refer to W. Whyte, 1943 – Street Corner Society.) Thus anomie (refer to Durkheim (1893) as well as mertonian (1957)) one, coupled with family disorganisation, bad companions hip factor, unemployment, poverty, deviance, delinquency set in. Thus this led to a spurt in the rate of crime in Mumbai and today what we see is the bludgeoning effect of the underworld controlling Bollywood, cricket, elections, extortion, retail housing, drugs smuggling, human trafficking and what not.

'D' Dawood Gang: Today 'Bhai' 'D-Company' have become synonymous with Dawood Ibrahim Kaskar—an ace underworld 'don' and son of a former CID constable and one of the most powerful gangster involved in transnational crime, narcotics, smuggling extortion, contract killing, financing bollywood films, cricket betting, real estate (his brother Iqbal Kaskar and sister (behana) Hasina Parkaar are very active in Nagpada area, threatening extortion of money control of buildings; thus mafias have entered into real estate business. He graduated into the business of crime at a very young age by smuggling silver, *vasuli*, extortion, forgery and cheating. He also tried to legitimise his illegal business by starting travel agencies, 'D' company and what not.

His most infamous dastardly act was the Mumbai Bomb Blast Jan 6th 1993, March 13th, 1993 as a revenge of Babri Masjid Demolition in December, 1992. His gang is extremely strong and powerful and killed 257 people so far and injured more than 700 people in 1993. At present, it is suspected that he has links with international crime (terrorism) such as Laskar e-Taiba, Al-Qaida and is very much an 'India's most wanted list and is a prime suspect in the July 11th, 2006, Borivali Train Bomb Blast. Till recently his right hand man was Chota Rajan Nikhalje (new gang) the street smart boy from Chembur who began his career by black marketing tickets at Cinema Hall in Tilak Nagar (a semi-slum area of Chembur suburb). Dawood had a secular gang but after 1993 blasts, Chota Rajan parted ways and for some time honey-mooned with Shiv Sena. At present, he has his own gang-extortion, real estate scandals and now his wife too has joined hands in their family businesses. Dawood in fact managed to escape to Dubai in the 1980s and from Dubai he controls everything through his three brothers Anees, Noora and Iqbal and sister Haseena and other close aides. Earlier Abu Salem used to help him especially in financing Bollywood films, *vasuli* job, extortion, contract killing (supari) at present in jail.

Many films such as 'Don', Murder, Company, Gangster, Satya, shootout at Lokhandwala depict the mysterious life of these gangsters. In fact, the film *Vastaav* is based on the life of Chota Rajan Producer N. Chandra stated, "Reel life and Real Life are incommensurables". Truth is in fact stranger than fiction. Selling of arms, RDX drugs, AK-56, etc., are also a part of the business of Dawood and Co. About 10-15 years ago there was an advertisement in a leading Mumbai newspaper vacancy for graduates (chemistry, science) and some of the shortlisted candidates were put up in five star hotels pay was about Rs 20-25,000. Many of the graduates were hired, but few were lucky enough to realise the hidden job and managed to escape by the skin of their teeth.

There are two-three other gangs operating.

1. *Arun Gawali Gang*: He was originally a textile mill worker, now he is an MLA of his party *Akhil Bharatya Sena* and is a frequent visitor to the jail. His gang is involved in extortion, collection of protection money from rich businessman, contract killing. He lives in a safe haven called 'Daagdi Chawl' (stone chawl) and is considered to be 'A big daddy' of all the slum dwellers.

2. *Amar Naik*: A son of a textile mill worker and an earlier friend of Dawood. He began his career as a collector of

protection money from vegetable vendors in Dadar Area, collection of *hafta* and extortion money, etc. Amar Naik was daggers drawn with Arun Gawali Gang and finally was killed on August 9th, 1996 and his brother Ashwin Naik an engineer took over the gang since Amar's death.

The crime situation in Mumbai has worsened over the years and it has assumed an international global terrorism dimension to it. Today, crime is no longer considered to be for personal vendetta but has become more an international and global domain.

Crime in Mumbai

Its prominent types, (*Source:* A. Shaban, 2006)

1. Crime against life, murder is a result of personalised/ personal disputes and altercations (Clinard Meier, 1975). The Rate of murder differs according to country region, local area, caste class, race religion. In 1975, Mumbai had 1/10 out of 9 per cent cases in Maharashtra. In 2003 only 0.74 per cent, it is really after 1993 that the murder rate declined. Post 1995 police efforts to eliminate big gangs, small gangs too in the process were eliminated. The use of fake encounters by the police resulted in the decline.

Table 2. Top 10 Police Stations in Terms of Reported Murder Cases and Murder Rate in Mumbai Average in 2002-02

Sr. No.	*Police Station*	*Cases*	*Sr. No.*	*Police Station*	*Murder Ratio*
1.	Sakinaka	12	1.	J.J. Marg	13.81
2.	Antop Hill	9	2.	Nirmal Nagar	11.38
3.	Malavani	8	3.	Colaba	10.75
4.	Dharavi	7	4.	V.P. Road	8.70
5.	Shivaji Nagar	7	5.	Pant Nagar	8.60
6.	Mulund	7	6.	Juhu	8.40
7.	Oshiwara	6	7.	Aare (sub)	8.36
8.	Kurla	6	8.	L.T. Marg	7.51
9.	D.N.Nagar	6	9.	Bandra	7.37
10.	Agripada	6	10.	Shivaji Park	8.14

Places/police stations such as Sakinaka, Antop Hill, Dharavi, Shivajinagar, Mulund, Oshiwara, Kurla, Agripada, D.N. Nagar, Agripada all have slums dominated by lower middle class people, the density of population is very high here and murder rate is very high in J.J. Marg Nirmal Nagar. At the same parts of South Mumbai, such as Colaba V.P. Road is where upper middle and high income group people live, hence high murder rate. It is relative deprivation/poverty which contributes to high murder rate.

The case of violent crime like murder has significantly increased in big cities. Mumbai till 1993, used to be ranked second city in murder rate but then it started declining and was mainly confined to five hotspots South Mumbai, South Central Mumbai, Mahim Creek, Pant Nagar, Shivaji Nagar axis in eastern suburb. In Goregaon, where more slums are located and major transport lines (railway tracks) run from south to north direction of Mumbai. At the same line in south Mumbai areas with low population density and high floating population, there is a high risk to life. In Colaba, particular, mostly old people stay alone, and there are major offices located - economic crimes are committed to a very large extent.

Source: Crime Branch Mumbai

Table 3. Top Ten Police Stations: Reported Cases of Attempt to Commit Murder Cases and its Rate in Mumbai August 2000-02.

1.	Dharavi	5	Bandra	11.97
2.	Sakinaka	5	J.J.	10.34
3.	Vakola	5	Malabar	8.32
4.	Malavani	5	Mahim	7.44
5.	Mulund	5	Dongri	6.51
6.	Oshiware	5	Kherwari	5.33
7.	Bandra	4	R.A.K. Marg	5.08
8.	Chembur	4	Pant Nagar	4.72
9.	Trombay	4	Shivaji Park	4.07
10.	Shivaji Nagar	4	Juhu	3.89

Source: Mumbai Crime Branch, 2004.

2. Property crime includes dacoity, extortion, robbery, house burglary, theft, chain snatching and pick pocketing.

Now-a-days extortion has increased which has a positive correction with the underworld. Besides the underworld muscle men with political nexus, local goons and *goondas or dadas* along with *bhailogs* are also involved in this crime. Very often we hear/read news that prominent businessman's son was kidnapped and a ransom of Rs 20 crore demanded or threats, demands over mobile phones from builders. We often hear of '*haftas*' being asked not only by goons but also by policemen, e.g., passport/license renewal.

There has been a sharp rise in extortion cases. Years 1998-2004 i.e., when the underworld dons took over eversince 1985-92, there has been a steep rise. Big underworld gangs like Dawood, Chota Rajan, Shakeel operate through youngsters hired who are mostly school dropouts, unemployed and earn about Rs 3,000 per case, whereas the real 'don' earns crores of rupees. Now-a-days even girl and women have become 'extortionists' '*behenas*' as they are popularly called are often lovers, sisters of '*bhais*' (dons). To cut a few examples, Rubina behena C/o Shakeel gang. It is lucrative business for them.

Table 4. Top 10 Police Station Extortion Rate

J.J. Marg	18.98
V.P. Road	12.21
Bandra	11.26
Malabar Hill	11.05
M.R.A. Marg	10.40
Mahim	10.30
D.B. Marg	9.16
Nirmal Nagar	8.12
Worli	7.19

Source: Crime in Mumbai and Abdul Shaban, 2006).

Table 5. Dacoity

There were 41 cases reported in 2004.

L.T. Marg	23.79
Bandra	8.29
V.P. Road	7.87
Dongri	5.58
Pant Nagar	3.91
Byculla	3.71
D.B. Marg	2.81
Pydhoni	2.53
MRA Marg	2.20
Kasturbha Marg	2.18

Very often robbers belong to ex-criminal tribes (Bhatkya Vimukta Jamatis). For them, it was a hereditary castewise occupation each in villages. Most of them are uneducated, poor and often live on railway platforms, under flyover. During British period, they were classified as criminal tribes. (Noted Anthropologist Oscar Lewis (1968)). In the study of Slum Culture – Backgrounds for Le Vida (Mexican Studies in the Culture of Poverty), Lewis tried to posit a correlation between poverty and its associated traits as a culture, or more accurately, as a subculture with its own structure and rationale, as a way of life that is passed down from generation to generation along families.

The 'concept of culture of poverty' can come into being in a variety of historical contexts.

In the case of India, to be Maharashtra specific—the *Pardhis* (ex-criminal tribes) were compelled to follow their traditional occupation, i.e., of looting robbery pickpocketing, theft. Sociologically speaking, it was a hereditary occupation (caste-tribe wise) based and had to be followed strictly according to traditional customs. Parsonian term would be 'ascriptive status' which was passed on from generation to generation. The peculiarity of Indian society was that they were also treated as 'outcastes' 'stigmatised'. (Refer Irwin Goffman 'The stigma' (notes on management of a spoilt identity or socially labelled, branded (1973)). (Howard Becker) Caste wise residents, Lewis stated that 'culture of poverty is both an adaptation of poor to their marginal position in a class-stratified highly individuated capitalistic society. It represents effort to cope with feelings of hopelessness and despair that develop from the realisation of the improbability of achieving success in terms of values and goals of larger society. Thus as Lewis had stated that landless rural migrants are more likely to develop culture of poverty when they migrate to cities. The concept of anomie (Durkheim) (state of normalessness, isolation, estrangement, alienation (from their villages, families, communities) to a strange new place where there is a literal struggle (survival of fittest) in a big city. Hence, it is survival and subsistence which must be met here so their old skills. Most of them are hired by local *goondas* and dons for robberies thefts at times even shooting, due to their sharp aim.

Police Encounter (2005)

Table 6. *Goondas* Killed in Police Encounter

Year	*Dawood*	*Chota Rajan*	*Arun Gawli*	*Amar Naid*	*Others*	*Terrorists*	*Total*
2000	39	19	5	3	7	0	58
2001	30	42	0	7	15	0	70
2002	7	26	0	1	13	0	35
2003	2	15	3	0	15	5	27
2004	1	5	0	0	4	5	12
2005	1	2	0	1	9	0	12
2006	1	2	0	1	10	1	15

Source: www//Mumbai police.org (2005).

Comparative Statistical Analysis

Table 7. Extortion Crimes Related to Gangs and Other Types of Petty Crime

Year	*Total Crime*	*Gang*	*Petty Crime*	*Total Arrested Accused*
2000	344	338	238	576
2001	290	212	369	581
2002	175	135	138	273
2003	142	86	147	227
2004	190	66	185	251
2005	210	59	258	317
2006	137	42	185	227

Table 8. Action Taken Under MOCCA Its Analysis

Year	*Dawood*	*Chota Rajan*	*Arun Gawli*	*Amar Naid*	*Others*	*Total*
2000	54	0	0	4	7	65
2001	51	0	5	18	11	85
2002	05	0	0	14	12	31
2003	6	0	0	0	6	12
2004	23	0	6	10	51	90
2005	7	0	2	56	69	134

* In the case of Arun Gawli figure is '0' because he was arrested and now even though released has become an MLA floated at new political party called 'Akil Bharatiya Sena' in 1997. At present he is lying low. He was recently arrested on 1st December, 2006 by Mumbai police in connection with extortion demand of Rs 4 crore from a prominent builder in Mumbai, and later released after paying Rs 1 lakh as bail for getting out of jail.

Table 9. Use of Fire Arms during Murder

Year	*Total Cases*	*Total Crime Organised*	*Local Goondas*	*Total*
2000	24	3	22	25
2001	18	11	7	18
2002	13	3	10	13
2003	10	1	11	12
2004	16	0	16	16
2005	6	0	6	6

Another aspect of city crime is the growing incidence car/ auto theft. The concept of the relative deprivation, invidious comparisons and relative poverty generates this type of crime. One of the chief reasons attributed is growing consumer's craze in equality which often leads to desperation in the marginalised sections of the society hence resorting to illegal means stealing. Mertonian concept of anomie disjunction between cultural goals and institutionalised means the type of adaptation would be that of innovation. Very often auto theft takes place in areas inhabited by middle/rich class places take Shivaji Park, Juhu people own more than 2-3 cars, faculty of pace, park cars hence are often parked on the roads there by leading to thefts. A closely related type of crime to auto theft is chain snatching which is carried out by gangs. Many times women resort to it splashily inside crowded buses, trains, markets. Anonymity and overcrowding facilitates crime. It is quick money and is very similar to pick pocketing.

A major type of high profile crime is Economic/Corporate/ white collar which rocked the crime of Mumbai in 1992, Harshad Mehta Shares Rigging Market/ Stock exchange scandal. Evasion of taxes counterfeiting manipulation or by hiring influential people to gate work done illegally bribery, corruption constitutes it. Majority of such crime occur in south central Mumbai. The last type of crime is against women-rape, molestation assault. Recent rape-case at Marine Drive Police Chowkey More, a sub-inspector on a teenaged college girl sent shock waves thought Mumbai. Rape is a type of moral crime areas of occurrence finds associated which help density of population, congestion slums hotspots such as J.J. Marg, Dongri, Bandra, Mahim, Kherwadi, Matunga, Shivajinagar, Chembur, Mankhurd, Deonar, Pantnagar, Vikhroli spatially speaking area scheduled locally spots are also rape/ crime prone Colaba, Juhu, Malbar hill, Bandra Reclamation pomerenade near Bandra bus stand. Today, a lot of moral policing has started and lonely couple lovers are discouraged from sitting at beaches on park benches and police even go to fashion shows in civilian clothes.

Conclusion

Although Mumbai is the financial capital of the country, alas all that glitters is not gold. The ugly face of crime is present and makes its presence felt everywhere. One is saddened, when one opens the newspaper early morning and the crime news just spills over. The push and pull factors (see Evert Lee.) the unchecked migration—majority from BIMARU states into the city. The chief causes of migration are employment, marriage and family feud. The latest figure i.e., out of every five migrants to Mumbai, one from U.P., only 37.4 per cent were from Maharashtra. (refer to D.P. Singh (TISS), Migration in Mumbai: Fifty years review) Today 24.3 per cent of the migrant population in Mumbai is from U.P. i.e., during the last fifty years it has moved from 12 per cent to 24.3 per cent and from Bihar 0.2 per cent to 3.5 per cent, 81.5 per cent of rural migrants were from U.P., 79 per cent, Bihar in 2001.The factor of anonymity, heterogeneity, size and density of the population contributing to sense of loneliness, alienation, estrangement contributing to sharp rise in deviant, criminal anti-social behaviour. The socio-economic disparity from high rise buildings, pent houses, malls to slums, squatters, hutments. The lack of jobs, growing unemployment. The ghettoisation of Muslim population 17 per cent, who migrated from U.P., Bihar in the city especially post 1992-93. Last but not the least, the underworld gangsters, credit card extortion, its internationalisation and globalisation of terrorism has all contributed to hike in the crime and lastly the inability, connivance, ignorance and collusion and criminalisation of politics and politicisation of crime and lastly corruption contribute to crime. As stated by Home Minister, after finance department, it is police department which is the second most corrupt one, in Mumbai/Maharashtra. As once Lalu Prasad stated, 'Maharashtra and Bihar have a lot in common to share, unfortunately after Bihar it is Maharashtra (Mumbai) where the crime rate is very high. It is the pathetic plight of law and order situation that makes Mumbai go closer to Bihar. Bollywood and crime-underworld financing films entertainment industry are the other aspects of crime.

References

Boudon, Raymond. 1974. *'The Sociological Explaination'*, Penguin Books Ltd., Great Britain.

Crime Analysis and Over View: pp. 253-254. 1995 from International Encyclopedia of Sociology Vol. 1 and pp. 1025-1027, Vol. 2, edited by Frank Magill, Fitzroy Dearbon publisher, London. U.K.

Davis, M. 2004. *'Planet of Slums'*. New Left Review 26, pp. 5-34.

Dickens, C. 1846. *'The Adventures of Oliver Twist'* Bradbury and Evans', London.

Floor, J. 2002. *'Secure tenure: global definition and measurement'.* Paper presented to the European Housing Network Conference', Vienna, July 2002.

Gerth, H.H. and Mills. C.W. 1958. (English Translation) From Max Weber: *'Essays in Sociology'*, Galaxy publication, New York, USA.

Gilbert, Alan. *'The Return of the Slum: Does Language Matter'?*

Hadded Lawrence, Ruel. T. Marie and Garrett James L. April 1999. *'Are Urban Poverty and Under Nutrition Growing?'* Food and Consumption and Nut*rition Division, International Food Policy Research* Institute, 2033, K. Street, N.W., Washington D.C, Publication, USA. Hawkins, J.M. and R. Allen (ed.). 1999. *'The Oxford encyclopedic English dictionary'*, Clarendon Press, Oxford.

J. S. Mill's Methods, source. www.wikipedia Books 1843. *'A System of logic'* www.wikipedia.com. J.S. Mills, 'Methods Cannons of Agreement'.

Marris, P. 1979. *'The Meaning of Slums and Patterns of Change'.* International Journal of *Urban and Regional Research 3, 419-41.*

Max, Scheler. 1968. *'International Encyclopedia of Social Sciences'*, Vol. 14, edited by David. L. Sills, published by Macmillan Company and Free Press.

Max Scheler, 1912. 1961. (English Translation of German book) 'Resentment (edited) Free Press publication, New York, USA.

Mehta, Suketu. April 2006. *'Maximum City: Bombay Lost and Found.'* Penguin Books India Publications, New Delhi. India.

Mumbai Police. 2006. *'Crime Report'*, At a glance.

Oxford Economic Dictionary online. www.document. URL http://dictionary.oed.com/cgi/entry/50228106?query_type=word&queryword=slum&first=1&max_ to_show=10&sort_type=alpha&result_place=1&search_id=hEbF-5jy7Uw-1159&hilite=50228106(accessed in February 2007).

Prunty, J. 1998. Dublin Slums, 1800-1925; *'A Study of Urban Geography'*. Irish Academic Press, Dublin.

Ravallion M. Feb. 2001. *'On the Urbanisation of Poverty'* World Bank Publication, Washington D.C., USA.

Times of India, Mumbai. 19th December, 2007. *'Crime and the City'*

UN-Habitat. 2003a. *'The challenge of slums: global report on human settlements 2003'*, Nairobi.

UN-Habitat. 2003b. *'Slums of the world: the face of urban poverty in the new millennium'*, Nairobi.

Vebler, Thorstein. 1925. *'The Theory of Leisure Class: An Economic Study of Institutions'*. George Allen and Unwin Ltd. Publication. London. Great Britain.

World Bank/UNCHS (Habitat). 2000. Cities 'Alliance *for Cities without Slums: action plan for moving slum upgrading to scale, special summary'* edition www. Document. http://www.citiesalliance.org/activities-output/topics.

Yelling, J.A. 1986. *'Slums and Slum clearance in Victorian London'*, Allen and Unwin, London.

Zetter Berg. Hans L. 1954. *'On theory and verification in Sociology.'* Stockholm. Almquist and Wiksell/Tressler press, New York. USA.

6 Deviant Behaviour of Children in the Age of Globalisation

P.K. Chaudhary

Introduction

The human behaviour is described in two forms. First form helps in the preservation of social structure and organisation, and the second one brings about the disorganisation. The first type of behaviour is found in consonance with the social values while the second type of behaviour is contrary to norms and values of the society. Those, who behave in accordance with the rules of the dominant culture, are called conformists. Those, who violate the codes of conduct, are generally known as non conformists or deviants. In general deviate means to stray from an accepted path. The deviance consists of those acts which do not follow the norms and expectations of a particular group of the society as a whole.

Sociologist has defined deviance as a part behaviour that violate is an essential social norm or set of norms. Deviants are those who go beyond the limits of socially acceptable behaviour.

An American Sociologist Marshall B. Clinard suggested that the term deviance should be reserved for "those situations in which behaviour is in a disapproved direction and of a sufficient degree to exceed the tolerance limit of the community. In terms of Clinard's definition, crime and delinquency are the most obvious forms of deviance, but this definition has not been accepted by others, because crime refers to those activities which break the law of the land and are subject to official punishment; delinquency refers to the criminal activities of youth. However, many other psychologists, and sociologists, approved that deviant acts go beyond the limits which come under the definition of crime.

Deviance is a relative concept. Whatever is deviant at one

place are at one time, be acceptable behaviour elsewhere or at any another time as well, Behaviour is defined as acceptable in one culture can be off limits in another. At certain times in western society, it has been considered deviant for women to smoke and consume alcoholic drink in public. Now-a-days such case is not longer. In the same way behaviour accepted as normal in western society may be defined as deviant in other society.

On the basis of above explanation—discussion, deviance refers to those activities which do not conform to the norms and expectations of members of a particular society. It usually refers to those activities which bring general disapproval from members of society. Action is only deviant in relation to the standards of a particular society at a particular time in its history.

Children are the blooming flowers of the garden of society and a valuable asset of the nation. Nation, state and family members should take proper care of their development. To some extent effort has been made for their development. But due to various processes of change i.e., modernisation, westernisation and globalisation children underwent change in behaviour. Deviant behaviours of children is not recent phenomena. Before globalisation and modernisation, there was deviant behaviour, but the nature of deviant behaviour underwent a great change.

The whole world has been facing problem of deviant behaviour of the children below the age of 10 years. Deviant behaviour of children is known in various names in different countries. They are the teddy boy in England, the '*nozem*' in the Netherlands, the "*raggar*e' in Sweden, the '*blusons noris'* in France the '*tsotsis*' in South Africa, the '*bodgies*' in Australia, the '*halbstaken*' in Austria and Germany, the '*tai-pau*' in Taiwan.

Factors Responsible for Child Deviation

There are different opinions regarding the cause of deviation. They are usually oversimplified, explanations such as slum living, broken homes, films and moral deprivation fail to provide us universal and realistic reasons of deviation. The cause of children deviation may be divided into following categories.

1. Social Factor

The determining factors of children deviation are social. As observed by Dr M.J. Sethna, "undesirable condition at home, particularly quarrels with parents, desertion, intoxication, immorality of the parents, poverty and lack of employment, overcrowded in one room lodgings, lack of proper sanitation or inconveniences, cruelty of step parents, desertion or lack of care in the case of an unwanted children these are the main causes. In fact, warm and secure family ties are essential for mental, moral, and physical growth of children. Further, more boys in comparison to girls are apprehended. The reason for this may be that in Indian set-up, girls lead a very sheltered life and are therefore, less likely to come in conflict with the law of the land than boys. The police as well as the public are also likely to be more lenient to girls than boys, and may not apprehend them."

2. Economic Factor

"Many writers have drawn the attention to the fact that most children belong to the downtrodden class due to which crimes increase with economic depression and unemployment and that crime stands against poverty are more common in a capitalistic organisation of the society. There can be no question as to these facts. The problem is in their proper interpretation. Does it mean that they steal because they are hungry? Do girls enter in to life of prostitution, because of need? For both cases the question can be answered 'yes' and 'no'. Some persons steal because they are hungry or because of their families in need. Some girls enter into the life of prostitution or to that cause of conduct which may lead to prostitution by reason of the pressure of necessity. On the other hand, some people in very deepest distress do not also commit crime and some girls in the direct need do not stray from the path of virtue. It is therefore; very much clear that in most cases they act indirectly rather than directly.

It is observed that most of the social thinkers agree to the fact that poverty is a major cause of deviation. Some writers, however, do not think that poverty alone is responsible, but it is almost a unanimously agreed conclusion i.e., the poverty which forms the soil on which deviation may germinate in the shape being determined by individual personality. It may also be pointed out here that poverty is not synonymous with a state of hunger or starvation. A section of population or an individual may have enough to eat, but if there is economic disparity in the society, if a section of population possesses all textures objects of comfort, while the other section do not have, then a state of social starvation is created, a starvation of hunger for the comfort commodities, which our modern society has created, therefore, hunger is not from food alone, but hunger, widely prevalent in our society, hunger is not from food alone, widely prevalent in our society, due to lack of commodities which is also responsible for increasing the number of deviation.

3. Psychological Factor

Psychological factors are also important for the causation of children deviation. Lack of affection and insecurity are bound to create mental conflict in the child, among the children during childhood the mind set up is very sensitive. Hence overcrowding is very bad for the children. The child sleeping in the same room with his parents sees and overhears all things from parents. It creates very bad effects. Further, the emotional disturbances also create deviant behaviour. Generally mental suffering and emotional disturbances lead to deviation.

4. Biological Factor

The biological factors are also involved in the causation of deviation. Physical ailments create inferiority complex and as a result of this complex there is deviation in the behaviour.

According to Healy and Bronner, the main cause of deviation are (1) Bad Company (2) Adolescent Instability (3) Mental Conflicts (4) Early Sex Experiences (5) Emotional Conflicts (6) Motion Pictures (7) Poor Recreation (8) Vocational Dissatisfaction (9) Physical Condition.

5. Globalisation Factor

The process of globalisation, liberalisation, information technology is being taken place in our society. It has under gone changes almost all traditional norms and values of the society. The different channels of T.V., i.e., H.B.O. M.T.V., ZMZ, Zoom and so on are also responsible to expose give young generation about the new culture.

When parents return home, there is a little interaction between the parents and the kids, except for homework and studies which makes the kids tenser. Experts also pointed out that the pressure in schools is very high. There is little or no interaction between teachers and students, while parents are shifting duty to the teachers, the teachers are shifting it to parents. Patterns of delinquent behaviour arise in the texture of modern society.

Films and pornographic literature have also aggravated the situation. Social scientists Walter Beels thinks, "what better media than the cinema and lately the television from early child is initiated into lustful scenes, and becomes habitual later on to suggestive innuendoes laughs at bolts and bares and bars and eats the worlds as his oyster."

Following are the findings of recent studies:

(a) Dr. Ashum Gupta leading professor of Psychology in Delhi University made a classic explanation about child deviation. He said that the Attention Deficit Disorder with Hype activity (ADDH). In technical terms, this is a neuro-chemical disturbance in the brain found in a large number of children for deviation. Dr Gupta said that only this disorder is behind aggression in kids. It certainly could be one of the major contributory factors. Sometime, the feelings of alienation may join an anti-social gang just to gain peer acceptance that may be self-gratifying sometimes, they may turn towards deviation. Petty thieves indulge in stealing or committing more heinous crime.

(b) Riyata Kaffshoma, social scientist of To Hokuu University Japan, said computer game playing frequently more for than one hour destroy the brain cells, which control the human behaviour

(c) The Research Report of Michigan University U.S.A. enlighten that violent video game playing is very serious for children, because children placing themselves as actor in game. Report also enlightens that children who are watching violence movies also become violent in their real lives.

Some important incident of child deviation in the age of Globalisation:

- On March, 1999, a 24 year old allegedly battered to death by their three year old friend and left her body in a nullah.
- On October 27th, 1999, Hemant, a 16 year old student of DAV school in Vasant Vihar in New Delhi was bludgeoned to death allegedly by four neighbourhood

boys in a school compound in R.K. Puram, where they all live because the boys mistakenly believed that Hemant's father owned a petrol pump (he was a manager there) and wanted to abduct him for ransom but panicked and killed him.

- On 7th May, 2000 a 14 year old boy from Vikaspuri in Delhi killed his mother, when she accused him at stealing her Jewellery.
- On 24th May, 2000, a 10 year old Rajesh from Saharsa at Purnea District in Bihar allegedly shot his classmate Munna after a quarrel when they were watching T.V. Munna apparently did not give Rajesh enough space to sit before the screen in the crowded room. The two had a fight. An enraged Rajesh went out, returned with a revolver and shot Munna dead at point blank range.
- On 26th June, 2000, an 11 year old boy named Badal of Std. IV student and a resident of Sahibabad was on his way to his aunt's house, he came across a little boy cradling his six-month old baby sister. Badal snatched the infant Shweta, ran off with her towards the big nullah, and allegedly drowned her. Why did he kill them? Because he liked to see the bubbles in the water and the kids struggle as he drowned them? Apparently, the idea had struck him after he watched a television serial, "Captain House."
- A 14 year old student of the Army Public School in Delhi reportedly killed his classmate because the latter one had refused to give him Rs 10.
- In September, 2004, a 11th class student of Delhi Public School, R.K. Puram, New Delhi reported that he was indulging himself in oral sex with girl classmate in the classroom and his friend was made video recording. His friend sent the said video recording to other friend through Blue-tooth technology; it was displayed in all modern cell phone and in computer.
- There was the six year old child of Luckhnow, who left off the balcony of his second floor, trying to imitate a bungee jumping drop shown in a soft drinks commercial aid.

- According to the report of Alcohol Atlas 2006, said that 13.5 year old average children started consuming alcohol in Kerala.
- On 6th Oct, 2007, a 10th and 11th Class student assassinated the three year old child.
- On 11th Dec., 2007 a 8th Class student of Uro International School of Gurgaon Shot dead his friend.
- On 30th Jan., 2008, a Xth Class student of Satna, M.P. reported shot dead to VIIIth class student.
- A 12 year old Subin Kumar, who claimed to have been severally thrashed and confined to hospital bed by a couple of other same aged teenagers practicing their latest World Wrestling Federation (W.W.F.) move or dwelling into the darker and more sinister story.

There have been reports all over the country of children hurting themselves while trying to ape the superhuman feats of *Shaktiman* (the superhero of Indian T.V.)

Apart from above deviation, children have started another deviation: Children have invented various new types of deviant behaviour in modern society and those deviations are unknown to their elder people. For example, Iodex ointment which is a medicine for muscular pain relief and corex a cough syrup, but children are found of eating with slice bread and at a time consume full bottle of corex cough syrup, drinking for getting intoxication. Likewise, Dendride is type of gum but, children who are engaged in surrounding railway areas found that Dendride could be purchased by paying only Rs five and pour on any cloth or handkerchief and inhale by mouth, then they feel very relaxed and intoxicated. It is also found that Disprine, a medicine for headache is used by younger school going and college going students putting it in cold drinks. In five minutes disprine dissolve in cold drink, they drink and feel intoxicated. Some of the school children found to be eating slice bread with whitener for intoxication.

Analytical Description of Child Deviation

The social scientists and media experts have been searching the answer for decades that what is the main cause of child deviation in the modern age and thousand of studies have been done on it. Most of them reached the same conclusion; media violence is responsible for deviant behaviour in children. Some of them are having supportive argument and a few of them are having negative argument.

Mr. P.N. Vasanti, Director Centre for Media Studies, said, an overdose of screen violence can have lifelong detrimental effects on the health of the kids.

In the age of globalisation, the situation is worse that children today are viewing more violence and conflict than ever before.

A study of violence on Indian television and its impact on children commissioned by UNESCO accused the idiot box is "bombarding young minds with all kinds of violent images, cutting across channels, programmes and viewing times."

The researcher identified 759 distinct acts of violence across five channels over a period of nine days. The report pointed out that in one episode of *Shaktiman,* there were as many as 17 acts of violence in approximately 25 minutes. These include assaulting, slapping, punching, shooting, strangulating, burning, pushing stabbing etc., important for deviant behaviour.

Not only research, but also incident go to prove that children who watch violent episodes show increased deviant behaviour says Kanta Choudhary, a parent of two young boys, whenever the boys watch W.W.F. there is half-an-hour wresting competition at home.

Abhilasha Kumari, a media researcher at Jamia Mila University said that "Millions of Kids Watch t.v. The very fact is that every child does not imitate the violence, therefore t.v. goes to prove the relationship between media violence and human behaviour is still quite weak: it does not prove a direct cause and effect relationship."

Dr Vasantha R. Patri a counsellor said that, anger, aggression and anti-social tendencies are already quite high for so many reasons. So, parental attitudes and reaction to aggression are probably equally important. She further said that, in most cases media is only the fourth most important influence in a child's life, while parents, teachers and peers being the first three.

Conclusion

Deviant behaviour of children is not a recent phenomenon, but nature of deviation underwent a change in the age of globalisation. There are contradictions between close society and modern society. We are living in close society, but due to process of globalisation, the mentality of open society (Western Society) has developed in our society.

To some extent media is responsible for deviant behaviour of children. Media exposes all knowledge and information about modern and traditional society, that is why children are behaving premature behaviour.

In this context, it not good assumption that media is only responsible for deviant behaviour of children, in fact parent, teacher, friend, culture and family environment of society is also equally responsible.

Sometimes T.V. provides an opportunity to discharge the pent-up, aggressive, feelings of anger, hostility and frustration. So, media is not problem for children, but lack of media education is a problem for children. Parent should teach them real status of T.V. programmes, for example children need to be told that T.V. programmes should be treated simply as entertainment. They should be told that violence is faked for T.V. shows, using special effects, stunts, editing and other techniques that make violence look realistic.

Prof Yogendra Singh, Emeritus fellow of J.N.U. said that present education system is valueless system that is why valueless education builds up moralless behaviour, therefore, value should be taught in modern education system.

K. L. Luthra, Chairman, A.S.N. Public School said that most of children are out of control from parent side. The parents are not supposed to beat for any type of deviation, and government has prohibited to child beating in school, therefore children are fearless. Fearless is also important reason for deviant behaviour. So, parent should beat their child only when their child does major deviation that will create fear in children, and teachers also be given freedom to beat their students.

The careless parents are also responsible to make their child violent. In modern society, parent don't have time for love and affection with their children. So, parent should give love and affection and spare proper time for their children. Don't accept all demand on the basis of rationality, fulfil their demand parent should teach them what is right and what is wrong, respect to elder person, make some restriction to bad accompany.

Dr (Prof.) P.D. Singh said that kids should be taken care of since pregnancy period. If mother reads religious text at the time of pregnancy period, that will make good effect on kid's moral and character.

Sex-education is not proper in our school stage and whatever knowledge acquired is not sufficient. So, they have built up wrong image about the sex and trying to fulfil in school age—that is why healthy sex-education is required in school age.

Referencs

B. Chakraverty, *Education and Child Labour,* Chugh Publication, Allahabad.

Dave A.B. (1988), *Extent, Forms and Cause of Child Abuse in India.*

Suman, Somen K. '*Child Abuse in India, Social Welfare*", Nov.-Dec. 1985, p. 22.

Glueck S. and Gluek E. (1950), '*Unraveling Juvenile Delinquency*', Cambridge, University Press.

Kulshreshtha, Jinesh C. (1994), *Indan Child labour*, Uppal Publications Delhi.

Prohl S. (1994) *Images of Deviance and Social Control: A Sociological History* (2nd ed.) New Yourk, McGraw-Hill, Inc.

7 Legal System in India

Hanu H. Chavda

The Indian Legal System is one of the oldest legal systems in the entire history of the world. It has altered as well as developed over the past few centuries to absorb inferences from the legal systems across the world. The Constitution of India is the fountainhead of the Indian Legal System. It demonstrates the Anglo-Saxon character of judiciary which is basically drawn from the British Legal System.

The Primary Origins of Law

- The Indian Constitution
- Customary Law
- Case Law, and
- Statutes (Legislation)

Among these, the statutes are operated by the Parliament, union territory legislatures and state legislatures. There are mainly two categories under which the Indian legal system operates, these include, Indian civil law and criminal law.

India is a land of diversified culture, local customs and various conventions which are not in opposition to the statue or ethics. People of different religions as well as traditions are regulated by all the different sets of personal laws in order to relate to family affairs.

Classifications of Indian Legal System

The judicial system or Indian legal system is a unique feature of the Indian Constitution. It is an integrated system of courts that administer both state and union laws. The Supreme Court of India is the uppermost part in the Indian legal system. Under this, each state or a group of states possesses High

Courts. There are several subordinate courts under these High Courts.

Basics of Indian Legal System

The President of India appoints the Chief Justice and the other judges of the Supreme Court. The Supreme Court of India has its own advisory and appellate jurisdiction that extends to the enforcement of primary rights mentioned by the Indian Constitution and to any argument in between the Government of India and all the states of India.

While the Indian legal system is measured fair, a large backlog of different types of cases can be found and regular dissolutions can effect in the delay before the closing of a particular case, though, matters of precedence and public interest are dealt with efficiently. Besides these, interim relief is also allowed in other cases where it is necessary.

Judicial System in India

The judiciary is relatively independent and the legal system is based on English common law. India's independent judicial system began under the British, and its concept and procedures resemble those of Anglo-Saxon countries. The Supreme Court consists of a chief justice and 25 other justices, all appointed by the president on the advice of the prime minister.

The Supreme Court is the apex court in the country. The High Court stands at the head of the state's judicial administration. Each state is divided into judicial districts presided over by a district and sessions judge, who is the highest judicial authority in a district. Below him there are courts of civil jurisdiction, known in different states as *munsiffs*, sub-judges, civil judges and the like. Similarly, criminal judiciary comprises chief judicial magistrate and judicial magistrates of first and second class.

Supreme Court

The Supreme Court has original, appellate and advisory jurisdiction. Its exclusive original jurisdiction extends to all disputes between the Union and one or more states or between two or more states. The Constitution gives an extensive original jurisdiction to the Supreme Court to enforce fundamental rights.

Appellate jurisdiction of the supreme court can be invoked

by a certificate of the High Court concerned or by special leave granted by the Supreme Court in respect of any judgment, decree or final order of a High Court in cases both civil and criminal, involving substantial questions of law as to the interpretation of the constitution. The President may consult the Supreme Court on any question of fact or law of public importance.

The Supreme Court of India comprises of the Chief Justice and not more than 25 other Judges appointed by the President. Judges hold office till 65 years of age.

High Courts

There are 18 High Courts in the country, three having jurisdiction over more than one state. Bombay High Court has the jurisdiction over Maharashtra, Goa, Dadra and Nagar Haveli and Daman and Diu. Guwahati High Court, which was earlier known as Assam High Court, has the jurisdiction over Assam, Manipur, Meghalaya, Nagaland, Tripura, Mizoram and Arunachal Pradesh. Punjab and Haryana High Court has the Jurisdiction over Punjab, Haryana and Chandigarh.

Among the Union Territories, Delhi alone has had a High Court of its own. The other six Union Territories come under jurisdiction of different state High Courts. The chief justice of a High Court is appointed by the President in consultation with the chief justice of India and the Governor of the state. Each High Court has powers of superintendence over all courts within its jurisdiction. High Court judges retire at the age of 62.

The jurisdiction as well as the laws administered by a High Court can be altered both by the Union and State Legislatures. Certain High Courts, like those at Bombay, Calcutta and Madras, have original and appellate jurisdictions. Under the original jurisdiction suits, where the subject matter is valued at Rs 25, 000 or more, can be filed directly in the High Court. Most High Courts have only appellate jurisdiction.

Lok Adalat

Lok Adalats are voluntary agencies for resolution of disputes through conciliatory.

Facts about the Indian Government:

India is one of the Asian countries that follow a federal system of governance and the Prime minister takes care of the

Central Government affairs. The Central Government acts on the behalf of the Indian President, who is designated as Head of the State. More important facts about the Indian Government have been mentioned below.

The Parliament of India is located in New Delhi at Sansad Marg. Total members of the Parliament include 250 Rajya Sabha members' and 552 Lok Sabha members.

A bill becomes an Act only when the Parliament, both the Rajya Sabha and the Lok Sabha, passes it and the same is given assent to by the Indian President.

The Executive, the Legislative and the Judiciary: Under the Indian Constitution, there are three bodies that can exercise its powers for the betterment of the nation. They are classified into three categories:

- Legislative
- Judicial
- Executive

The Union Executive comprises the President of India, the Vice-President and the Council of Ministers, headed by the Indian Prime Minister. The Indian Parliament forms the legislative body of the country. The Union judiciary is ruled by the Supreme Court of India. A similar executive, legislative and judiciary structure also exists within the individual states in India.

The history of Indian government:

- The first Prime Minister of India was Jawaharlal Nehru
- The first Indian President was Dr Rajendra Prasad
- India became a federal, democratic republic on January 26, 1950
- Dr Zakir Hussain was the first Indian President to die in office

Indian Penal Code Facts: Indian Penal Code Facts relate all the crimes, offences and wrong-doings to the articles and their sections under which the criminals and the offenders are punished by the court of law. Every Indian citizen is entitled to be punished under Indian Penal Code according to the nature and intention of the offence committed. The Indian Penal Code or IPC also covers the crime committed on a ship or an air-craft within Indian boundaries.

The Indian Penal Code was put into effect in 1862, during the British rule. Since then, it has been undergoing several amendments at regular intervals. The IPC was first drafted by the first Law Commission under the chairmanship of Lord Macaulay. While preparing the draft, helps were sought from Livingstone's Code of Louisiana and the French Penal Code. Later, the draft of the IPC was put under careful revision by Sir Barnes Peacock, Chief justice of the then Calcutta Supreme Court.

The spectrum of Indian Penal Code is very wide. Some of the common offences which are dealt by the IPC include:

- Offences Affecting the Human Body
- Offences against Property
- Offences Relating to Marriage
- Offences against the State
- Offences against Religion

Offences Affecting the Human Body

There are several offences which affect the human body. These offences are committed either intentionally. Some of the popular forms of these kinds of offences include.

Culpable homicide: If a person causes death to another person with an intention to cause him or her body injuries, he or she is found the guilty of culpable homicide.

Murder: If a person causes death to another person with a prior intention to get him or her finished, he is implicated under the charge of murder.

Culpable homicide (death of person other than the intended person) : If a person who is found a guilty of culpable homicide but he or she has not intended to cause the death of the dead is implicated under this charge.

Punishment for murder: It comes under Article 302 of the IPC. Anyone who is found the guilty of murder will get death punishment with fine.

Indian Constitutional Facts

Indian constitution can be well said as the written guidelines to monitor a nation in every possible way and to restrict it from adhering to any bad and looking up to the best. The Indian constitutional facts will focus on some of the important aspects of the Indian Constitution and will focus on some facts about India.

Date: The Indian Constitution came into effect on January 26th, 1950 and that is the day which is observed as the Republic Day of India.

Inspirations: The Government Act of India, 1935 has acted as the greatest inspiration to draw the final Indian constitution. Irish Constitution, Laws followed in U.S.A. France, Canada, Soviet and U.K. has played a significant role in determining the constitutional rules here in India. While borrowing from other nations it has been kept in view to take the best of all other nations, to set the constitution in India and run the country on the line of democracy.

Functions and Structure: The laws and rules set by the Indian constitution is regulated, carried out and enacted by the federal system of India which includes the judiciary, Parliament and the State Legislatures. The laws set are unitary and followed by all that these are administered separately for the Union and the States.

Power: Lays guidelines and issues laws as per the need of the situation.

Administers Civil and Criminal Laws: Parliament stands as the highest authority of the Indian Constitution and the Supreme Court is the body to carry laws set out.

The Constitution dictates certain fundamental rights, which are followed irrespective of legislative of any standard and the executive and the judiciary.

Unique feature of the Indian Constitution: Under the Indian Constitution comes the following and all of these are administered and monitored by the Constitution of India:

- Indian Preamble
- Indian States and Union Territories

- Indian Panchayat Raj
- Indian Citizenship
- Indian Fundamental Rights and Duties
- Indian Directive Principles of State Policy
- Election Commissioner of India
- Amendments in Indian Constitution
- Relation within States of India
- Emergency Provisions in India

India Constitution is the longest written constitution in the world for any independent nation. There are 444 articles in all where in 395 are main articles and 49 sub-articles. Apart from this, there are numerous amendments and 12 schedules.

Amendments: Constitutional laws can be amended as per need and necessity of the changing situation without violating basic constitutional structure, and that can be done by special majority of the Union Legislature.

Terrorism and Indian Legal Policies

Policing terrorism in India is fraught with difficulty. India is a large, heterogeneous democracy that is surrounded by countries experiencing their own intense problems with terrorism. The legal structure, inherited from the colonial past, is struggling to cope with the demands placed upon it by a country of 1.6 billion. India is a federation and this also complicates the structures needed for counter terrorism. Despite the democratic framework, policing in India is largely an inheritance from the non-democratic colonial past that paid scant regard to the doctrine of separation of powers. Given these problems, India's performance in policing terrorism has been mixed. We should not look for an early resolution of the problem of terrorism, either through preventive investigation or political amelioration of the issues that contribute to terrorism. But, India has done well to adhere to basic democratic norms in the face of what is, by Western standards, a major terrorism problem.

Conclusion

Indian Legal System though very well—structured due to the deficiencies in the taking steps at the right time we are facing hardship and the events of terrorism so often and other events of stealing, murder etc.

Indian government requires to evaluate the system and improve through passing the resolution and most importantly execute the thing urgently.

References

Ahuja Ram (2000), *Criminology*, Rawat Publication, Jaipur.

Dubber, Markus D. (2002), *Criminal Law, Model Penal Code*, Foundation Press.

Hale Chrisetal (2005), *Criminology*, Oxford University Press, New Yourk.

Reiner R. (2007), *Law and Order*, Cambridge, Polity Press.

Sharma Urmila and Sharma S.K. (1999), *Indian Constitution*, Atlantic Publication, Delhi.

8 Social Defence Approach in Correctional Perspective in the Prison System

Bira Kishore Dash

Introduction

In the common parlance, the term Social Defence is usually understood as protection of society against social deviance. Social deviance in forms of crime is as old as the origin of society. Every known human society is crippled with ramifications of crime, criminality and criminalisation process that are posing great threats to the social setting. The modern criminologists and sociologists accept the views of societal factors contributing to crime and its growing incidence. Social control mechanisms exert pressure on individuals through persuasive and repressive methods for conformation to the norms of the society. Social Defence, on the other hand, adopts preventive and rehabilitative methods to safeguard the society from crime and its repercussions. Social Control and Social Defence are the two conceptual frameworks through which the gamut of social deviance may be understood both in punitive and reformative perspectives. The concept of Social Defence is largely based on the concern for protection of society from the potential threats and effects of offence and offenders, treatment of offenders devoid of retributive methods and application of human treatment to offenders considering them as humans. Prison system as the institutional mechanism is supposed to safeguard the society in facilitating the justice delivery system in a grater way by providing safety and security to the offenders as well to the victims through which social order can be maintained, reforming the offenders to conform to the norms of the society, rehabilitating them with capacity building and preventing further crimes. Hence, prison has a greater role to play in areas of social defence.

Social Defence

The idea of social defence is as old the Greek philosophy. Plato, the Greek philosopher advocated the concept of the prevention of crime with penal philosophy which should aim at not punishing the offenders on the basis of past injustice but safeguarding the future of society through avoidance of crime. The exponents of positivist school of thought in criminology, particularly Enrico Ferri, widely used the term social defence and suggested it to the prime objective of criminal justice. Social defence in narrow view is considered punishment, treatment and welfare of the persons in conflict with norms of the society. But in a wider view, social defence is treated as a broad conceptual framework which covers the entire process of preventive, therapeutic and rehabilitative services. It tries to protect the society from the state of disorganisation not merely by treating and rehabilitating offenders but by creating such conditions for conducive, healthy and wholesome growth of human life. It also tries to eradicate the problems arising out of socio-economic deprivations, which are associated with commitment of offences as measures to reintegrate the offenders into the mainstream of social life. It firmly subscribes to idea of inalienable and inherent human rights by accepting the view that a person does not cease to non-person if he commits a crime.

Prison System

Prison is a formal institutional system through which deviance is dealt with in both punitive and reformative approaches. The punitive approaches of the prison system aim at deterrence of offenders to safeguard the social order as well as facilitate the criminal justice system in delivering the justice for both victims and the victimisers. Prison as the end part of the criminal justice system works in collaboration with other two parts i.e., Police and Judiciary. It may not be value loaded to argue that prison is bestowed with ever increasing works compared to other two parts. This argument finds justification with overcrowding of prisons. A lot of people awaiting trial are lodged in the prison apart from the sentenced prisoners. It is ironical that the Prison Administrators do not have any say on number of persons they can accommodate in the prison, but have to manage them as the functionaries of the criminal justice system.

The paradigm shift from punitive to reformative approaches is the outcome of humane approach adopted by the developed and developing societies. Offenders are sent to prison not for punishment, but as a punishment in consonance with the Human Rights approach. Prison is a complex institution which is overburdened with different works in achieving social goals of the criminal justice system. It mainly performs two broad roles in providing safety and security to the inmates and corrective intervention to reform the offenders with a view to reintegrate them into the mainstream of the society. The societal goals achieved in the process are mainly prevention of further crimes and rehabilitation of offenders.

The paper approaches the subject from both theoretical and practical view points. It proceeds with explanation of various concepts that are in currency in the field of correctional administration. It approaches, therefore, two methods of correctional treatment involving both individual and collective tools. The paper also tries to have a clear understanding of the collective roles of prisoners, prison keepers and other agencies involved in the process of prison reforms. In the conclusion, the paper tries to focus on issues of correction in a social defence perspective. Under the above backdrop, this paper tries to unravel the intricacies of the prison system vis-à-vis various correctional interventions adopted in Orissa prisons. The objectives of this academic exercise are mainly to find out the efficacy of prison system in achieving societal goals in purview of social defence and suggest the remedial measures. The findings of this exercise can be useful in criminal policy formulations. The paper is the outcome of an on-going research by the researcher adopting exploratory and descriptive designs through appropriate techniques and tools.

Study Area

The study area covers all the 84 nos. of functional prisons and correctional institutions of the state of Orissa. The different categories of prisons include four Circle jails, nine District jails, two Special jails, one Open Air Ashram, one Female prison, six Special-sub jails and sixty one Sub-jails. Apart from this, two Observation-cum-Special Homes functioning under Women and Child department have been included in the study area. It may be mentioned that convicted prisoners along with prisoners awaiting trial are usually accommodated in the Circle jails, District jails, Special Sub-jails, Female prison (*Naribandi Niketan*) and Open Air Ashram because vocational training and production units are available there. The Sub-jails are mainly meant for the under trial prisoners. However, in some cases—the short-term sentenced prisoners are being accommodated in these jails depending on short distance of their native area from the jail. The Female prison located in Sambalpur only accommodates the sentenced and under-trial-fémale prisoners. The only Open Air Ashram (Biju Pattanaik Open Air Ashram, Jamujhari at the outskirt of Bhubaneswar) accommodates the relatively reformed male prisoners from the other closed prisons in order to facilitate further reforms in a conducive environment.

Sample

The prisons in Orissa are functioning with the administrative control of Home (Jails) department of government of Orissa through Directorate of prisons and Correctional Services. The guiding principles of prison administration are laid down in the Orissa jail manual, Government orders, circulars issued by the prisons Directorate. Hence, the functioning of these prisons is similar with variations of facilities and infrastructures, categories of prisoners and scheduled capacities. The sample was drawn up from the entire study area with systematic random sampling method. The sample includes one Circle Jail, one District Jail, one Special Jail, one Special Sub-jail, one Female Jail, one Open Air Ashram and five Sub-jails. Apart from this, one Observation-cum-Special Home was also chosen for the sample in order to collect data from the juveniles.

Data Collection

Data collection works have been done from both primary and secondary sources. The primary sources include prison officials, correctional officials, prisoners and inmates of prisons and observation home. Statistical information has been collected from the secondary sources like prisons Directorate and prison Statistics from NCRB, New Delhi. Interview schedules, questionnaires and case studies were some of the tools used for data collection.

Correctional Perspectives in Orissa Jails

The entire process of correctional administration involves three approaches. They are 'pre-care', 'care' and 'after-care'. The 'pre-care' is mostly connected with the probation of offenders who commit such crimes for which punishment like life imprisonment or death penalty is not awarded. Usually, these offenders are first timers and when found guilty by court of law, are released on probation under the supervision of probation officer. Hence, these offenders are not sent to prisons to serve the sentence and those who are already in the prison as under-trial prisoners are immediately released with a view to give them a chance to reform themselves in their own communities. The 'care' component of correctional administration revolves around prison institution with emphasis on institutional care and treatment. The 'after–care' component is another device of treatment through which released prisoners are taken care of by the correctional officers with the help of other agencies. The 'after care' centre acts as a transit house for the released prisoners who do not have anybody to accept in their own community.

The vital phase of correctional intervention takes place in prison where a lot of care and treatment are provided. The most common and general corrective measures undertaken in Orissa prisons are (a) social contact, (b) individual therapy, (c) group therapy, (d) vocational training and (e) review of sentence. A brief description of such measures is given below.

Social Contact

The sentenced prisoners are allowed to make social contacts through interview with family members, relatives and advocates. They are released on furlough and parole to visit native places and interact with their family members. The furlough and parole are leaves granted to the prisoners for two weeks and one thirty days respectively. The parole leave for thirty days are deducted from their sentence. Apart from this, a prisoner is allowed to avail leave to attend urgent occasions like to see the ailing family member, performing the last rites of a deceased person of his family of course with escort from the prison authority. The very purpose of social contact lies in motivating the prisoners to renew the love and respect for the society in general and strengthen the family ties in particular. As a result, the offenders will not revert back to the crime world after their release—instead they would prefer to stay in family and community as law-abiding citizens.

Individual Therapy

All prisoners are not alike. Every prisoner has his own

problems and need individual treatment. A trained counsellor can have the patience and expertise to diagnose the problems of the individual prisoner with corrective measures At times help of psychiatrist and clinical psychologist is needed to correct the prisoner to be ready for further correction. Most of the prisoners develop psychological problems in a confined place like prison. This is due to the guilty feeling for the offence committed as well as for remaining cut off from the family and community. Provision for land phone inside prison acts as a medium of family contact and gives them solace and happiness. Prisons in Orissa are not well equipped to provide individual therapy in a scientific manner due to the non-availability of trained counsellors and psychiatrists.

Group Therapy

Prisoners in many cases are treated like a homogenous group in so far as some correctional measures are concerned. This is done beyond the individual therapy in order to undertake certain activities in a group to change the mental state of the prisoners. Spiritual discourse, yoga, *pranayam*, meditation, cultural programmers, educational activities, games and sports etc., are some of the general measures adopted in Orissa prison to have long lasting impact on the mind of the inmates. These programmers are undoubtedly effective ones but due to lack of follow-up do not yield expected results in some prisons. This therapy is effective only in case of prisoners who are first timers and have committed offence in spur of moments.

Vocational Training

It is true to all of us that 'empty mind is devils workshop'. If the prison authority does not keep the prisoners engaged, they would keep the prison administration engaged by creating various problems. Vocational training to the sentenced prisoners is effective measures to skill development and capacity building while serving the sentence. These training inputs are motivating and creating sense for value of works among the prisoners. The vocational training prepares the prisoners to take up some productive activities after their release from the prison. Training inputs in textile, smithy, tailoring, phenyl making, agriculture, horticulture, cultivation of medicinal plants, computer operation and printing and binding works are provided in Orissa under vocational activities. The prisoners are paid incentive money in lieu of their labour Rs 40 per day. Apart from the monetary gains, they also earn remissions to lessen the sentence period. Utilisation of prison labour and implementation of Court decree in enforcing rigorous imprisonment are the positive outcome from these vocational training.

Sentence Review

There is a Sentence Review Board in Orissa comprising members like principal Secretary, Home department, Secretary, Law department, I.G of prisons and director of Correctional Services, District and Sessions Judge, Khurda I.G of police (Crime and Law and Order). The board meets to review the sentence period of prisoners whose cases have been favourably recommended by the prison authorities and District administration to release the prisoners before the expiry of total sentences awarded by the Court of Law. This provision is well known to the sentenced prisoners and acts as a motivating force among them to reform and exhibit good behaviour in prisons for a favourable recommendation from prison authorities. The prisoners of open prison are in a better position for lessening of sentences because of reformed behaviour during their stay in closed for which they were sent the open prison.

The above measures are some of the regular activities in Orissa prison. Besides, prison authorities facilitate in providing higher education to prisoners. The youthful offenders who are the dropouts from High Schools or above level are being encouraged to continue their study through distance education.

Drawbacks in Prison

1. Overcrowding—Prisons in Orissa are overcrowded due to more under–trial prisoners (66 per cent). Prison authorities find it hard to manage such large number of inmates with limited infrastructure and resources—both material and human. This seriously affects the correctional intervention process for the convicts. The recently concluded National Mission for reduction of under-trial prisoners in Orissa has achieved its target and due to collective efforts of three parts of criminal justice system, Orissa got second position in national level.

2. Overstressed Prison Officials—Prison official in Orissa are overstressed due to increasing burden of routine works, threat from gangsters and nasal prisoners, shortage of adequate guarding and supervising staff and disproportionate financial supports from government.

3. De-motivated Staff—Prison officials in Orissa are mostly de-motivated due to less pay package compared to police and other personnel. This has created a sense of inferiority complex among them even though they are overburdened with complexities of prison administration in handling dreaded offenders in a confined area. All the jail reform committees formed by the Union and State Governments in different times have recommended for higher salary for jail officials, but yet not been implemented for which jail officials feel de-motivated.

4. Lack of Inter—Segments Coordination; Coordination among the various segments of the criminal justice system is in declining trend. This has affected the correctional perspectives of Orissa prisons. Efforts should be made from higher level of the government to restore the expected coordination among three segments to achieve the societal goals of criminal justice system.

Conclusion

Prisons are certainly institutions of social change in discharging the over encompassing roles in reforming and rehabilitating offenders. The handicaps and bottlenecks should be removed to achieve the expected goals with greater sensitivity from government, prisons officials, civil society and other concerned agencies to make prison system an effective mechanism to deliver the expected results in social defence.

References

Dr Kurt Neudek, *Imprisonment Today and Tomorrow – International Perspectives on Prisoners' Rights and Prison Conditions*, Kluwer Law and Taxation Publishers, Netherlands, 1991.

Govt. of India (NCRB), "*Prison Statistics*", 2007.

J. Guha Roy, *Prisons and Society: A Study of the Indian Jail System*, Gyan Publishing House, New Delhi, 1989.

Lali, U., "*Need for Alternatives to Imprisonment, Case for Community Sentencing*", Indian Police Journal, Vol. L VI, No. 1, 2009.

Srivastava S.P., "*Rehabilitation in the prison community*", Indian Journal of social Work, Vol. 37 i. No.1, 1976.

Sinha Nupur, *Prison Reforms*, Centre for Social Justice, Ahmedabad, 2005.

Workshop on Prisons and Human Rights, Commonwealth Human Rights Initiative, New Delhi, 1998.

9 Cyber Crime in India

Jyoti Upadyay

Introduction

Deviance is any behaviour that violates cultural norms. Deviance is often divided into two types of deviant activities. The first, crime, is the violation of formally enacted laws and is referred to as formal deviance. Examples of formal deviance include: robbery, theft, rape, murder, and assault, just to name a few. The second type of deviant behaviour refers to violations of informal social norms, norms that have not been codified into law, and is referred to as informal deviance. Examples of informal deviance might include: belching loudly (in some cultures), or standing too close to another unnecessarily (again, in some cultures). Robert K. Merton, in his discussion of deviance, proposed a typology of deviant behaviour. A topology is a classification scheme designed to facilitate understanding. In this case, Merton was proposing a typology of deviance based upon two criteria: (1) a person's motivations or adherence to cultural goals; (2) a person's belief in how to attain goal as. According to Merton, there are five types of deviance based upon these criteria.

Conformity involves the acceptance of the cultural goals and means of attaining those goals (e.g., a banker).

Innovation involves the acceptance of the goals of a culture, but the rejection of the traditional and/or legitimate means of attaining those goals) (e.g., a member of the mafia values wealth, but employs alternative means of attaining the wealth).

Ritualism involves the rejection of cultural goals but the reutilised acceptance of the means for achieving the goals.

Retreatism involves the rejection of both the cultural goals and the traditional means of achieving those goals e.g., homeless person who is homeless more by choice than by force or circumstance).

Rebellion is a special case wherein the individual rejects both the cultural goals and traditional means of achieving them but actively attempts to replace both elements of the society with different goals and means e.g. a communist revolution.

Now a days in the twenty-first century information and technological development creates new types of deviant behaviour in youth like cybercrime and it creates many national international problems.

The first recorded cybercrime took place in the year 1820. That is not surprising, considering the fact that the abacus, which is thought to be the earliest form of a computer, has been around since 3500 B.C. in India, Japan and China. The era of modern computers, however, began with the analytical engine of Charles Babbage in 1820, Joseph-Marie Jacquard, a textile manufacturer in France, produced the loom. This device allowed the repetition of a series of steps in the weaving of special fabrics. This resulted in a fear amongst Jacquard's employees that their traditional employment and livelihood were being threatened. They committed acts of sabotage to discourage Jacquard from the further use of new technology. This is the first recorded cybercrime! The use of a computer as an instrument to further illegal ends, such as committing fraud, such as trafficking in child pornography and intellectual property, stealing identities, or violating privacy. Cybercrime, especially through the Internet, has grown in importance as the computer has become central to commerce, entertainment, and government.

Defining Cybercrime

"Cybercrimes are criminal or harmful activities that are informational, global and networked and are to be distinguished from crimes that simply use computers. They are the product of networked technologies that have transformed the division of criminal labour to provide entirely new opportunities and new forms of crime which typically involve the acquisition or manipulation of information and its value across global networks for gain. They can be broken down into crimes that are related to the integrity of the system, crimes in which networked computers are used to assist the perpetration of crime, and crimes which relate to the content of computers." (*Source:* David S Wall (2007). Cybercrime, Polity Press Cambridge, p. 221)

The use of a computer as an instrument to further illegal ends, such as committing fraud, trafficking in child pornography and intellectual property, stealing identities, or violating privacy. Cybercrime, especially through the Internet, has grown in importance as the computer has become central to commerce, entertainment, and government.

Defining Cybercrime

New technologies create new criminal opportunities but few new types of crime. What distinguishes cybercrime from traditional criminal activity? Obviously, one difference is the use of the digital computer, but technology alone is insufficient for any distinction that might exist between different realms of criminal activity. Criminals do not need a computer to commit fraud, traffic in child pornography and intellectual property, steal an identity, or violate someone's privacy. All those activities existed before the "cyber" prefix became ubiquitous. Cybercrime, especially involving the Internet, represents an extension of existing criminal behaviour alongside some novel illegal activities.

Most cybercrime is an attack on information about individuals, corporations, or governments. Although, the attacks do not take place on a physical body, they do take place on the personal or corporate virtual body, which is the set of informational attributes that define people and institutions on the Internet. In other words, in the digital age our virtual identities are essential elements of everyday life: we are a bundle of numbers and identifiers in multiple computer databases owned by governments and corporations. Cybercrime highlights the centrality of networked computers in our lives, as well as the fragility of such seemingly solid facts as individual identity.

What is Computer Crime?

An important aspect of cybercrime is its non-local character: actions can occur in jurisdictions separated by vast distances. This poses severe problems for law enforcement since previously local or even national crimes now require international cooperation. For example, if person accesses child pornography located on a computer in a country that does not ban child pornography, is that individual committing a crime in a nation where such materials are illegal? Where exactly does cybercrime take place? Cyberspaces simply a richer version of the space where a telephone conversation takes place, somewhere between the two people having the conversation. As a planet spanning network, the Internet offers criminals multiple hiding places in the real would as well as in the network itself. However, just as individuals walking on the ground leave makes that a skilled tracker can follow, cybercriminals leave clues as to their identity and location, despite their best efforts to cover their tracks. In order to follow such clues across national boundaries, though, international cybercrime treaties must be ratified.

In 1996 the Council of Europe, together with government representatives from the United States, Canada, and Japan, drafted a preliminary international treaty covering computer crime. Around the world, civil libertarian groups immediately protested provisions in the treaty requiring Internet service providers (ISPs) to store information on their customers' transactions and to turn this information over on demand. Work on the treaty proceeded nevertheless, and on November 23, 2001, the Council of Europe Cybercrime Convention was signed by 30 states. Additional protocols, covering terrorist activities and racist and xenophobic cybercrimes were proposed in 2002. In addition, various national laws, such as the USA PATRIOT Act of 2001, have expanded law enforcement's power to monitor and protect computer networks.

Short mentioned is a robust open source tool which exists for monitoring network attacks. Its development started in 1998, and through years, it has evolved into a mature software (defector standard) and even better than many commercial intrusion Detection System. Short mentioned monitors network traffic to detect unusual behaviour based on rules established by the administrator such as unauthorised applications, viruses and intrusions.

Global Distribution of Cybercrime

Cybercrime is a global industry but the combination of poor economic opportunities and high skills is driving many developing regions to surface as major players in cybercrime Mr Mane was speaking that cybercrime also called computer crime, hi-tech crime or electronic crime, deals with the use of a computer as an instrument to further illegalness, such as committing fraud, trafficking in child pornography and intellectual property, stealing identities or violating privacy he mentioned that Cybercrime especially through the Internet has grown in importance as the computer has become central to commerce, entertainment, and government.

On the forms of Cybercrime, he mentioned hacking, denial of service attach, virus dissemination, software piracy, pornography, IRC (Internet relay chart) crime, credit card fraud, net extortion, phishing. Spoofing, cyber stalking, defamation, and salami attack.

Cybercrime in India: In harvesting data in call centres, India is the world leader in business process outsourcing (BPO). The country's top ten BPO firms hire up to 25,000 new employees per year, and financial services are one of chat rooms. The fastest growing segments, however, low salaries and fast turnover in the industry might provide an incentive to make extra money through cybercrime. Call centre cybercrime is becoming popular. A recent article in *India Daily* stated that for locals in Pune and Bangalore in India, the biggest incentive to work in a call centre is to be able to back the bank accounts and illegally withdraw millions from bank customers. During the last five years, the number of reported cases has multiplied and undercover investigations have revealed the large flow of stolen personal data that is moved through call centres in financial services. Amid fears of losing international customers, local companies have tightened security measures. Although these cases have been labelled as isolated cases of fraud, certain investigations have suggested that there is evidence of some operations being carefully, designed and very organised. Russia, China and Brazil are world leaders in cybercrime, with groups and individuals in India powering up to compete.

Cybercrime Statistics from the 2006 Internet Crime Report: In 2006, the Internet Crime Complaint Centre received and processed over 200,000 complaints. More than 86,000 of these complaints were processed and referred to various local, state, and federal law enforcement agencies. Top contact mechanisms for perpetrators to victims were e-mail (74 per cent) web page (36 per cent) and phone (18 per cent) (There was some overlap).

(Cybercrime Statistics from the Online Victimisation of Youth, Five Years Later study.)

Reports of online sexual solicitations of youth decreased while reports of aggressive sexual solicitation of youth did not perhaps indicate that some prevention and education measures may be working, while the most serious offenders may not be deterred. Increasing numbers of children are being exposed to unwanted sexual materials online. Online child solicitation offenses are rarely reported to any authority. Incidents of online harassment and bullying increased. This is an empirical study based on approximately 1,500 surveys conducted with online youth in 2005, that were compared to the results of a similar study in 2001. The study was conducted by the National Centre for Missing and Exploited Children, the Crimes against Children Research Centre, and the Office for Juvenile Justice and Delinquency Prevention at the United States Department of Justice. The complete results of the study can be found here (http://www.missingkids.com/en_US/publications/NC167.pdf)

Types of Cybercrime

With the growing use of computers, cybercrime is becoming more and more predominant into days' world various types of cybercrimes that can be encountered over the net are:

Spam

Spam or the unsolicited sending out of junk e-mails for commercial purposes, which is unlawful, New anti-spam laws are being passed in various countries which will hopefully limit the use of unsolicited electronic communications.

Fraud

Computer fraud refers to the fallacious misrepresentation of fact conveyed with an intention of inducing another to do or refrain from doing something that will ultimately lead to some major kind of loss.

Obscene or Offensive Content

The contents of some of the websites and other electronic communications over the net can be really distasteful, obscener or offensive for a variety of reasons. In many countries, such communications are considered illegal. It can be very troubling if your children are exposed to adult content.

Harassment

This cybercrime encompasses all the obscenities and derogatory comments directed towards specific individual or individuals focusing for example on gender, race, religion, nationality, and sexual orientation. Harassment is the cybercrime most commonly encountered in chat rooms or through newsgroups.

Drug Trafficking

Drug traffickers use the Internet as medium for trading their illegal substances by sending out enciphered e-mail and other Internet Technology. Most of the drug traffickers can be found arranging their illegal deals at Internet cafes, using courier websites for the delivery of illegal packages constraining drugs, and sharing formulas for amphetamines in restricted access chat rooms.

Cyber Terrorism

Due to the increase in cyber terrorism, the hacking into official websites or the crashing of official websites, government officials and information Technology Security specialists have recently begun a significant increases their mapping of potential security holes in critical systems in order to better protect information sensitive sites.

Profile of Cyber Criminal

- Disgruntled Employees
- Teenagers
- Political Hacktivist
- Professional Hackers
- Business Riva
- Ex-Boy Friend

Common Sources of Cybercrime

Researchers at Siphons Labs claim to have created language software that can figure out the host country of malicious software by tracing the default language of the computer on which it was programmed. According to their analysis of the default language linked up with about 19,000 samples at the end of last year, Americans and other non-British English speakers, surprisingly, produced a large proportion of malware. China produced 30 per cent, Brazil with 14.2 per cent and Russia produced 4.1 per cent of the world's malware.

The Future Trends for Cybercrime

Involvement in cybercrime is likely to continue on the path of low risk and high gain. New business models and new entrants encouraged by low barriers to entry are already emerging. The organisational and technological capabilities of cyber criminals, particularly with no global counter-strategy, will likely go deeper and wider into the foreseeable future. As cyberspace develops further, new opportunities will open up. It remains to be seen how the current global financial crisis will affect this situation. If it is deep and prolonged, this may hit the emerging and educated middle classes in developing countries harder than most and encourage a new generation of under or unemployed youth with IT skills to seek entry into the profitable and comparatively low risk world of cybercrime. The BRIC countries have already seen the start of such a growth. Countries in South East Asia, the Middle East and Central and Southern Europe cannot be too far behind the further expensive diffusion of IT capabilities into Africa, Asia, Latin America and parts of Europe. As more countries gain substantial economic power, global solutions to global problems will become more difficult to attain genuine, broad based consensus will replace the viewpoint of single superpower. In the absence of effective global governance and leadership, loose networks will proliferate to pursue convergent goals and interests. This can also be seen within the cybercrime ecosystem end. Moreover, the ecosystem perspective permits a clearer view of multiplicity within the cybercrime universe, with no dominant force.

Unlike traditional organised crime models, ethnicity appears to be neither a barrier nor an advantage. Cybercriminals will make common cause with anyone where such links are of mutual benefit. Age, sex, religion, location, ethnicity all seem to be irrelevant which could define the world of cybercrime a pure form of meritocracy. As the opportunities for qualitative and quantitative expansion occur, the only barrier to entry will be the skills required. The implications for victims, analysts and law enforcers could not be more daunting. Crimes such as electronic theft and fraud will occur more rapidly, reducing the likelihood of being caught. Information about how to compromise with a system will be available more quickly and to more people, which means that opportunistic criminals linked into organised networks will no longer be controlled by organised crime—if indeed they ever were and these components will come to dominate and define the ecosystem.

The education and ability of criminals to use new technology will also have a major impact on the nature of crime. In cyberspace, we can expect this to be further magnified. The relationship between the offender and victim may change, as neither sees the other as a person. The lack of such awareness may see online offenders committing more extreme crimes equally, if victims have no contact with the offender, their attitudes to punishment may change. Whether this will see a reduction in demands for punishment, or increases in those for harsher penalties, is not clear. The constraints on cybercrime are unlikely to be as comprehensive as for some other forms of crime. Whereas narcotics and human trafficking have immense implications for the welfare and safety of vulnerable groups, this is not perceived to be the case with low level fraud. When identities as credit cards are stolen, the relevant authorities tend to react quickly to replace and compensate. As such, the resources available to law enforcement agencies will tend to be channelled into programmes to combat the types of illegal activity that pose the greatest threat to vulnerable groups. Therefore, the environment in which cybercriminals operate is likely to remain benign and increasingly attractive to a growing number of people, not least from within states and regions where law enforcement is weak. Both the international system and its component parts lack the comprehensive instruments to tackle cybercrime in all its forms. And there is no evidence that they are doing anything about it. The growing immunity for cybercriminals and the promise of easy gains against a backdrop of global recession will surely fuel the supply side of what threatens to become a global criminal industry. But we do need to respond and we need to do so at three levels: international, national or institutional, and individual.

Remedies

Now the cybercrime has become the one of gravest problems of our times. So, it is very necessary to check before it worsens further. Government has constituted new laws to prevent the cybercrime. Experts of the field also provided some useful tips so as to avoid cybercrimes. The government has made certain uses for the cyber care owners. They must be observed by the cyber café owners.

The various safety tips as displayed on websites by the various department and government agencies are listed here under:

General Tips

If on line citizen takes certain precautions, the cybercrimes can be avoided. So, it is necessary for abusers to take certain precautions to prevent their credit or debit card from being misused—both online and offline.

1. Do not provide photocopies of both the sides of the credit card to anyone. The card verification value (CVV) which is required for online transaction is printed on the reverse of the card. Anyone can use the card for online purchases, if the information is available with them.
2. Do not click on links in email seeking details of your account: they could be phishing emails from fraudsters. Most reputed companies will ask you to visit website directly.
3. While using a credit card for making payments online, check if the website is secure the CVV will also be required.
4. Do not give any information to persons seeking credit card information over phone.
5. Notify your bank credit card issuer, if you do not receive the monthly credit card statement on time. If a credit card is misplaced or lost, get it cancelled immediately.

Online Safety Tips

It is needless to say that Internet is a fine and fantastic place to chat and to search new things. But, it must be born in mind that it offers peril and risk. So, it is a thing to be done with great care and caution. Here are some suggestions on what you should and shouldn't be doing online to help protect you against the bad stuff.

1. Never reveal personality identifiable information online. A lot of creeps use the Internet to take advantage of

other people especially kids and teens. Never reveal any personality identifiable information online, whether it be on your profile page or in a blog, cartoon, and instant messenger chat or email.

2. Never share your password with other people (except for your parents).
3. Never arrange meeting with strangers.
4. Don't believe everything you read or see online.
5. Don't download files or software without your parents' permission
6. Don't respond to inappropriate messages or emails.
7. Don't post inappropriate content.
8. Be leery of personal questions from strangers,
9. Don't be bullied into fights.
10. Don't use adult sites.
11. Understand what you put online will be there forever.

References

Duffal Pavan, *the Internet: Legal Dimensions*

Duggal Pavan, *Cybercrimes*

Kapoor G.V., *Byte by Byte*

Kumar Vinod. *Winning the Battle against Cybercrime*

http://www.cybercellmumbai.com

http://www.expressindia.com

10 Cyber Crime: Impact on Society and Juveniles

Kaushik C. Raval

Introduction

> *To look into special aspects of the future, we do not need projection by super computers; much of the next millennium can be seen in how we care for our children today. Tomorrow's world may be influenced by science and technology, but more than anything, it is already taking shape in the bodies and minds of our children.*[1]

As we know that, child is a basic unit of family and society. So, we accepted that child is a National Asset. But looking to the age he is not in a position to take care for him. In this context since ancient time child were taken care by state and many laws enacted in favour of child. After independence, we specifically protected child interest through inserting Article-15(3), 21, 21A, 23, 24, 39 (e), 39 (f), 43, 45 and 51A (k) etc....

As per our democratic system, constitution provided legislative body, executive body and judicial system separately. We continued Acts which enacted before independence but consonance with the Constitution of India. We have general laws and specific laws, i.e., Indian Penal Code, 1860 and specifically newly enacted and also amended Information Technology Act, 2000, to protect the interest of nationals. Apart from this, we also enacted special legislations in favour of child which are in consonance with International Conventions, Covenants, Treaties and Declarations. Some of them are, The Young Persons (Harmful Publications) Act, 1956, Juvenile Justice (Care and Protection of Children) Act, 2000, National Charter for Children, 2003 and The Commission for Protection of Child rights Act, 2005. These Acts protect child rights and child interest.

Twentieth century is the century of science and technology.

Lot of research is being carried out by many experts on various subjects. Ultimate use of research and invention are needed to provide conveniences, sophistication and relax from hard labour and relief from many problems which put human life in danger. Transportation and communication change the whole scenario of the world. Cyber is a term for electronics communication and such communication makes possible that all operations of business can be carried out at very small place even on palm.

Invention of computer took place during the year 1952. People are believed that only three people can purchase. Now computer became part of our life. At the same time Internet also add more facility towards the fulfilment of human requirement in various fields.

At early stage, the Internet user population was dominated by young men who had high income and plenty of education. We know that, every coin has two sides. Same way, the computer and Internet produce/provide good and bad thing. No doubt about that, cyber is a tool, a device for electronic communication, it depends on who and how used. There are so many articles with references to this problems in newspaper, magazines on the Internet etc.

Their aim is to educate the parents, elders and guardians so that they keep a vigilant eye on the child and his/her surroundings. Due to nuclear family and various emotions like anger, irritation, restlessness, excitement and enthusiasm are released through the source of entertainment and a regular splurging of emotions forms into a habit. Not only war game but kids grow up and learn to explore the net on their own and then the major threat begins. Early information on adult site and hacking also spoils a child's mental set up. The search engine doesn't distinguish between an adult's hit and child's hit. Children became vulnerable because they are not able to distinguish malware. Children mostly value 'free' over 'safe'.

Modus Operandi

When children get busy on net, chat with strangers and make photos and personal details publicly accessible, predator use clues about vulnerabilities and get emotionally and physically close in contact. In addition, some web browsers automatically open to display images that may be pornographic and also distributing is the fact that child can be automatically switched to an adult web page-exhibiting sexually explicit images-without even clicking on the link.

Predator initials conversation and not disclosed his real age, and show his age which is similar to child. First, they engage the child and try to get confidence and trust of the child. Visiting regularly the children gradually talk about sex to teenager. Also send pornography and convince the child that other children are sexually active. Finally agree, face to face meeting and above the sometime shows video of sexual act which corrupts mind easily.

Many time children want to release their anger, irritation, restlessness, excitement and enthusiasm through this source of entertainment and a regular splurging of emotions forms into a 'habit'-a habit lose control.

Net is good for educational purpose. Britannica and Library to search for information on topic of one interested.

Some time music, song and entertainment also available. We can get and send many information and card and greeting etc. It is true that Internet is a powerful tool to be remaining in context with whole world on our finger tips.

Hazards of Cyber

Common practice of pornographer is to posting of free teaser images on their sites as enticement to solicit new subscriber. Everyone can view these free though accidentally accessing such sites or deliberately searching out-even-without clicking on the link. Such sites use popular terms. Search engine has not found the age of users.

Twenty-five per cent of porn sites are estimated to misuse popular brand name and use such famous/popular name likewise Disney, Barbie etc.

There are more than 5, 00,000 website containing pornography literature and 60 per cent of children admits that they are busy with surfing such pictures on Internet, as these are for adults.

Social and National Interest

More access are high rise of acting out what they visualised, it may be sexual assault, rape, or theft, cheating, molestation etc. Such surfing habits converted in strong desire for such acts. The expose of such acts promote kids to act out accordingly.

Student came in school with weapons increase eight times more in USA. (2006)

Now a days, Cyber, Internet or Computer emerge as a new growing form of social cruelty.[2] It produced e-wastage also. It is true that computer provides global connectivity and it make easier for criminals who are busy with organised crime at various remote places and it is also difficult to determine jurisdiction of court, i.e. High Sea. Internet enables the producer and worldwide dissemination of information and knowledge which could be potentially harmful, threatening or liable to entice violence and create problems related with internal and external security.[3] Recently CBI website was also hacked.

Adverse Effect on Health and Mind

Many research on adverse effect on health and mind while sitting or using computer for long time, where Professor Kawalima of Tokyo University of Japan found that computer gave activated vision and movement points and restrict development of other areas. "Compupsyco" syndrome increase four per cent among child and it develops loneness and irritating nature. Sitting and busy with computer for long time adversely affect our intellectual sensibility and loses control over violent behaviours.[4]

Place

Children access the net at school, home, friend's home or cyber cafe and cell phone, where they came in contact with others who are busy with such activities.

New Marketing Strategy in Cyber Era

When children visit commercial site, they tempted to fill up form for free gift or free membership. Such information sends children to favourite fictional hero or hobbies, by e-mail to be from that 'person'. Actually, the person is not real at all.

Earlier, it was available in hard copy or form now due to technological development it is available in soft form. So, it require no shops or vendor or printing machinery and easily circulated to many persons without any expense. By this way, predators quickly transmit pornography world at large in no time.

Difficult to Identify Predator

Survey found that many convicted or not, but it is true

that they are educated may be young or old. And they also have respectable job in society.

Their targets are 9 to 15 years of children because such age child trust stranger easily. Children who are curious or rebellious by nature loneness and care for love easily attracted.

Some Examples on Online Child Abuse

- Rober U Carey, 52 employees at National Oceanographic and Atmospheric Administration (NOAA) since 1974 used government computer at office and home found 1,000,000 images of pre-pubescent girls and early teen in erotic or sexually graphic posses. There are images where he was busy with sexual acts with minor girls.
- Mother fixed up date with 15 years boy for her daughter, when they met 'boy' was 50 years old.[5]
- Once Romanian predators to stalk the 1,00,000 abandoned or orphaned children. Some of them are street children and poor who live on the street of Bucharest. George Roman from Save the Children in Romania assists the police.
- George Chamberlain (57-manager of Insight, Inc) was in USA prison, serving 23 years sentence for molesting girl was found to be trading pornography over Internet from prison. He had 2,000 children photos and address. The man was sentencing seven year more on his original sentence of 23 for molestation and not allowed to use computer in prison.
- USA live pornography found by police via Orchid club. In 1996, 10 year, girl told her mother that she had been sexually abused by her friend's father, while spending night at friends home. While investigating police found first time that, the club engaged in live Internet transmission of sexual abuse of children ranging in age of five to 10 years. Orchid club have number in nine states and four countries. They were busy with such practice in Finland, Canada, Australia 19 defends are sentenced, ranging from 12 months to 30 years.
- Zalatarou and Boika extradited from Europe has started company and charging 2-5 million to seven million dollars fees and busy with child-pornography websites

1,200 arrested for buying and selling pornography by net.

- On 18 May 2005, 10 million dollars law suit filed by victim's father because on yahoo.com group for trading child pornography.
- In the month of February-2007, an open talk show has discussed Online Sexual Solicitation with various teenagers who were at least once in their pre-puberty stage had been victim to such a perverting experience. Predator had asked the child to strip himself so that he would give him some amount of money as gift. All this without the knowledge of the child people all over world watching him.

Cyber Misuse

- 17 years old Surdeep of college was caught for sending e-mail. The reason was he wanted to avenge, over the insults meted out to him by his teacher.
- December 2007, five students made a club and they are savvy. One day, they decided to play game 'Pass Out'. The game was stirning the oxygen supply to the brain, was stopped for few seconds and that gave certain feeling of 'high'. The process was explained in mail. They all decided to experiment this. This boy asked to do first—he ended up losing this life.[1] Cybercrime by Child: Danger for future.
- In USA, 15 years boy studying in Std. VIII mailed the information about shares, which are not transacted since long and artificially rate of such shares go sky high and earn 272,828$. By this act, security exchange commission got shocked.[2]
- One student of computer engineering from Kerala sent treating mail to chief minister of State of Gujarat.[3]
- One student put teacher's photo in gay-people group.
- In Singapore, 15 years old sent 161064 massages to his teacher's mail account to take revenge for punishment.[9]
- 17 years old child hacked 2000 websites to prove his efficiency.[10]

- First cyber criminal was 16 years old, son of ex-air force officer for creating obscene website.[4]
- Twenty million $ fraud from bank accounts through cyber/Internet by 18 years old boy.[12]

Child pornography is leading industries on World Wide Web. The word Internet itself becomes synonym with pedophilia and child abuse.

Urgently Require Online Protection to Child

India has no specific law in relation with privacy of child through net. USA has Children Online Privacy Protection Act, 1998 (COPPA), the federal law came in to effect on 21 April, 2002. Website operator must include privacy policy and seek consent of parents or guardian of the child whose is age be less than 13 years. It should be dealt with severely.

First Time in India: Action Taken by Police Commissioner of Ahmedabad

Earlier the Police Commissioner of Ahmedabad issued the notification that all the Cyber Cafe owners had to maintain one register of Cyber use and get registration. Cyber Café operators filed a writ petition on Gujarat High Court challenging the notification. The High Court found that notification is valid in law and welcome the decision taken by Home Department for protection of the interest of society in general.

New Zealand is supposed to be first nation to detect and track Internet user, who are busy with child abuse.

It is true that the cyber is a device as well as the material for communication and business transaction. Now, the duty caste on state to make law in favour of certain vulnerable groups and duty caste on society in general and parents in particular to take care of citizen and their kids respectively.

UNESCO started movement, "World movement of citizen to protect innocence in danger." According to study, 40,000 hunters came to chat-room. UNESCO gave information through website regarding abuse through net.[13]

Conclusion

Duty of Parents

Children and parents certainly need to be still more cautious and vigilant while using Internet. Before we use any device or instruments, we should educate our kids about dangers and risk in the device and how we can be safe and not be victimised or tempted for getting free. Also watch and make sure that their kids and youngsters remain out of trap of sexual predators. The best way to assure that your children having positive online experience is to stay in touch with what they are doing.[14]

Multi-battle War

Looking to above mention facts and circumstances it is not a simple issue, which can be dealt by one department or one subject. It is multifaceted and complicated problems. But it is related with subjects of education, economics, sociology, psychology, criminology, penology technology and law also. To cope with this issue, inter and multidisciplinary approach and research can be more benefited and we can be arrived on a probable solution.

Future of any nation is largely determined on how its children grow and develop.

References

Kofi Annan (Secretary-general, UN, 1999).

William Kirk, University of California.

Navy War Room-Air HQ. November 20, 2006.

The Times of India, April 4, 2001.

The Hindu, dt. August 11, 2002 .

News published in The Times of India.

Sandesh daily, Ahmedabad, 23 August, 2000.

Sandesh daily, Ahmedabad, 6 April, 2000.

Divya Bhaskar daily, July 13, 2003.

11 Increase in Youth Crime : Ticking Time Bomb in India

Kamini B. Dashora

Introduction

Youth is a critical stage in life, full of challenges confusions and insecurities. It is a phase that acts as a bridge between childhood and adulthood. It is a change-oriented and a 'questioning' phase and includes concepts like identity, role and dynamism. Soares (2000) defines youth as both a social concept created to define the particular way that human beings see themselves and others at a particular point in their lives, and a useful sociological concept. Today, there is a crisis of confidence and feeling of unrest in large sections of youth in the country. The issue of youth in crime is an area of increasing concern in the context of the fact that crime rates have been steadily rising in urban India. With liberalisation and growth of a consumer economy, newer avenues in the illegal sector have emerged, which have direct absorption and income generating avenues for the educated and semi-educated youth.

There has been a disturbing increase in criminal incidents involving young people in India in the past few years. The trend is not confined to the poorer quarters of our cities and towns but even afflicts well-to-do sections of society. According to the latest figures from the National Crime Records Bureau, youth in the age group of 18-30 were responsible for 41 per cent of the total heinous crimes—murder, rape, burglary, dacoity and kidnapping—in 2002, up from 35 per cent in the previous year violent behaviour can have several triggers. Parental conflict, broken families, child abuse, poor parental supervision and delinquent peers, coupled with the carefree attitude of youth in schools and colleges are often the precursors to youth involvement in crime.

Social anthropologist Ashish Nandy strikes a note of

caution. "Youth crime is an inevitable part of urban growth," he says. "The giant uprooting in the name of development has led to a breakdown of community ties and as a consequence results in spiraling crime." The disconnect between aspiration and opportunity causes social disruptions that ultimately lead to youth turning to crime.

Sociologists believe that the breakup of community ties in rural community is responsible for the economic and social stress amongst youth. Due to the massive migration from these areas, there are few able-bodied men left in the villages who can be role models for the youth. In the absence of an iconic figure, migrant youth who move to cities are sucked into crime easily. TV too has shaped the attitudes of youth.

A recent UNESCO study reveals boys' fascination for aggressive icons. For instance, Arnold Schwarznegger was known by 88 per cent of the boys living in high-crime environments in India, Brazil and Japan. "There is desensitisation to violence. Some youths see it as a solution to day-today problems," argues Dr Rajesh Parikh, psychiatrist at Mumbai's Jaslok Hospital. Influenced by these violent images, many young people feel they can get away with anything. "This mistaken notion that crime is low risk and high gain is their motto".

Another theory puts the blame on biology. It says Generation Next is growing up faster physically. Girls and boys now attain puberty at a younger age than previous generations did, but emotional development has not kept pace with physical maturity. The hormonal disturbance often makes young people turn violent. Akila Sivadas, director of the NGO Centre for Advocacy and Research, describes the problem as a "crisis in gate-keeping". "Parents have to stop being gate-keepers and be facilitators. High expectations of ambitious parents can lead to volatile behaviour." For India—which has about 550 million young people —it is a ticking time bomb it can't afford to ignore. If the factors leading to youth crime are not curbed, the country could slip into anarchy. (http://indiatoday)

Rationale

The shortage of research in India in the area of youth offender studies, and especially those involved in serious offences and organised crime, may stem from a general lack of focus in the country on youth as a social category. Criminal justice processing may convert young offenders into 'criminals'. The consequent subsuming of identity could lead to obfuscation of valuable data about what happens to them, once they join the ranks of socially excluded population in our society. It is in this context that there is a need to look at who constitutes this group? It is important to find ways to re-integrate this group in the mainstream in the light of the fact that the illegal sector is ready and waiting to re-absorb them. These issues constitute largely the concerns of this study.

Objectives

1. To study the socio-economic, family, education and work background of the male youth offenders purportedly involved in property offences of serious nature.
2. To examine from the alleged male youth offenders' viewpoint, the factors that contributed to his entry into the criminal nexus leading to his arrest and re-arrest and his views on family, peer and gender relations, religion and the criminal justice system and processing.
3. To study the social supports available to the youth prisoner to address his imprisonment related and post-release problems.
4. To understand the legal, social and livelihood-related processes that unfolds in the life of the alleged youth offender after his release from police prison custody.

Methodology

This study is essentially qualitative in nature, but uses a combination of both quantitative and qualitative research methods. The attempt is to understand the lives of youth offenders who have a history of arrests by the police in cases related to extortion over time from the insider's perspective.

The universe of this study is male youth in the age group of 18 to 30 years in the city of Anand and its suburbs, with a history of arrests related to cases of extortion against their name. For arriving at the profile of the group, the structured interview method was used. Respondents for the interviews were initially identified from official data supplied by the Anand Police. The sampling technique used was theoretical and convenience sampling method from the population of the youth offenders arrested in extortion related crimes. Apart from these interviews, legal data pertaining to 50 youth arrested by the Crime Branch, Anand Police for the years 2005, 2006 and 2007 was collected and quantitatively analysed to understand the trends and patterns of arrests made by the Anand Police. To understand reasons and the process of entry into the criminal nexus, the social supports available to the respondent youth to deal with arrest and post-arrest problems, his views on family, peer and gender relations, religion and the criminal justice system and processing and to study the processes that unfold in the post-arrest phase, in-depth interviews were used with selected respondents. Two life histories were developed on the basis of the in-depth interviews, which were qualitatively analysed using narrative analysis.

Review of Literature

A comprehensive survey of literature on criminological theories was carried out, as they have developed over time. This is followed by a review of literature on the effect of urbanisation processes on crime trends with specific reference to Mumbai city, followed by a brief review of literature on criminal justice system and process in India and its possible impact on youth. This is followed by a survey of literature on the specific category of youth crime that this study aims to study, beginning with an introduction and concepts related to the professional criminal. This is followed by a discussion on what constitutes organised crime, its definition, history, nature, scope and magnitude of activities. Subsequently, there is a discussion on extortion as a form of organised crime. The chapter concludes with a discursive sub-section on youth gangs and youth involvement in organised crime. The review of literature has highlighted the fact that while youth involvement in organised crime and gang behaviour in youth is a well researched subject in the West, there are very few studies on this issue in the Indian context. Some of the theories on crime causation such as the social disorganisation and subculture theories of the Chicago School, the social attachments theory and the labelling theory of the radical school seem to emerge as having relevance to the urban youth crime scenario in India. Similarly, studies on organised crime, its changing nature and youth involvement in organised crime and gangs seem to co-relate with similar phenomena in the urban milieu, especially with a city like Mumbai. The review of literature helped the researcher to firm up research questions and the objectives of the study, and was also very useful to develop the methods and tools of the research process.

Data Analysis

More than half of youth arrested in extortion cases were between the age group of 18 to 24 years. Most of them were literate with a majority educated up to secondary level. Most of them were skilled, semi-skilled or unskilled workers in the informal sector. An overwhelming majority of the youth were unmarried or single. Most youth arrested for extortion offences belonged to families settled in slum area of the city. The distribution of the residences of the youth arrested in extortion crimes in this study conforms to the social disorganisation theory of Shaw and Mckay (1942), which propounded that the highest rates of delinquency are found in areas characterised by low rents in old dilapidated buildings, low family incomes and a high percentage of immigrant populations. Most youth described their families as 'normal', i.e., absence of conflict between the parents. However, there were a few youth who came from families where conflict was a defining feature. The tensions and conflicts at home led to the youth remaining outside home for long hours each day or even leaving home altogether at an early age. An interesting insight that can be gained from the family situation is that youth who came from conflict-ridden families were more deeply entrenched into gangs than those who gave relatively happier accounts of the family situation during their childhood. While majority of the youth belonged to working class and 'normal' areas, a few came from areas which corroborate Cloward and Ohlin's (1960) description of criminal or conflict sub-cultures. Those from criminal or conflict sub-cultures were found to be leading and organising extortion as an activity, were into extortion as a full-time activity and were part of the upper hierarchy of the gang. The work place and the area or the neighbourhood have emerged as the two prime 'scenes' or sites of crime. Another site that has emerged in terms of cementing a youth life in crime is the prison environment, which acts as an ideal platform for criminalisation of the youth, especially in the absence of strong family supports.

A significant percentage of the youth have revealed a history of arrests. However, most of these youth were arrested for the first time in cases related to group fights or violent incidents, and not extortion. Subsequent developments including imprisonment (for the first offence) led them to extortion related crimes, thus corroborating Tannenbaum's (1938) labelling theory Lemert's (1951) theory of primary and secondary deviance: It also emerges that most of the youth held rather traditional and patriarchal views with regard to gender relation, a humanistic and secular view of religion and a view about the role of the State advocating its protector (of the weak) and provider (of goods and services) functions. These perceptions create an image about the youth having 'larger than life' view of themselves and a very strong sense of 'right and wrong', justice and fair play. Most of the youth had rather negative experiences with the criminal justice system. On a comparative scale, the police came across as the most negative followed by the prison. The image of the judiciary was mixed, but it had negative connotations.

The need to bring reforms in the criminal justice system emerged clearly. The trigger for attempting to get out of crime is marked by the entry and presence of a person in the individual's life, to whom he feels a strong sense of attachment and accountability. This finding corresponds with the social attachment theory propounded by Hirschi (1969), which linked offending behaviour to the level of commitment and attachment to belief in society. The death of a mother, the birth of a child, an 'encounter' with a police or prison officer or a social worker, or the period spent in prison are events that can prove to be turning points or life-changing incidents. The entry of a social worker or a rehabilitation agency in the life of the individual has emerged as an important factor in one's attempts to get out of crime. The role of the police and prolonged association with gangs can have a positive and/or negative impact on the youth as far as chances of getting out are concerned. Finding stable and 'meaningful' employment is an important indicator of rehabilitation. Finally, finding supportive relationships outside the immediate family and the lived environment of the youth and getting involved in social work are good indicators of rehabilitation.

Criminal Careers

The life-time likelihood of acquiring at least one criminal conviction is greater than commonly realised. More than four out of ten males and one in ten females are likely to be found guilty or cautioned for an indictable offence at some point during their lives. However, it is also true that a comparatively small proportion of the populations - about 5 per cent of males are chronic offenders who account for about half of all known offending. Official records and 'self-report' studies also show that individuals more often break the law when they are young. The 'peak' ages at which they are most likely to be found guilty or cautioned are between 15 and 19. Criminal involvement typically starts before the age of 15, but declines markedly once young people reach their 20s. However, young people who become involved in crime at the earliest ages—before they are 14 tend to become the most persistent offenders, with longer criminal careers. Young offenders tend to be versatile and rarely specialise in particular types of crime, including violence. Longitudinal research has identified features in the childhood and adult lives of violent offenders and non-violent persistent offenders that are very similar, suggesting that violent offenders are essentially frequent offenders. Studies have also found that young offenders are versatile in committing other types of antisocial behaviour, including heavy drinking, drug-taking, dangerous driving and promiscuous sex. Delinquency is, therefore, only one element in a much larger syndrome of antisocial behaviour. Interviews with young offenders, meanwhile, suggest that their crimes are most commonly committed for material gain. However, a minority of offences, especially vandalism and taking vehicles without the owner's consent are committed for excitement, enjoyment or to relieve boredom.

A Theoretical Discussion

There are three sites of criminalisation of individuals as already discussed above. These are (1) the area of residence or the neighbourhood which corroborates the conflict or criminal sub-cultures described by Cloward and Ohlin's (1960), propounded in their sub-culture theory; (2) the work place characterised by an informal sector which offers a range of jobs for individuals coming from poor education and semi-skilled or skilled backgrounds and (3) the prison environment which leads to prisonisation of individuals. Let us call the first two as primary and the third as secondary criminalising site. These sites are marked by routine law violations, flourishing of illegal practices and exploitation by the powerful individuals and/or interest groups. They offer opportunities for 'acting out' behaviour and have the capacity to absorb the tensions within individuals, by directing their energies in a crimogenic direction. There are recruiting agents who are part of the criminal nexus and are connected with criminal elements or gangs. There may manifest some factors in an individual youth's life such as family conflict, dropping out of school due to financial problems, peer influence leading to lifestyle problems, addictions, and personality factors such as anger outbursts and need to prove oneself. These factors often appear to be the cause for the person's entry into crime. However, in the absence of the criminalising sites, the factors do not find expression in the individual's life in terms of criminal behaviour. There is an inter-play of factors with either one or more of the criminalising sites, leading youth into crime. However, while making attempts to get out of crime, it is the factors which become primary and significant compared to the criminalising sites. The sites are hurdles to be contended with, and are difficult to cross without family support, re-education, employment, counselling, determination and emotional maturity and presence of a social worker. These factors have a crucial bearing on the outcome of the getting out process.

It has emerged that extortion is largely a group offence (as opposed to an individual crime) and therefore needs to be viewed as an illegal activity embedded in the political economy rather than as an aberration of individual behaviour with psychological overtones. The study reveals that extortion per se and as a form of gang-related activity is on the decline in Anand city.

This could be linked to the crackdown by the police on violent gang activities in the nineties, the application of tough laws like the MCOCA and the changing nature of criminal or illegal activities of gangs in the last decade or so. The history of criminal gangs reveals that the first generation of gangs started off and built the foundation of their organisations through violent crimes such as extortions and supari (contract) killings. These gangs invested the money earned through extortion and supari killings into subsidiary illegal businesses such as land grab, betting and gambling rackets, and illicit liquor trade. A few also diversified into drug trafficking and fake currency rackets. These gangs flourished during the eighties and nineties and built large and expanded empires. They developed contacts with business partners and started or invested in legal businesses such as real estate, films and the stock markets to further strengthen their organisation and financial power. This financial power helped them to build a nexus with those in power the police, local officials and politicians who now form powerful cartels which are mutually beneficial to all parties concerned. As this process gained pace, gangs have increasingly changed from an 'actor' orientation to a 'network' orientation. This shift in their activities has led to leaner organisations with upper echelons in the hierarchy becoming agents and wheeler-dealers, but backed by a small team of youth who can be asked to use force if and when required. In the changed scenario, the predominant and violent face of crime in the mega polis whose protagonist was the dreaded gangster is giving way to an image of the criminal who is corrupt and violates laws and procedures with impunity, in collusion with vested interests for financial gain.

Major risk factors for youth crime are:

1. Low income and poor housing
2. Living in deteriorated inner city area
3. A high degree of impulsiveness and hyperactivity
4. Low intelligence and low school attainment
5. Poor parental supervision and harsh and erratic discipline
6. Parental conflict and broken families

Evaluative research suggests that the most promising techniques for reducing the risks of young people's involvement in drug misuse, crime and other antisocial behaviour include:

1. Frequent home visiting by health professionals during pregnancy and infancy
2. Education in parenting
3. High quality nursery education
4. Training children to 'stop and think'

The most hopeful strategy for reducing youth crime is to identify the main risks and ways of reducing these within a community. This knowledge can be used to apply prevention techniques whose effectiveness has been demonstrated by research.

Risk Factors

Research concerned with the backgrounds, circumstances and attitudes of future offenders has identified thousands of factors that point to an increased risk that children and young people will become criminally involved in the future. The major risk factors for juvenile offending are:

- **Prenatal and Parental:** Early child-bearing increases the risks of such undesirable outcome for children as low school attainment, antisocial behaviour, substance use and early sexual activity. An increased risk of offending among children of teenage mothers is associated with low income, poor housing, absent fathers and poor child-rearing methods.
- **Personality:** Impulsiveness, hyperactivity, restlessness and limited ability to concentrate are associated with low attainment in school and a poor ability to foresee the consequences of offending.
- **Intelligence and Attainment:** Low intelligence and poor performance in school, although important statistical predictors of offending, are difficult to disentangle from each other. One plausible explanation of the link between low intelligence and crime is its association with poor ability to manipulate abstract concepts and to appreciate the feelings of victims.
- **Parental Supervision and Discipline:** Harsh or erratic parental discipline and cold or rejecting parental attitudes have been linked to delinquency and are associated with children's lack of internal inhibitions against offending. Physical abuse by parents has been associated with an increased risk of the children becoming violent offenders themselves in later life.
- **Parental Conflict and Separation:** Living in a home affected by separation or divorce is more strongly related to delinquency than when the disruption has been caused by the death of one parent. However, it may not be a 'broken home' that creates an increased risk of offending so much as the parental conflict that lead to the separation.
- **Socio-economic Status:** Social and economic deprivation are important predictors of antisocial behaviour and crime, but low family income and poor housing are better measurements than the prestige of parents' occupations.

- **Delinquent Friends:** Delinquents tend to have delinquent friends. But, it is not certain whether membership of a delinquent peer group leads to offending or whether delinquents simply gravitate towards each other's company (or both). Breaking up with delinquent friends often coincides with desisting from crime.
- **School Influences:** The prevalence of offending by pupils varies widely between secondary schools. But, it is not clear how far schools themselves have an effect on delinquency (for example, by paying insufficient attention to bullying or providing too much punishment and too little praise), or whether it is simply that troublesome children tend to go to high delinquency-rate schools.
- **Community Influences:** The risks of becoming criminally involved are higher for young people raised in disorganised inner city areas, characterised by physical deterioration, overcrowded households, publicly-subsidised renting and high residential mobility. It is not clear, however, whether this is due to a direct influence on children, or whether environmental stress causes family adversities which in turn cause delinquency. One difficulty in explaining the development of offending is that most risk factors coincide and are interrelated. For example, adolescents living in physically deteriorated and social disorganised neighbourhoods tend, disproportionately, to come from families with poor parental supervision and erratic discipline, and to display a high level of impulsiveness and low intelligence. Moreover, while a great deal is known about risk factors, comparatively little attention has been paid to factors that may protect young people, especially those from high-risk backgrounds, against offending. Those factors that are known include having: a resilient temperament; a warm, affectionate relationship with at least one parent; parents who provide effective supervision, pro-social beliefs and consistent discipline; and parents who maintain a strong interest in their children's education. An understanding of how to build on the positive features influencing individuals, their families and communities can be used to increase the effectiveness of prevention strategies.

Prevention Techniques

Strategies for preventing crime, drug abuse and other antisocial behaviour among young people should be designed to counter specific risk factors and, where possible, to enhance known protective factors. A combination of interventions may be more effective than a single method. On the basis of well-designed experimental research, mostly conducted in the United States and Canada, the most hopeful methods of preventing youth crime are outlined below.

- Frequent home visiting by health professionals to women during pregnancy and infancy provide advice about prenatal and postnatal care of the child, infant development, proper nutrition, and avoiding smoking, drinking and drug use in pregnancy. Studies suggest that this can lead to a reduction in child abuse by parents as well as a longer term reduction in delinquency among the children concerned.

- Pre-school 'intellectual enrichment' programmes are designed to stimulate thinking and reasoning ability in young children, and hence to increase their school success. The High/Scope Perry Pre-school Programme in Michigan provided high quality nursery education for an experimental group of children in a disadvantaged African-American community, including a curriculum that encouraged children to plan, implement and review their play activities. A long-term follow-up of former participants at age 27 found that they were less likely to have been arrested than a control group of similar children, and more likely to have completed their secondary education, to have reasonably well-paid jobs and to own their homes.

- Parenting education programmes encourage parents to notice what their children are doing, to praise good behaviour, to state house rules clearly, and to make rewards and punishments contingent on children's behaviour. A number of programmes have demonstrated success in reducing children's antisocial behaviour, although reduction in stealing and other delinquent activities have in some instances proved short-lived.

- Cognitive and social skills training teaches children to stop and think before acting, to consider the consequences of antisocial behaviour, to understand other people's feelings, and to solve interpersonal problems by negotiation rather than aggression. Some of these techniques intended to strengthen children's own inhibitions against antisocial behaviour, have also been used to reduce re-offending among juvenile offenders.

- Peer influence strategies offer young people advice on how to resist pressure from friends to engage in antisocial behaviour ranging from underage drinking and smoking to drug abuse and other crimes. Research suggests that advice is most likely to be heeded when given by specially trained, high-status peers rather than by parents or teachers.

- Classroom management and other training can help teachers to communicate clear instructions and expectations, to notice and reward children for socially desirable behaviour and to be consistent in their use of discipline.

- Anti-bullying initiatives in schools include implementing explicit rules that encourage children to report bullying incidents and offer help to victims. Playground monitoring and supervision may also need to be improved. Programmes in Norway and Britain have demonstrated success in reducing bullying, which is itself associated with an increased risk of delinquency. Efforts to modify the risk factors associated with delinquency have also included community crime prevention programmes, with a focus on achieving physical improvements in disadvantaged neighbourhoods and providing recreational facilities for young people. Unfortunately, there is a shortage of convincing evidence for the effectiveness of these programmes. Crime prevention in the United Kingdom has, meanwhile, tended to emphasise measures designed to reduce the opportunities for crime in particular situations. Techniques include increased surveillance by closed circuit cameras, improving physical security, and protecting individuals against re-victimisation. The major difficulty with such programmes is that they may merely displace crime to other places or victims rather than preventing altogether. Priorities for research and development, the most important knowledge about the causes and development of offending in the United Kingdom derives from rather old longitudinal data. New follow-up studies are needed to investigate the development of antisocial behaviour from childhood into the teenage years, and from the teenage years into adulthood. Such research should be closely concerned with protective as well as risk factors. Although well-designed evaluations of preventive projects have been carried out in America, there is an urgent need to evaluate the replicability and effectiveness of such strategies in the United Kingdom. The available evidence suggests that prevention programmes are best implemented as elements of a larger programme targeted geographically on high crime areas. The aim should be to carry out a systematic assessment of the main risk factors in a community and to adopt effective strategies for reducing or eliminating them. A programme should also identify protective factors and other strengths within a community with a view to enhancing them. Communities that care programme for reducing antisocial behaviour among young people has been devised by researchers at the University of Washington, Seattle and is one of the most promising strategies to emerge in America. Its combination of flexibility and a systematic approach would lend itself to adaptation in the United Kingdom. Described as 'a risk and protection focused programme', it is based on a social development strategy that can be tailored to the specific needs of a neighbourhood, district or city.

Its main features are:

- **Community Mobilisation:** Key leaders are brought together and a management board set up consisting of representatives from local agencies and the community. The board's task is to arrange a detailed assessment of local risks and resources and to agree an action plan.
- **Implementation:** Prevention plans address the priority risk and protection factors by implementing techniques

from a menu of strategies that research has shown to be effective.

- **Evaluation:** Detailed monitoring is carried out to ensure that the programme's progress and effectiveness can be evaluated.

Conclusion

The time is now ripe to mount a large-scale community-based programme against crime that adopts the most promising prevention strategies to tackle risk factors that are problematic within particular communities. Such an approach would have similarities with public health programmes that seek to reduce illnesses such as coronary heart disease by tackling the known risk factors (smoking, a high-fat diet and lack of exercise, for instance). The programme's aim should be to promote community safety, pro-social behaviour and healthy development as well as to prevent drug misuse and crime.

References

Allen Francis (1964), *Borderland of Criminal Justice*, University of Chicago Press.

Carey, James T. (1978), *An Introduction to Criminology*, Englewood Cliffs, Prentice Hall.

Gurumukh Ram Madan (1967), *Indian Social Problems*, Alliad Publication Pvt., Bombay.

NCRB (2009), *Crime in India*, Compendium, Ministry of Home Affairs, GOI, New Delhi.

Siddique A. (2007), *Criminology*, Eastern Book Company, Lucknow.

Sparks R.G. and Dodd D. (1977), Surveying Victims, Chichester,Wiley.

Walterc, Reckless (1971), *The Crime Problem*, New York, Appleton-Century-Crofts, Inc.

Void George B.and Thomas J. (1986), *Theoretical Criminology*, Oxford University Press, New York.

12 From Gender-Biased to Gender-Sensitive Policing: A Sociological Analysis

Sudeshna Mukherjee

Introduction

In a democratic country like India, the police, an enforcement machinery of the state owe their existence and derive their authority from the public, at large. The constitution and the various laws that govern police work, serve both as clear parameters for police functioning as well as limits of their authority. Considering the historical background of police in India, it has been difficult to transform the system from a type of ruler-appointed force to a people-appointed service. (Baxi, 1982) Most critics feel that the people themselves have not understood and accepted this transformation. However, it is not very encouraging that even after 66 years, we are still in the process of attempting this transformation. We are still trying to work together, the police and the people, to make the system more responsive and sensitive towards the citizens of a democracy, particularly those who are traditionally oppressed, dominated, violated against or ignored—women, children, minorities, people from SC/ST communities, the disabled and so on.

We have a police force to provide citizens with a sense of safety and security. The police are there to maintain peace and order in society as well as prevent and detect crime. They are there as the law enforcers—to make sure that everyone, including the police force itself, follows the law at every step. The police force has several duties. It must prevent and control crime, detect and investigate properly whenever it happens. It must also prepare an honest, evidence-base case for the prosecutor to present at court. The police force has a responsibility for maintaining overall law and order; and for this purpose also gathers information about what is happening in and around the community it serves. The police have all sorts of different powers, all of which are given by law and they must use them only according to the procedure laid down in the law. They can make arrests, carry out search and seizures, investigate offences, question witnesses, interrogate suspects, disperse unruly crowds and maintain order in society, but they have to do it strictly in the way the law lays down and not in any other way. They cannot act just as they wish or want to. Any abuse of power or negligence of duty will amount to a breach of discipline, civil wrong or a crime and the police officer is liable to be punished.

Indian independence has not made any substantial difference to the functioning of the police. (Baxi, 1982) This has been the conclusion of a large number of state police commissions appointed by state governments, National police commissions and reiterated by scholarly studies. But according to Bayley, 'if the police retain its repressive colonial profile, it is due to the fact that the governing elites wish it so". Independence brought revolutionary changes in political structure of the government; it brought none of any consequence to the structure of police administration. (Bayley, 1969) Bayley has opined, "People get the government they deserve." By extension, people must get the police they deserve. According to the theory implicit in this popular formation, government reflects the character of its society. The police can only be what the public will allow. Government passively reflects societies, the police, as an agency of government, are the creatures of both (Bayley, 1969). But after analysing in detail on structure and organisation of the police force, and its relationship with political establishment as well as the other administrative structures, Bayley had opined that police too can influence its social and political environment in following manner.

First, they are thoroughly and widely visible, since they are uniformed, their activities are difficult to disguise. Since their responsibilities permeate all corners of social activity, they are brought into contact with everyone. Other government servants deal with very specialised parts of human life and when they do so they attract little public attention.

Second, police possess a near monopoly on the instruments of force. They are societies, regulators, imbued with power denied to everyone else.

Third, they have responsibility for safeguarding the most

basic elements of human life. There is the power to protect or not to protect, to save or not to save. Moreover, they intrude into individual's lives at moments of stress and tribulation. Policemen are identified with the greatest of life's crises.

Fourth, Police are immediately identified with law. In many respects, they are more important law, for they implement its structure and decide when it is to be applied. Whether government is by men or by law depends to a marked extent on the nature of police. (Bayley, 1969)

The relationship of police and civil society is far from being cordial. David Bayley in his empirical examination of Indian public attitudes towards police show a strong no contact, no recognition dimension. For the majority people, the police are faceless and nameless creatures with whom they never had any contact. (Bayley, 1969) One of the issues most frequently debated is the use of unwarranted physical force by the police on those under their custody or control.

Police, the Abuser of Human Rights: Police culture and public image of police are inextricably linked with each other. Ideal police culture would also correspond to this ideal image of the police. But unfortunately, there is a wide chasm between ideal and reality and the image of the police, instead of being glamorous, is tarnished.

The reasons are:

- **Barking Cognisable Crime:** It is common knowledge that police evade registration of cognisable crime. They register cases of cognisable crime only when they cannot avoid it.
- **Misbehaviour:** The known categories of misbehaviour by police are found to be
    - (i) Rude and discourteous conduct.
    - (ii) Refusal to certain complaints.
    - (iii) Overbearing attitude.
    - (iv) Beating.
    - (v) Harassment.
- **Corruption:** Demand and acceptance of bribery for doing or not doing things by the police.

- **Favouritism:** Doing or not doing things for obliging people in power or people who matter.
- **Neglect of Duty:** Not doing things which the law requires them to do.
- **Ignoring the Poor and Non-influential:** Polices' refusal to entertain the plights of the poor and work in favour of people who are influential either by virtue of their money power or political position.
- Fabricating evidence and padding up evidence.
- **Proportion of Wrong–doers:** There is no dearth of right thinking, right doing, and cool, courageous and conscientious police personnel. A thousand instances of courage and coolness must pass unnoticed. There are indeed few jobs as demanding integrity, wisdom and courage wise as that of a police administrator.
- Custodial deaths and encounter is unique contribution of the police in India to the vocabulary of Human Rights. No doubt, police has been given the power to shoot but it is subject to restrictions, limitations and circumstances. It cannot kill a person under its custody. Custodial death and encounter are gruesome acts, which is the violation of fundamental rights enshrined in the constitution of India.

Police Atrocity and Women

Police interact with women in various capacities, as a victim, complainant, eye witness, offender and so on. In many situations, police action can really deliver well to women. It is important to note that when the inmates of the custody happen to be the women, the vulnerable section of society face additional unspeakable mode of torture including molestation and rape. Women are often faced with following problems while interacting with police:

1. Initial complaint is disbelieved and action is contemplated only on proper verification and after a value judgment as to whether the woman is deserving of appropriate police response.
2. Discouraged from pursuing complaint.

3. Intensive, bullying and callous interrogation and aggressive and sexist questioning.
4. Succession of officers interviewing the victim.

Table 1. Incidence and rate of Crime Committed Against Women in State, UTs and Cities during 2012

Sl. No.	*State/*	*Incidence*	*Percentage of Contribution to All-India Total*	*Rate of Total Cognisable Crimes*
1.	Andhra Pradesh	28171	11.53	66.05
2.	Arunachal Pradesh	201	0.08	33.67
3.	Assam	13544	5.54	89.54
4.	Bihar	11229	4.60	23.41
5.	Chhatisgarh	4228	1.73	34.38
6.	Goa	200	0.08	23.01
7.	Gujarat	9561	3.91	33.58
8.	Haryana	6002	2.46	50.31
9.	Himachal Pradesh	912	0.37	27.13
10.	Jammu & Kashmir	3328	1.36	58.60
11.	Jharkhand	4536	1.86	29.16
12.	Karnataka	10366	4.24	34.92
13.	Kerala	10930	4.47	61.21
14.	Madhya Pradesh	16832	6.89	47.75
15.	Maharashtra	16353	6.69	29.87
16.	Manipur	304	0.12	24.64
17.	Meghalaya	255	0.10	19.38
18.	Mizoram	199	0.08	40.20
19.	Nagaland	51	0.02	4.70
20.	Idisha	11988	4.91	58.79
21.	Punjab	3238	1.33	24.98
22.	Rajasthan	21106	8.64	63.75
23.	Sikkim	68	0.03	23.29
24.	Tamil Nadu	7192	2.94	21.23
25.	Tripura	1559	0.64	86.95
26.	Uttar Pradesh	23569	9.65	24.25
27.	Uttarakhand	1067	0.44	21.50
28.	West Bengal	30942	12.67	70.30
29.	A&N Islands	49	0.02	20.08
30.	Chandigarh	241	0.10	37.60
31.	D&N Haveli	16	0.01	9.30
32.	Daman & Diu	11	0.00	11.22
33.	Delhi	5959	2.44	69.75
34.	Lakshadweep	2	0.00	5.13
35.	Puducherry	61	0.02	8.87
	Total (All India)	244270	100.00	41.74

Source: National Crime record Bureau, 2012.

5. Medical examination delayed and conducted in unpleasant or threatening surrounding.
6. Women are not supplied with basic information about their legitimate rights and available support services.

Since gender based violence constitute 41.74 per cent of all cognisable crimes the table below justifies the need for gender-sensitive policing to ensure gender-justice for women by the main law enforcement agencies of the nation.

Police and Gender-Justice: Police function today is more than just to maintain law and order situation. "Police goals are constantly changing with the change of time and as a consequence, traditional police functions are not enough to cover all aspects of police functions. The concept of police function in our society expressed a varying set of emotions ranging from fear to relief". (Chakrabarti, 1989)

Contextualising narrow question concerning crime control or the protection of the community against crime, raises the fundamental political questions about the nature of the social order that police are expected to protect. The social order is characterised by patriarchal power structures that divide and hierarchically structures assorting the community into classes, races, sexual groups and by gender. As the police are accorded a front line position in the maintenance of society, as constructed presently, their role is essentially political (J. Hanmer, J Radford, E A Stanko, 1994)

Defining the problem of policing in terms of the maintenance of public order is socially legitimated by the belief that the police can adopt a gender-neutral social role. This is guaranteed by local or community accountability. But, for example if racist and sexist ideologies predominate in a community, then community accountability cannot guarantee progressive change in police policy or practice. (Hanmer, Radford, E A Stanko, 1994)

The conceptual division of social life into public and private is a social construction which arises out of gendered social relation. The reification of the public and the private is an ideology that explains and fortifies the decriminalisation of men's violence against women. This means that not only the police are engaging in a world inhabited by gendered subjects in unequal power relationship but the police are also gendered and constitute a part. They are not above or outside the system and struggles around gendered-relation. Identifying the police as gendered-subjects, provide insight into their public order and crime prevention activities. (Hanmer, Radford, E A Stanko, 1994)

As a part of their crime prevention role, the police are accorded with a formal responsibility for citizen's safety that includes offering protection from violent crime. While citizen is an apparently engendered term, it would be a mistake to assume men and women are treated the same. Understanding about citizen safety is mediated by the assumption of gender. By and large, men are regarded as capable of self-protection and women are protected through their dependency on men. Women outside of men's protection are then defined as deviant women, provocative women, undeserving of protection. Progressive changes are required in police policy or practice (J Hanmer, J Radford, E A Stanko, 1994). The disposition of the criminal justice system towards women shows two contradictory trends. One of paternalism/chivalry (preferential treatment) and the other is sexism/penalism (discriminatory treatment). The bottom line in paternalism/sexism debate is that women are treated leniently or harshly by the criminal justice system—not because they are women, but because they conform to or deviate from the "appropriate feminine behaviour and demeanor" (Panigrahi,1991).

Thus a major task ahead is to find a way by which feminists can promote the view that woman should be free of violence without compromising women's independence. This is not easy, but failure to engage in the debate on policing and to secure benefits for women will leave many women open to further abuse and even death. Thus prerequisites of gender-sensitive policing are:

(A) Need for more women in the police force.

(B) Better work environment and other professional requirements for the police personnel.

(C) Increasing reliance on technology for crime detection.

(A) Need for More Women in Police Force

Policing in India has traditionally been considered as a male bastion as the policing activities require physical powers. The rising trend of crimes against women, increasing involvement of women in various crimes, and the problems in handing juveniles, have stressed the need for women police in India.

The need for women police in India was felt during the labour strike in Kanpur, in 1938. The state of Travancore also experimented with the appointment of women as special constables in 1939. One woman head constable and twelve women police constables were appointed. It was however, only after Independence that women have been regularly recruited in state departments, and an organisational pattern of specialist service has been evolved. Although, women police in India have multifarious duties to perform, the number of women police in India is much lower in comparison to the strength of the male police members.

Table 2. The Percentage of the Women Police in India out of the Total Strength of the Police during the Last Few Years is As under

Year	*per cent of police Strength*
1979	0.4 per cent
1985	0.61 per cent
1988	0.71 per cent
1989	1.05 per cent
2001	2.08 per cent
2009	3.65 per cent
2011	5.65 per cent

Source: NCRB.

The induction of more women in the police force has been acknowledged as an essential component of the ongoing police reform efforts in India. Beyond making their presence felt in the force, encouraging more women to access its services without inhibition, should serve as a precursor to many other positive outcome in the policing process.

However, since the princely state of Travancore appointed women as Special Police Constables in 1933, for the first time in modern India, progress on this front has been tardy. While repeated recommendations state that women should account for at least a third of the civil police force up to the level of sub-inspectors, as of 2011, of a total of 16.6 lakh personnel, only 93,887 were women. This accounted for a mere 5.65 per cent, marking an increase of 4.6 percentage points over two decades since 1991.

Among the states, Maharashtra has made a late surge. As of 2011, in absolute terms, it had the highest number of women personnel, doubling the number in two years since 2009. It had 12,813 women in 2009 and the number doubled to 24,219 in 2011, which is 13.2 per cent of the 1.82 lakh-strong forces. Tamil Nadu, an early starter, followed with the figure of 15,864, also having doubled the number in the two-year period. Yet, at the other end of the spectrum is Mizoram, with not one woman in a force of 10,861 and the Union Territory of Daman and Diu. (The Hindu, March 24, 2013)

Likewise, the representation of women in the central police forces remains dismal. Women personnel and officers constituted a mere two per cent of the more than two lakh troopers recruited by paramilitary forces in the last three years and in the initial few months of 2013. While 20,73,48 personnel were recruited in various ranks in the CRPF, the BSF, the ITBP, the SSB, the CISF, Assam Rifles and so on between 2010 and 2013, the number of women among them was a mere 4,733. (The Hindu, March 24, 2013)

Moreover, 13 States and Union Territories have no all-woman police stations. According to data from the Bureau of Police Research and Development, there were just 442 such police stations across India as on January 1, 2011. Tamil Nadu had the maximum number of stations (196), followed by Uttar Pradesh (71). Beyond the numbers for the women who are already in, there is a range of issues that need to be addressed to mainstream and empower them for the full gamut of policing functions. A lot remains to be done also in terms of working conditions and facilities that are oriented to their needs. It is a long haul ahead to correct the gender-imbalance in policing. (The Hindu, March 24, 2013)

In principle, women police officers have the same tasks as their male counterparts. Legally also, there is no distinction between the duties of a policewoman and a policeman. In practice, however, the police women are frequently used for certain 'specialised' or selected tasks, for which they considered to be more suitable. These very concepts of "special duty" are very much gendered in nature and confer a kind of inferior status to the women police force. Even their male colleagues also do not consider them competent.

The main duties generally performed by the women police officers in India as under:

In view of the special needs and requirements of women, the need for women police has been accepted all over the world in both developed as well as developing countries. The functions of women police are mainly to protect the honour of women and to save them. In case of victims of crimes, especially those involved in cases of rape, harassment by husbands, in-laws, women police have special role to play and it is here that they can help in bringing a subtle social change. The women police can also play a very constructive role as an agent of social change in establishing truth in case of unnatural and dowry death, rape, bride burning, etc. It is a known fact that truth is always suppressed in such cases and unless extra-ordinary pains are taken, culprits cannot be punished which will make the very purpose of social legislation defeated. Thus, National Police Commission has rightfully highlighted the role of women police as social workers. Acceptance of the role of women police as social worker is a clear indication that women police is expected to be an agent of social change.

They are generally engaged in:

(a) Help in the investigation of offences involving women and children.

(b) Assistance to the local police in tracing missing women and children.

(c) Keeping watch over places of ill-fame.

(d) Recovering minor girls from brothels and escorting them to rescue homes, courts and hospitals and recovery of women and girls involved in abduction and kidnapping cases.

(e) Collection of intelligence.

(f) Interrogation of Juveniles, women offenders, under trials and witnesses, interrogation of juvenile victims of sexual offences.

(g) Arrest, search and escort of women offenders.

(h) VIP and other security duties.

(i) Work relating to women passengers at airports and search of their persons and belonging.

(j) Conduct of enquiries in connection with passport applications, etc., of "*Purdahnashi*" ladies, family investigation etc.

(k) Assistance to the local police in evaluating women and children from disturbed areas during emergencies.

(l) Keeping order in women's meetings and processions.

(m) Dealing with women agitators, *satyagrahis* and labour troubles in which women are involved.

(n) Looking after women and children in fairs, places of pilgrimage and during festivals.

(o) Guiding women passengers at big Railway stations and important bus stands in large towns and cities, and

(p) Performing traffic duties.

The demand for women police arise from the assumption that the shared gendered experience of life will make it easier for women officers to understand what has happened, but in practice some report that women police are even less sympathetic than their male colleagues. The explanation for this lies in the power of masculinity within the organisation of policing. An institution that rigorously reinforces a gendered-male view of policing can overshadow women who enter the force. As an individual, a woman officer may have and show understanding and empathy with women, victimised by male violence but such attitudes run counter to the dominant ideology of her profession. There may be explicit or implicit criticism of style of working and even a questioning of her suitability for the police work. The presence of a small number of women in contemporary police forces cannot dent a male-dominated institution committed to secure the gendered *status quo*. (J Hanmer, J Radford, E A Stanko)

The presence of a few women officers cannot alter the fact that in most policing situations, police officers intervene as male-gendered subjects. My field experience and my interaction with women police officers corroborate that this cult of masculinity is affecting the police organisation.

- Women police were very hard and rude to women suspects. They even beat them and use very abusive language.

- Instead of encouraging, they rather discourage even rape victims to launch their F.I.R. as they believe in the lengthy process of justice they will win nothing but humiliation.
- They behave discriminatingly with people on the basis of their social status.
- Rather than being sympathetic, polite and patient they assert rude and rough behaviour.
- Very assertively they support the use of third degree method like their male counterpart.
- Many of them (overwhelmingly in the rank of constables) have never heard of anything like human rights, or human rights. Those who knows, human rights to them is a good concept but difficult to follow in day-to-day policing.

Although women police can serve as agent of change in many ways, it needs drastic changes in the recruitment and training policies. As things stand today, the recruitment policy puts emphasis on physical strength of the candidates. The various tests for the recruitment of women police try to test the stamina of the candidates. There is no method to test other qualities, which are essential for women police to perform their functions as women, e.g., patience, politeness, sympathetic attitude, better understanding of the human nature etc. The environment in which they are trained make them tough police officers. The net result of this scabbed type of training is that it turns soft polite women into hard police officers.

Better Work Environment and Other Professional Requirements for the Police Personnel

The guiding principles of criminal justice administration in a democratic society recognise the centrality of human rights in the enforcement of the rule of law. Accordingly, detailed standards for the protection of the rights of the accused and convicted persons are prescribed. (S.P. Srivastava, 1998) The situation, on the contrary, is that those who are meant to uphold the law quite often violate, and seek to justify their actions on the ground that such steps are necessary to maintain law and order. Police are not a bunch of sadist or psychopaths. Thousands of policemen have given their lives to protect and safeguard the integrity of the nation and have rendered valuable service in crime prevention, putting down organised crime and giving relief to the people affected by natural calamities. Some basic structural functional anomalies and incongruities contribute to police inefficiency and encourage errant behaviour on the part of the force are:

Outdated Organisational System: One of the most potent reasons for the inability of the police system to conform to the demands of the human rights mandate, as also to the demands of the democratic polity, is the continuance of an obsolete and outdated Organisational system. The system is governed by an Act of 1861, which British rulers had drafted to constitute a civil force that would perpetuate their rule by controlling rebellion and containing the Indian people through the modes of repression, retribution and revenge. The police, as per British design was a force to suppress people's aspirations, silence their dissent and disobedience. (S. P. Srivastava, 1998) All piecemeal and cosmetic efforts to reform police system, have yielded little result.

Job Stress: Stress is a multi-causal, complex, psychological phenomenon created by insidious, long range, continuous pressure, strains, threats and demands on the individuals much beyond tolerance limits. Stress can be caused by social factors, job demands, organisational factors and intra-psychic human factors up to a limit. Individual can cope with stress by extra-ordinary efforts, aggressive coping techniques, and relaxation methods. But when an individual fails to cope with cumulative stress, it causes psychological breakdown. National Police Commission (Dharam Vira Commission). Report has rightly noticed that an average constable works 14 hours every day without any respite under extreme conditions of stress and strain.

The causes of stress in police are due to the following factors:

(a) Long hours of work without weekly off or any holiday even during holidays and festive times.

(b) Poor living conditions in police quarters where available and where not available, they live at the mercy of the house owner.

(c) Police stations lack basic facilities like toilets and even chairs for the constables to sit and relax.

(d) Courts, including frequent appearances and lenience by court.

(e) Administrative back up including lack of support in different situations.

(f) Lack of support from the public.

(g) Lack of career planning opportunities.

(h) Inadequate rewards and non-recognition of achievements.

(i) Excessive paper works.

(j) Ineffective measures against criminals and fear for security.

(k) Distorted press reports.

(l) Inadequate resources and inequalities in pay and job status.

(m) Working in isolation and under hostile environment with old, outdated, dysfunctional weapons.

(n) Strains of tours and travelling and time management problem due to too many VIP visits.

(o) Conflict with social /family commitments.

(p) Traumatic events like witnessing dead bodies (sometimes of their colleagues), involvement in armed encounters and constant threat of physical injuries to life.

(q) Irregular grant of leave and refusal of grant of leave.

(r) Lack of adequate emotional support from peer group and superior.

(s) Lack of clarity of orders, unresponsive administrative set up and conflicting values of the Organisation. (K.M. Mathur, 1994).

Public Apathy and Ambivalent Public Attitude: Police violence often takes place when police are performing their role as crime fighters. Our legislators churn out laws at an alarming rate to satisfy their conscience and entrust the enforcement to police. Many of these laws, though noble in their aims have not been accepted by the public. In our country, we seek to achieve social reforms through punitive measures, enforced by the police instead of through persuasion and education. Benefit of modem means of crime detection, devoid of public co-operation, utilising archaic judicial procedure and working with a sluggish and non-responsive judiciary, police tend to attain quick result through the third degree methods. Surveys reveal that general public are also not averse to the concept of police using violence against 'Criminal'. People cannot distinguish between a suspect, an accused and a criminal. Since criminals come mostly from the disadvantageous sections of the society, violations of their human rights by the police seldom attract people's attention, unless death takes place in custody. The public is not bothered whether human rights of these criminals are respected or violated.

Political Interference: Growing political interference in the day-to-day working of police has turned the force to become the agents of the party in power. The pressure, which the politicians in power use to harass their adversaries, contributes in the practice of torture. Ethos of democracy lies in control of people's representatives over administration. Once the politicians and the police become partners, the former are compelled to overlook the misbehaviour of latter. Subramanian comments "when quick decisive results are demanded of police and no questions regarding the means are raised, law enforcers, the police, in their eagerness to achieve the results take law into their own hands." When ends become important and the means are not questioned human rights become the first casualty. (Subramanian, 1992)

Limitations and Compulsions of Criminal Justice System: The criminal justice system consists of four elements namely, legislation, police, judiciary and jails. The police are only a cog in the wheel. All parts are required to work well for the smooth functioning of machine. When approximately 15 to 16 lacs or even more I.P.C cases are pending in criminal courts, how can the criminal justice system work? Justice delayed is justice denied, is a well settled doctrine. The entire criminal justice system needs some daring reforms. The functions of the judiciary and the police are complementary and criminal justice system needs the abolition of hiatus between justice and social positioning. (K.M. Mathur, 1994)

The Confused and Dehumanised Forces: The Indian police system has been facing a crisis as it is unable to cope with pressure of work, increasing demands from politicians and public, growing criticism from the media, and an unending stream of court verdicts on human rights violations. An under-manned (police-public ratio in India: one police/761 person, as per UN: one police/450 person) and ill-equipped force is being subjected to daily denigration for its failure to arrest the awesome crime wave, increased lawlessness and mounting socio-political tension. The pressure of political and bureaucratic masters to keep the alarming law and order situation under control at any cost in disturbed areas are enormous, or else they face the consequences in the form of transfers, suspensions, and punishment posting. This compels police to keep the crime situation by resorting to indiscriminate arrests and oppressive unlawful activities and in doing so; they are roundly criticised for committing a variety of human rights violation. The policemen's acclimatisation to this hostile environment of profession leads to his dehumanisation.

Police Sub-Culture: Cynicism and pessimism, defensiveness, suspicion and secrecy, conservatism, alienation, machismo are part of the police sub-culture and one consciously indoctrinate himself or herself into this rigid hierarchical structure based on authoritarianism to be a successful police person.

Increasing Reliance on Scientific Methods of Investigation

Often police excess is justified, both in cases of gender-based violence and other cases of violation of human rights, for the sake of crime prevention and detection. This deplorable trend can be curbed with increasing use of modern technology.

Some of them are:

Cellular Technology: Cellular technology is increasingly becoming the most sought-after tool for the policemen to catch criminals. Though no formal training has been given with regard to cellular technology, a few police officers have become experts in nabbing the criminals with the help of tracking mobile phones. In fact, none of the accused in the multi-million stamp paper racket in Karnataka has been subjected to third-degree methods by stamp investigation team. All the arrests have been affected on the basis of interception of telephonic conversation, the accused had with the kingpin, Abdul Karim Telgi.

Forensic Science: Forensic medicine was earlier known as 'Medical Jurisprudence'. In 1958, Sir William Herschel of the Indian Civil Service first used 'Modern dactylographic' or application of finger prints for personal identification. In fact, it was the government of India which first adopted identification or persons by finger print comparison methods. Thus a finger print bureau was established in 1897, in Bengal. Only later, this method was introduced in Scotland Yard in 1901. Now, for the last two decades with the changing crime scenario and the high professionalism and integrity shown by forensic scientists, there have been more interactive and productive analytical sessions taking place between police officials, forensic science experts, investigating agencies and forensic medicine experts. The popular tele-serial C.I.D shows how forensic science can be handy in crime detection and solving.

In cases of sexual assault, the assailant usually inflicts multiple injuries on the victim. During the tussle, the assailant may also suffer bite marks and other injuries inflicted upon him by the victim. Trace evidence materials on the victim of the assault, on the weapon, on the person of the suspect and the scene of crime are analysed by sophisticated laboratory methods. They examine the bloodstain patterns, edges of the dried up stain—both at the place of the offence and at the place of disposal of the body. From the scene where crime may have taken place, if the victim's body has been shifted, forensic scientists inspect the clothing for stains of semen and blood. The clothing may have also carried soil, hair samples of both the victim and the offenders and other residues. All these trace evidence materials are scientifically examined.

Criminal Psychology: Clinical or criminal psychologists further help forensic scientists in their marathon task of interpretation of the crime. In order to interpret the behaviour of the criminal (or the suspect) and corroborate the investigating officers' observation and the saying of the suspect, psycho analytical tests such as polygraph test, narco analysis and brain mapping is carried out.

Polygraph: A lie detector or a polygraph test depends on the assumption that there is an interaction between the mind and the body. When a deceptive examinee is subjected to this test, his or her intrinsic pattern of reacting to stressful situation will elicit certain body responses. Their responses are recorded by the three components or the sensors of a polygraph machine, which are attached to the subjected (or the suspect). The "pneumograph" records respiratory variations such as a subject's rhythm, depth and rate of breathing, a "Galvanometer", records the skin responses of electrical stimulation and a "Cardio-Spymograph" records a subject's blood volume, pulse rate and blood pressure.

Polygraph test is conducted in three phases—a pre-test interview, chart recording and diagnosis. During the pre-test interview, the psychologist clarify the purpose of the test with the suspect. The examiner (a clinical or a criminal psychologist) would have prepared a set of test questions depending upon the relevant information about the cases provided by the investigating officer, such as the criminal charges against the person and statements made by the suspect. Lying by a suspect is accompanied by specific perceptible physiological and behavioural changes and the "guilt consciousness" in a suspect is exposed by the 'sensors', which record various parameters such as the blood pressure level, respiratory rate, pulse rate and a wave pattern in the graph. The findings of a polygraph test are open for a judicial scrutiny.

Narco-Analysis: Another 'criminal – assessment' scientific test is the 'Narco analysis'. The accused person's detailed medical examination is carried out. Only if the accused is medically fit to undergo the procedure, small doses of intravenous infusion of sodium pentothal is administered. This is an effective non-hazardous method of inducing hypnosis in the subject. Due to lack of inhibition produced by the drug, the accused talks freely and responds truthfully to verbal questions. Psychologists make sure that all the emergency medical measures are available to the person while undergoing the test, including the presence of an anaesthetic to monitor the vital body functions.

Brain Mapping: Recent research has shown that electrical brain responses can be a reliable indicator or information processing activities in the brain. This method called the "Brian-wave finger-printing" was researched and patented by neuro-scientists Dr Lawrence Farwell (Director and Chief Scientist Brian wave science IOWA). Dr Farwell has published that a MERMER (Memory and Encoding Related) is an in-built programme, which automatically removes responses obtained due to 'tensions' unrelated to the crime. The accuracy rate is

99.99 per cent and in U.S.A., the FBI has been making use of 'Brain-mapping' technique to convict criminals. Studies have shown that an innocent suspect's brain would not have stored or recorded certain information, which an actual perpetrator brain would have stored. Indeed, from finger printing and DNA analysis to brain mapping, forensic science has made rapid strides and made investigation much easier.

Conclusion

While preparing the paper, I have interacted with the victims, social activists, and women's organisation and media persons. The invaluable insights of these interactions are:

Police responses to victims are characterised by sexism, bias, victim's culpability and social stereotypes regarding crimes against women. Police are generally accused of being rude and impatient. A gender-sensitive police response would be patient and emphatic listening. A patient hearing sometimes work as a good healer as mostly people meet police when they are in distress. They should try to identify themselves with women's viewpoints and put on efforts to make them feel at ease. Because there is a tendency among police men that in the very first instance they try to unnerve the person, so that they feel intimidated. They always talk from the above. They treat both offender as well as the victim alike.

Female criminality offends the social conscience more severely, because it challenges the ideological constructs regarding gender roles. Police response to female offenders is not very different from "sexist" societal perception. Not only they are straight jacketed as loose and disrepute, police custody and restraint contribute to their further powerlessness and they are subjected to indecent and obscene behaviours, including custodial rape. A gender-sensitive police response to women offenders should include observance of due regard to their dignity, modesty and the procedural norms in all aspects of investigation, search seizure, arrest, confinement in police lockup, interrogation and forwarding in custody.

Another very significant aspect of police attitude is "differential treatment" on the basis of social positioning. Police response to women, who are on the margin of the society, whom they perceive as unrespectable and thus undeserving of protection, prostitute, women in the slum, domestic helps, women labourers, widows, single women, divorcees-ranges from indifference to intimidation, exploitation, hostility and violence. This is nothing unique of India, even in Britain and USA, black women and lesbians often are victim of coercive policing.

In view of the growing problems of crimes against women, the police leadership at the state and district levels should take adequate steps to sensitise and motivate their subordinates at the cutting edge level by utilising the services of women groups at the optimum level. This would inevitably enhance the performance of the force in prevention and control of crimes against women, as public support is the basis of good policing.

It should be the policy of the state government to encourage the formation of at least one women group in each district, who will work in close collaboration with the local police by taking various programmes for the care and protection of the women victims of various offences and also providing legal aid to them. But in reality the relationship with police and voluntary women's organisations are of mutual distrust and confrontation. Police perceive them as "trouble monger", "home breakers" who corrupt women and generate fake complaints and resent their interference in police-work. Women activists on the other hand complain on police inaction, harassment and victimisation.

Challenge for change has begun and the induction of more women in the force can thaw the ice of distrust existing between police and the civil society, better work environment and availability of scientific investigation method will instil confidence in the force and will motivate towards accomplishing a gender-just social order.

References

A. R. Desai (1986), *Violations of Democratic Rights in India,* Popular Prakashan, Bombay.

Anand Swarup Gupta (1979), *Crime and Police in India*, Vol. 1 and 2. Concept, New Delhi.

Bayley (1969), *Police and Political Development in India*, Princeton University press, New Jersey.

Baxi (1982), *Crisis of Indian Legal System*, Vikas Publishing House Pvt. Ltd , N. Delhi.

Bowden (1978), *Beyond the Limits of Law.*

Brewer, Hume, Brown (1990), *The Police, Public Order and the state,* Macmilliam Press, Belford.

Chan Janet. B.L. (1997), *Changing Police Culture: Police in a Multicultural Society.* Cambridge University Press, London.

Charles F (1952), *The Blind Eye of History: A Study of the Origins of the Present Police Era,* Faber and Faber, London.

Chakravarty N K (April-June 1989), *Non Crime Services,* BPR & D Journal Vol. XXXVI, No. 2, MHA, New Delhi.

Chakravarty N K (1994), *The Position of Women in Indian Society and the Role of the Police* in OC Sharma(ed), Crime Against Women, Ashish Publishing.

Deccan Herald 4th Jan. (2004).

G.C. Singhvi (1995), *Citizens Grievance against Police. In Dimensions and Strategies* IIPA.

Gobinda Mukhoty (May, 1994), *Torture, Human Rights, Legal Right, Economic and Political Rights.*

Hindu, March 24, 2013.

J Hanmer, J Radford, E A Stanko (1994), *Improving Policing for Women: The Way Forward in Women,* Rutledge, London.

Lorraine Radford (1987), *Legalising Women's Abuse,* in J Hamner and M Maynard (ed.), Women, Violence and Social Control, Macmillan, London.

K.M. Mathur (1994), *Indian Police Role and Challenges,* New Delhi.

K.D. Singh, *Criminal Justice and the Police,* papers for XIV police science congress, Delhi, 19-21st March.

Kalia. A.S (1995), *Job Stress of Indian Police,* Discovery Publishing House, New Delhi.

Krishna Iyer (1986), *Human Rights and Law,* Vedpal Law House, India.

Mahibul Haque (1996), *Police Atrocities in India,* Third Concept.

Mukherjee Sudeshna, (2005), *Police and Women's Rights: A Sociological Enquiry with Special Reference to Select Districts in Karnataka,* CSSC/SSS, Jawaharlal Nehru University, New Delhi (Unpublished Ph.D thesis).

National Crime Record Bureau Report, 2012.

Rajni Kothari (1988), *State Against Democracy,* Ajanta Publications, New Delhi.

Report of the Karnataka State Crime Record Bureau, (2007).

Statistics on Women in India , (2010) NIPCCD.

S.K. Ghosh (1991), *The Betrayal of Police*, Ashish Publishing House, New Delhi.

S.P.Srivastava, *Police and Human Rights the Independence Scenario*, Indian Police Journal, Vol. XLV, No 1 and 2 Jan-June, 1998.

Subramania, (1992), *Human Rights and the Police, Advancement of Police and Security Sciences*, Hyderabad.

Tomasevski K. (1993), *Women and Human Rights*, Zed, London.

V.R. Krishna Iyer (1979), *Law and Life,* Vikas, New Delhi.

13 Crime, Law and Prostitution: A Study on Female Prostitutes of Mangalore

Veerendra Kumar N.

Introduction

Prostitution is one of the oldest institutions of the world existed since the birth of the organised society. It is practiced in almost all the countries and every type of society. This system commodifies and dehumanises the bodies and persons of both sexes for the use and profit of man. After the 19th century the courtesan tradition seems to have been replaced in many parts of India by more exploitative systems of Devadasi and later commercial sex workers. Prostitution in different forms is widely rampant in India. The main form of prostitution such as 'women kept-in lodge' and 'Live-band artists' which have made the woman public property and deprived her of the right to independent choice. Indian law expressly prohibits social evils like prostitution, immoral traffic in women and others, but they do exist to some extent, more in cities than in rural parts. It is a system where prostitution is legally allowed to thrive, which attempts to hide it from the public.

This paper entitled 'Crime, Law and Prostitution: A study on female prostitutes in Mangalore city' has been prepared—based on the empirical research conducted in Mangalore city of Karnataka state. It provides an authentic analysis about the total number of prostitutes arrested and cases registered by police. Prostitute's opinion and problems are revealed as being in the profession they experienced at different levels of harassment, torture, exploitations at the hands of procurers, pimps, traffickers, law enforcement agencies and clients, due to their continuous contact with them. Their awareness about SITA or PITA, how Indian law treats prostitutes are also tried to give.

The approach and methodology adopted for this study

strictly adhered to typical sociological study. Primary data collected with the help of Observation, Interview-Schedule, Interviews, case studies and informal discussions with the respondents.

The cases registered and arrests made in six main police stations of Mangalore city under SITA and ITP ACT 8 (b) that was 1512. While the research went on, the researcher guessed that unlimited number of prostitutes might have been left without arrests.

Crime: A very accurate, comprehensive picture of prostitution either in world or in India is not available since sexual exploitation and sale of women and children are mostly unreported crimes. In India, criminalising women by forced entry into prostitution is different picture. Women and children are manipulated, forced, trapped, and enslaved in a variety of forms of prostitution. They are delivered into crime and prostitution by rape, battery, child sexual abuse, educational deprivation, poverty, race discrimination, sex discrimination, class discrimination, and war. Prostituted women and children comply with men's demands because they are promised food, clothing, shelter, money, drugs, safety, and companionship. The differences that set prostituted women and children apart are not of choice or morality, but differences of circumstance. The concept of choice assumes at least two options from which one choses. The difference between starvation, abuse, homelessness, loneliness, and death or prostitution can hardly be called a choice.

Prostituted women and children live lives of unlimited exposure. They are constantly exposed to disease, drugs and alcohol, homelessness, incarceration, mental illness, malnutrition, murder, physical abuse sexual abuse, sleep deprivation, torture, verbal harassment, and weather. Women and children suffer physical, social, emotional, and psychological damage from being prostituted day after day and year after year by man after man. Women and children sustain physical injuries, organ damage, infertility, and high-risk pregnancies. They are isolated from mainstream society, miss out on a normal socialisation process, and have difficulty establishing intimate relationships. The emotional effects of prostitution include anger, rage, deep pain, grieving, distrust and hatred for men, and feelings of humiliation, dirtiness, and shame. Psychological effects manifest in depression, dissociative disorders, drug and alcohol abuse, anxiety, post-traumatic stress disorder, and self-injuring and suicidal behaviours.

The Law and Prostitution

India is one of the nations signed the International Convention dealing with immoral traffic in women and girls, 1950. Before independence, prostitution was investigated and interpreted mainly in terms of the morbidity of the prostitute's life and the malignant effects of its in society. In effect, the prostitution was looked upon more as a cause than as an effect of the uncongenial conditions in society. The government of India in its report to the League of Nations in 1933, described its general policy towards prostitution and like questions as one of abolition. The states have, through the years, had legislations dealing with prostitution, have generally covered few areas.

The first law dealing with the status of sex workers is the law of 1956 referred to as 'The Suppression of Immoral Traffic Act (SITA).' According to this law, sex work in India is neither legal nor illegal; it is tolerated since prostitutes can practice their trade privately but cannot legally solicit customers in public. In particular, the law forbids a sex worker to carry on her profession within 200 yards of a public place. This Act does not criminalise prostitution, but only "commercialised vice". The focus is on the "larger interests of society" rather than on the prostitute herself.

Recently, the old law has been amended as 'The Immoral Traffic (Prevention) Act or PITA' 1986. The change in nomenclature from "suppression" to "prevention" is hard to explain. According to one commentary, the change in the name of the Act was effected "in view of the widening of the scope of the Act to cover all persons, whether male or female, who had exploited sexually for commercial purposes". Apart from a provision which empowers licensing authorities to suspend the licenses of hotels where children or minors are detected to be used for purposes of prostitution, there appears to be little else in the amendment which warrants the adjectival change.

From "abolition" through "suppression" to "prevention" has seen a legislative journey in law and societal reaction. It is hard to find in its midst concern for the plight of prostitutes or even for the reduction of its incidence. The law reflects a bias aimed at keeping out of the public eye and public mind the unsavory aspects of prostitution. Yet, it is commonly acknowledged that women in prostitution are subjects of exploitation. Protection to prostitution is the desideratum. ITPA attempts to deal with the problem, after person has already been inducted into the profession. They are the preventive measures assuring protection to the woman which should be the focus of the law and action.

The Indian Penal Code (IPC) that predates the SITA is often used to charge sex workers with vague crimes such as "public indecency" or being a "public nuisance" without explicitly defining what these consist of. Sections 366A and 366B of IPC are intended to punish the export and import of girls for prostitution. Section 366A deals with trafficking of minor girls from one part of India to another. Section 366B makes it an offence to import girls below the age of twenty-one (21) years for the purpose of prostitution into India from any other countries.

The approach was consolidated in SITA. The abolitionist trend continues with PITA currently in force. PITA's principal mandate is to prevent the traffic of women and children into prostitution. Unfortunately, the actual enforcement of the law has been mainly against the same women and the children it is supposed to protect. An examination of the records of the arrests and convictions under PITA in Mangalore shows that over 90 per cent of those arrested under PITA have been picked up under Section 8 (b) of the Act for seducing or soliciting—for purposes of prostitution, in a manner/place that makes her a public nuance. It appears that prostitutes may exist, but must not be seen. But thing is that women who have challenged their arrests under this section of PITA have invariably been acquitted due to lack of evidence. However, since most women are too ignorant and also frightened to go to court, they continue to be arrested in large numbers.

Section 4 of the Act says that any person over the age of 18 years who knowingly lives off the earnings out of prostitution of a girl or woman, either wholly or in part 'shall be punishable with imprisonment for a term which may extend to two years'. This obviously implies that the prostitute woman may support herself with her earnings, yet she herself is usually the one who is arrested and punished (Nataraj 2004:38).

Section 5, of the PITA 1986 defines procuring, inducing or taking persons for the purpose of prostitution. Section 6 of this Act, provides punishment not less than seven years for detaining a person in premises, where prostitution is carried out.

The study consisted 100 cases as it could satisfy with reliability and completeness of information generated through primary data collected with the help of observation, interview schedule, interviews, case studies and informal discussions with the respondents. As a first step, the observation was conducted across the city day and night visiting key places such as railway stations, live-band centres, lodges and circuit houses to know how prostitution is practiced. It was assumed that prostitutes could be found only on streets, but later realised this was just one form of prostitution. The evening dailies and fortnightly (*Hai Marutha, Karavali Ale, Special news, Patanga, Police news etc.*) have helped in gathering information about the places where the system prevailed in the city. The information gathered from other persons who are directly involved with the sex trade such as Hotel Managers, brothel keepers, pimps and clients have helped a lot.

Indeed, he succeeded in approaching the street-sex workers with the help of an auto-driver who was working as a 'pimp'. 'Pimps' had good rapport with many lodge managers for a smooth functioning of their activities. Managers supplied girls for the sexual satisfaction of their customers through 'pimps'. In the beginning, they were reluctant and suspicious about researcher's main objective. As they were convinced about the purpose of the study, they co-operated and assisted in collection of data essential for the study.

Prostitutes are not homogeneous groups. Their heterogeneity stands ratified by the typologies mentioned in the study of Mangalore. The streetwalkers have been identified in large number of the total respondents whose strength constitutes 31 per cent and who accept all clients. Call girls constitute 27 per cent, home-centred prostitutes form 23 per cent, sales girls make 8 per cent, women kept in lodges constitute 6 per cent and girls in live band cabaret constitute 5 per cent respectively. Most of these were engaging through organised set up.

Majority of prostitutes in Mangalore in all categories are from Karnataka (74 per cent) followed by from Kerala (22 per cent) as this city is very close to Kerala. Since this city is well connected with different types of good transport facilities, the researcher noted migrations from all over the state. The remaining few numbers of respondents are from Andhra Pradesh, Tamil Nadu and Maharastra, because they belong to either kept-in-lodges or live band artist-prostitutes. Based on the rotation system, they work through organised set-up, moving from one city to another throughout the year. Among the respondents, 47 per cent belong to different parts of the State especially from the rural areas. About 53 per cent of the respondents have originally come from different urban centres of both Karnataka and other Southern states.

There is an unequal distribution of prostitutes on the religious grounds could be seen in the city. Hindus (79 per cent) comprise the majority of respondents. Protestants constitute 10 per cent as the second largest in sample size followed by Muslims and Digambara Jains sharing 9 per cent and 2 per cent respondents respectively.

Literacy rates are very high (88 per cent) in almost all the categories of prostitutes in the city. Among the total respondents interviewed, 43 per cent have got primary education (most of whom are home centered prostitutes). Only 12 per cent respondents are illiterate, who mainly belong to home centered and street prostitution, as they are old-aged and have poor background. Due to the increasing migration especially from Kerala into the city, the Malayali speaking strength is high among the prostitutes. Where the rate of higher education is high, there the number of English speakers is also high. As this city has been more affected by the modern, western culture, than any other part of Karnataka, Mangalore city prostitutes are also well educated, among them call girls and sales-girls have completed their P.U education.

Based on the information available about the marital status of the respondents in Mangalore city, it is common that most of the prostitutes (41 per cent) are unmarried, because their age is below 25 years. In addition, they prefer the job first and then family settlement. Second highest numbers of prostitutes (19 per cent) are separated from their husbands and 12 per cent of them are widows. About 33 women respondents (separated, deserted and divorced) chose this profession because of their marital disintegration and because of the influence of bad company i.e., intermediaries, situational compulsions etc.

The call girls, sales girls, women kept in lodges, live band dancers and home-centered prostitutes seem to be mostly from nuclear families (78 per cent). The remaining (22 per cent) respondents, most of whom are common prostitutes and few others who are unequal in number have come from joint families. In Mangalore city transport facilities have developed very rapidly in recent years. It is easy for men from the surrounding villages to come and go very frequently. Most of the respondent families have no considerable property. Their economic condition is pathetic as they are unable to save much from their earning.

Causes of prostitution are manifold; they are rooted in the social, economic, religious, moral, political, psychological, biological, historical and civilisation aspects of the 'social' existence.

Where as in the case of Mangalore, there are 10 contributory causes to a girl's/woman's entry into prostitution have been identified. The data shows that the influence of prostitutes/ procurers/souteneur (pimps and touts) and desertion by husbands (41 per cent) are the two main contributory causes that come under social category for prostitution. Legal and administrative category includes three causes—(a) sold to prostitutes/procurers/souteneurs/by friends, relatives and neighbourers, (b) kidnapping by a prostitutes/procurers/ souteneur, (c) threat from sex C.D.brokers. Totally, it consists of seven per cent of the total respondents. Psychological and personal category includes three causes that consists of (a) lack of parental affection, (b) abandoned by lover and (c) own inclination. 26 per cent of the respondents fall under this category. Economic category consists of two causes—(a) Left a widow but no means of support (b) poverty and (c) destitution. 26 per cent of the total respondents interviewed belong to this. Thus, there is more than one factor contributing to women's entry into prostitution.

About 38 per cent of the respondents unequally engaged in different occupations prior to coming to the profession of prostitution. Of the total respondents who were previously engaged in different occupations nine per cent worked as agricultural labourers, eight per cent were house servants, two per cent were typists, six per cent were home centered beedi rollers, three per cent were dancers at live band, six per cent were sales girls, three per cent were nurses and one per cent was store keepers. The major portion of the interviewees (62 per cent) did not involve in any jobs, because they might have directly come to the profession during their early age by deception, own inclination and situational factors as most of them admitted.

According to this source, 36 per cent of the prostitutes have spent between eight to 30 years in prostitution. About 57 per cent have spent one to seven years where as the rest (seven per cent) are comparatively recent entrants and their involvement in prostitution ranges between 15 days to one year.

Operation of Prostitution

Majority of the prostitutes are found to be practicing through organised setup (53 per cent), as it is legally prohibited and publicly condemned. Second majority of them—call-girls, sales-girls and common categories—operate independently and that constitutes 33 per cent. Other prostitutes, especially home-centered and sales girls, constitute 11 per cent and functioning in the form of clandestine operations forms only 3 per cent. It includes especially married-women. It is so because in Mangalore, there are no tolerated areas to be described as red-light areas and the total sample was drawn from all categories of prostitutes and interviews were conducted at hotels and lodges, public buildings, private houses, houses of gharwalis, rented rooms and sometimes at street isolated places etc.

As many as 69 per cent respondents said that they have not left the home as they were working as a part-time prostitution (sales girls, call girls and home-centered prostitutes) and other time or days engaged in jobs that provides very low marginal salary. The two respondents said that they have missed their home since between their ages from birth to five years. About 27 per cent respondents did the same thing since between the 11 to 30 years. Only two per cent of them stated that they left their original home 30 years ago and never went back and they not interested at all to see the members of the family. Of the 29 per cent respondents (prostitutes for one to 30 years), few of them vocationally visited their parental homes and among them are live-band dancers, girls in-kept lodges and common prostitutes and others as they used to pay them.

65 per cent respondents expressed their opinion towards procurers and pimps. About 24 per cent of the total respondents

interviewed said that procurers or pimps were 'good', 18 per cent of them said they were 'money-makers', 15 per cent of them said they were' cruel and bad', eight per cent said they were 'good but money-minded'. The remaining 35 per cent women said 'they did not have any idea' as they were exception to this case and were engaging profession independently or clandestinely.

When researcher questioned them regarding their sickness, the prostitutes were very reluctant to say anything, though a few them had one or the other infirmity. It is found that, those who have spent more than eight years in the profession were suffering from HIV+.

Questions regarding their 'relation and number of warning they received' from the police roused suspicion and even fear in many of the respondents. Most of them evaded answering them or gave non-committal replies. Nine respondents received warning less than five times, four received five to ten times, 26 respondents received warning several times. Those who received warning said that they had received police warning for 'soliciting at public places' and 'operating from lodges' with the help of 'links' and complaints were given by the public.

However, most of them said that the police arrested them mostly for soliciting. About 23 respondents were arrested less than five times, seven respondents were arrested five to 10 times, two respondents were arrested 11 to 15 times and one respondent was arrested 16 to 20 times. Four respondents said that they have been arrested several times. The respondent who was arrested more than 10 times said that it was done out of sheer vengeance as she had refused to pay the weekly bribes to the police. Some of them were arrested red-handed in lodges with traffickers and pimps and released clients only. According to them, it is common in the city police stations that the arrested prostitutes were released only after the police were bribed.

About 37 arrested respondents stated that they were convicted at different ages. Only one respondent was convicted when she was below 18 years, another between the age 18 to 21 years, 21 between 22 to 25 years, four between 26 to 29 years, one between the age 30 to 33 years case, four between 34 to 37 years and five respondents said they did not remember the age at which they were convicted.

The police had arrested about 37 respondents at least once and the rest of them had escaped. All 37 arrested women had given their opinions about the police differently. 13 of them said they were 'cruel', 18 of them termed them 'cheats', six considered them 'bad'. According to one 19-year aged girl from kept-in-lodge category, she was forced to sexual relation with one police officer because he always gave threat of raids and arrests continuously for several days though she was in the cobweb of one pimp who brought her to the lodge and forced her to receive a series of clients providing nothing except good food for existence, dress and cosmetics for attraction. Most of the common prostitutes said they were simply arrested by the police of women's police station, as they required minimum arrest cases per month.

Mangalore city comes under the jurisdiction of six main police stations, which include one women police station at Pandeshwara. As the researcher collected statistical data chronologically for 10 years from all these six stations, it was found that most of the cases arrested and registered were under the PITA 8(b), because each respondent solicited herself at public place and after arrests were made, they would be released within 24 hours consequent to receiving penalty. If respondents were arrested on other grounds, after a thorough enquiry was made in police station, they were produced at the district criminal court in the presence of law-makers within 24 hours and the cases would be registered.

Unlike other main cities in India, there are no correctional agencies in the Mangalore city for the prostitutes. Since the number of women entering this profession is increasing manifold year by year, none of the Governmental or Non-governmental correctional agency concerned with prostitution is showing interest or coming forward for the upliftment of prostitutes and their families in the city.

For the welfare and rehabilitation of social victims, the NGOs play very important and remarkable role. When a researcher asked questions about their awareness towards NGO's, none of the prostitutes mentioned about the existence, and did not know the name of any Non-Governmental organisation, and its presence in the city. Due to this, it is very difficult to identify the prostitutes and find their numbers in Mangalore city.

Conclusion

Prostitution is, beyond doubt, a social evil. It has been an obnoxious feature of every society. Despite attempts made from time to time to check it, the evil of prostitution persists all the time. The PIT Act is one such attempt to check the evil. From the several study reveals that prostitution is a great threat to the institution of family and marriage. Hence, instead of banning it totally, the law in every country has tried to regulate it so that it may be kept within its legitimate bounds without unduly encroaching upon the institution of marriage and family.

The woman in prostitution is depersonalised two ways -- first by being forced into a position where she cannot make her own choice and then by being hounded by the state for being a prostitute. Social attitudes remain hostile towards single women. Most women who are deserted by their husbands are stigmatised and the state is unable to enforce payment of adequate maintenance. Kept-in-lodge prostitute Navya, describes her situation: "After I was rejected by my paramour, I was not taken in either by my family or my friends. When I was left free in the city, I got into the cobweb of intermediaries and they used me to learn decoration to support myself. I never dreamt that I would sell my body for sex; but at least here I get paid for sex."

In recent years, people's attention is focussed on the prostitutes because of the threat of STD. Few NGO's that started working with the women were also similarly motivated. However, they soon saw the enormous violence that the women were subjected to by brothel keepers, pimps and clients, and even by the police.

The text and spirit of the existing law does not allow anyone to take advantage of the helplessness and vulnerability of women and therefore it makes brothel keeping, procuring person for prostitution, living on the earning of prostitutes giving ones premises for prostitution, detaining anyone in brothel etc., illegal and punishable. But a total eradication of prostitution is impossible. Unlike other professions, sex workers are not protected under normal labour laws and are not entitled to minimum wage benefits, compensation for injury or other benefits that are common in other types of work. They do, however, possess the right to rescue and rehabilitation, if they desire and possess all the rights of other citizens. In practice, this is not common.

The fact is that, preparing framework for discussion on the welfare of women prostitutes is not easy. This is particularly true in the city of Mangalore, where an overwhelmingly equal number of prostitutes are from both rural and urban areas; a majority are from both middle and poor classes; a significantly high proportion have been sexually abused and ill-treated in their adolescent period. Very often, the trafficking of women has been facilitated by social, psychological and economic conditions in our country, rather than by organised criminal networks, it is also applicable to the female prostitutes of Mangalore. Unfortunately, the existing current laws target the prostitute and discriminate against her, instead of protecting her from the cobweb of law enforcement authorities and abuse by other state agencies.

With this as a justification for a law on the subject, PITA acquires the colour of being a cosmetic, moralising piece of legislative work. The Act is therefore concerned not with prostitution itself, but with the manner in which the activities of prostitutes and of those associated with them which offend public order and decency, expose ordinary citizens to what is offensive and injurious or involves an exploitation of others. "Legal action under the purview of the SIT Act of 1956 and PIT Act of 1987 should be strictly enforced against, procurers, brothel agents, and other intermediaries who are directly or indirectly supporting the system with vested interests. These elements are the important determinants of continuity in forced prostitution" (Shankar Jogan, 1990:209).

Recommendations

For control of prostitution, there should be a clear-cut understanding of law enforcing machinery regarding prostitution that it is a phenomenon arising out of socio-economic considerations having a human aspect. Law enforcers should be strict with those who are involved in prostitution as intermediaries or those who are responsible for the perpetuation of prostitution. The victimised women should be treated humanely and with compassion. Secondly, there is need for special legal and administrative measures which should check the forced entry of women and girls into prostitution. For controlling the 'demand' situation, there should be a way of checking the indiscriminate growth of cities, for plugging the 'supply' points it is equally important to provide comprehensive balanced developmental programmes after identifying the main supply centres. Thirdly, there is a need of orientation for the police and judiciary about the lives of prostitutes and circumstances that draw them into prostitution—so that they are sensitised enough to be able to deal with such issues in a perfect manner.

A lot could be done in the way rehabilitation of prostitutes. Rehabilitation programmes would apply to those women who are willing to come out of prostitution and re-establish themselves with the rest of the society. So, the identification of the beneficiary group is needed prior to taking up any further steps in this direction. For 'proper implementation of rehabilitation programmes,' there should be an integrated and comprehensive package aiming at both social and economic rehabilitation of the women and it is better to be provided through different NGO's working in their concerned areas. Inspiration to establish cooperatives for promoting economic activities of prostitutes is also essential.

Another important aspect of prostitution is rehabilitation and development of children of prostitutes. Measures for the children should be planned and systematised irrespective of whether their mothers are willing to leave prostitution or not. Such activities include—educational, economic, employment incentives, arranging institutionalised care, opening child guidance centres, provision of medical care etc. Authorities should be persuaded to accept mothers as legal guardians of the children and not insist for father's name. Existing childcare institutions should be encouraged to admit and take care of children of the prostitutes.

Further steps should be taken to improve the quality of life and living pattern of the prostitutes who are not able to come out of prostitution. This can be done by utilising health care facilities accessible and conduct regular health checkups, educate them about AIDS and provide them with condoms to protect from incurable diseases by providing clinical services in light areas through non-governmental agencies. Secondly, their literacy and general awareness should be improved by providing creche and day-care facilities to cover working hours of the women. Counseling services and legal aid should also be provided. It is essential to find out alternative livelihood opportunities matching to individual's qualification and aptitude.

It is essential to provide protection and restore confidence among willing prostitutes who wish to come out of their profession. While complete eradication of prostitution seems impossible, reducing the incidence of prostitution is possible. Similarly, rehabilitation of all the prostitutes is neither wanted, nor possible. What is possible is to make available all assistance and support to the prostitutes, willing to come out of the profession, and thereby helping them in their rehabilitation.

In case of prostitutes of younger group who are arrested during raid should be dealt with sympathy. They should be persuaded to get into state-homes, correctional or in-rehabilitation centres. Encouragement should be given to form organisations among prostitutes to lead movements. The experience in India, as in other countries, has shown that prostitution as a problem has to be tackled through the wider approach of social action. Raising the status of women in general and educating the community in particular would have a definite bearing on of prostitution.

References

Das R.M., 1962, *Prostitution in Women in Manu and His Seven Commentators,* Variance, Cinchona Publication.

George Ryley Scott, *A History of Prostitution,* Torchestream Book, 1954.

Joardar Bishwanath, *Prostitution in Historical and Modern Perspective*, Delhi Inter India Publications. 1984.

Jogan Shankar, *Devadasi Cult: A Sociological Analysis*, New Delhi, Ashish Publishers, 1990.

Kapur, Promilla, *Love, Marriage and Sex,* Delhi: Vikas Publishing House Private Ltd., 1973.

Punekar, S.D., and Kamala Rao, *A Study of prostitutes in Bombay*, Bombay: Lalvani Publishing House, 1967.

Shyamala Nataraj, *Women in Prostitution; Need for Informed Intervention,* MANUSHI, 2004.

S.I.T.W.G. Act, *Suppression of Immoral Traffic in Women and Girls Act, 1956*, New Delhi: Government of India, Ministry of Law, Publications division, 1958.

Sukumari Bhattacharji, "*Prostitution is in Ancient India,*" Social Scientist, Vol. 15, No. 2, (Feb., 1987).

14 Human Trafficking: A Human Rights

Avanish Bhai Patel, A.J. Mishra

Introduction

Human trafficking is a crime against humanity, which is a human rights abuse in its worst form and one of the most serious organised crimes of the world, transcending cultures, geography and time. Human trafficking is the illegal trade of human beings for the purposes of reproductive slavery, commercial sexual exploitation, forced labour, or a modern-day form of slavery. In India, the problem of human trafficking is a matter of grave concern. According to a report, the estimated annual turnover of human trafficking in India is around 20 billion rupee. Of the total number of persons affected by trafficking, there are 80 per cent women and 50 per cent children (*P.P.I., 2010:1*). Trafficking clearly violates the human rights. It violates the right to health, right to liberty, right to equality and security of persons. Besides, trafficking violates the right to employment and the right to self-determination (*NHRC quoted in 2003).*

Human trafficking flourishes in the poverty, distraction, inequity, corruption, scuttle hopes and broken dreams, deceit, violence, political conflict, criminality and domestic workers, personal service, factory, restaurant, farm, and agricultural labour. (*Shrivastava, 2007:65, Walker and Hunt, 2008:26*). The victim can be female or male child or adult and victims can be also found in any race or ethnicity and from any country of the world. Poverty and the lack of money play major role in the incidence of human trafficking. Where the financial system has shrunken, education creates false impression of opportunities abroad; family members are complicit in the victim's fate. The temptation for better life, crises in the home and the low value placed on women and children can push many towards waiting traffickers (*Shrivastava, 2007:65*). Trafficked persons become either unpaid or poorly paid. They are viewed as a commodity and they are used for gaining *(Esquibel, 2005:21)*. Poor parents sell their children to another country and blame their actions on poverty *(Monzo, 2005:398)*.

Child trafficking is the worst form of human trafficking which is affecting millions of children in the entire world. United Nations estimate suggests that globally trafficking in women and children is an operation worth $10 billion annually (*Shrivastava, 2007: 66*). In India, the volume of child trafficking has increased in last two decades. A large number of boys and girls are being trafficked every day. Children and their families are often lured by the promise of better employment and more prosperous life far from their home and others are kidnapped and sold. Trafficking violates a child's rights to grow up in family environment and exposes him or her to a range of dangers, including violence and sexual abuse. In India, a number of children are engaged in commercial sex due to religious prostitution, sex tourism and pornography. Briefly, religious prostitution is known as *devadasi pratha,* which is socially accepted in some parts of Indian society. Young girls from socially disadvantaged communities are given to God and they become *Devadasi (Sen, 2003:194). Davadasi pratha* is prohibited by the Prohibition of Dedication Act of 1982. Even today, religious prostitution is prevalent in Andhra Pradesh, Karnataka, Tamil Nadu, Kerala and Maharashtra *(Sen, 2003:42)*. Sex tourism may be defined as trips organised from within the tourism sector or from outside this sector, but using its structures and networks with the primary purpose of effecting a commercial sexual relationship by the tourist with residents at the destination (*World Tourism Organisation, 1995)*. Pornography is also worst form of human trafficking and close to sex tourism. Sex traffickers (sex tourists) are forefront of in the production of pornographic material in the forms of pictures, films depicting nude children and sex with the children. Traffickers are often found to be producing, collecting and circulating pornography (*(Sen, 2003:188)*.

Human trafficking violates the fundamental rights of a person. Article 23 (Fundamental Rights) of the Indian constitution prohibits trafficking of human beings that nobody can use any person in such works which are against the humanity. Human trafficking violates the right to health and health care, liberty and security of person, and the right to freedom from torture, violence, cruelty or degrading treatment. The trading and exploitation of human being is the most despicable violation of human rights by traffickers *(Sharma, 2007: 85)*. From the preceding lines, it is apparent that human trafficking is prevailing among the women and children in India and therefore, there is a dire need of scientific enquiry to analyse this issue from multiple perspectives and explore the factors which are responsible for trafficking among the children.

Definition of Concepts: Broadly, the first term human trafficking refers to "the recruitment, transportation, transfer, harbouring or receipt of persons (children), by means of threat or use of force or other forms of coercion, of abduction, fraud, deception, of the abuse of power or of a position of vulnerability or of the giving or receiving of payments or benefits, to achieve the consent of a person (child) having control over another person, for the purpose of exploitation *(Trafficking in Persons Protocol, 2000)"*. The second term "human rights are a generic term and it embraces civil rights, civil liberties and social, economic and cultural rights. All these rights which are essential for the protection and maintenance of dignity of individuals and create conditions in which every human being may develop his personality to fullest extent may be human rights (*Agarwal, 2010:2)"*.

Different Approaches to Human Trafficking: Criminological Approach to Human Trafficking

The goal of this paper is to focus on criminological approach. Criminology is the scientific study of crime and its treatment. There are three principles of criminology, namely, sociology of law, criminal etymology and penology (*Sutherland and Cressey, 2011:3*). Sociology of law is the study of crime as a social phenomenon and it is the scientific analysis of social conditions which are responsible for the criminal behaviour. Criminology sees that human trafficking is the criminal behaviour which violates human rights and breaks criminal law. No matter what the degree of immorality and indecency of an act, human trafficking is not a crime unless it is prohibited by the criminal law. Criminal etiology analyses the causes of crime including those conditions which lead to committing of crimes. Criminal etiology sees that poverty, deceit, distraction, unemployment, lure of job, migration, inequity and corruption are the major causes of human trafficking. Penology is the study of penal code and crime control and explores remedies which may help in the rehabilitation of victims.

Human Rights Approach to Human Trafficking

Human rights are those rights which belong to an individual as a consequence of being human. These rights are essential for all the individuals with their liberty, dignity, moral, spiritual and social welfare *(Agarwal, 2010:2)*. But, human rights violation is the serious issue in the entire world today due to human trafficking which include slavery, sexual exploitation, and child labour, forced labour, debt bondage and forced marriages. Human rights approach to trafficking means that "all those involved in anti-trafficking efforts should integrate human rights into their analysis of the problem and into their responses" *(United Nations, 2010:3)*. This approach judges the impact of law, policy and measure which are implemented for the protection and welfare of trafficked persons. Human rights approach to human trafficking directs to Government for protecting and promoting the human rights of all persons within their jurisdiction including non-citizens. It also emphasises on Government for legal provisions to eliminate human trafficking and related exploitation. There are so many human rights violations that take place on trafficked person such as deprivation of the right to dignified life, right to liberty and security, right to access to justice and health services, right not to be submitted to slavery and right not to be sold, traded or promised in marriage *(Nair,2007:8 and United Nations, 2010:52)*.

Review of Literature: Human trafficking is the most alarming issue around the globe today. We will have to review of literature to understand the human trafficking in deep. The nature and factors have been reflected through available literature. For instance, Esquibel (2005) has seen in her study that trafficked persons become either unpaid or poorly paid. They are viewed as a commodity and they can be used again and again for accumulating profit. Traffickers cheat the migrants taking in faith that they will earn many times more money abroad than they are able at home. Further, he claims that the global human trafficking is established due to increase of poverty level. Poor people are compelled into the arms of traffickers. Opportunity of transportation is given them by traffickers from one country to another country. Moreover, she has explained that human trafficking is composed of many crimes such as fraud, kidnapping, assault, rape, and sometimes murder.

Manzo (2005), has found in his study that poverty is the root cause of trafficking. Trafficking flourishes where poverty is itself a symptom of a structural problem. Here, a better life is not signalled by education and training, but by the lure of a wage, whereas children are more likely to emigrate to find work away from their parents. Further, he explains that a close relationship between poverty and trafficking, poor parents sell their children to another country and blame their actions on poverty. Sharma (2007), has done her study in Maharashtra. She has examined in her study that trafficking of human beings clearly violates the fundamental rights. It also violates the right to health and health care, liberty and security of person, and the right to freedom from torture, violence, cruelty or degrading treatment. The trading and exploitation of human being is the most despicable violation of human rights by traffickers. The violation of human rights is not only within the countries but also across the borders, regions and continents. This study provides an analytical framework of various factors responsible for trafficking of women and children in India.

Walker and Hunt (2009), have done their study in U.S.A. and examined that human trafficking is a crime that affects individuals, groups of individuals, and the communities in which the crime is occurring. Human trafficking is flourishing in the society in the various forms such as labour sectors including commercial sex work, domestic-personal service, factory, restaurant, farm, and agricultural labour. Further, they have discussed human trafficking includes poverty, immigrant status, hope for a better life, being female, being young, and being isolated.

Lutya (2009), has established epi-criminological theory to explain human trafficking which is derived from two disciplines namely public health and criminal justice system. He has provided a scholarly synthesis of epi-criminological responses to human trafficking of young women and girls for involuntary prostitution in South Africa. He has revealed in this paper that despite criminological and public health challenges facing South Africa due to human trafficking of women and girls for involuntary prostitution. Further, he claims that a linear progression of epi-criminological vulnerabilities that give rise to human trafficking of young women and girls for involuntary prostitution can be observed among the vulnerable groups in South Africa.

Yuko (2009) has developed criminal and human rights models to define human trafficking. The criminal model provides that those who violate criminal laws are viewed as criminals and they are punished. The criminal model also incorporates the rights of any person accused of a criminal offence. According to criminal model, human trafficking and its related crimes create a threat in the state. Human trafficking must be criminalised in every state on both a national and transnational level. This model also ensures that there are no geographic regions in the world void of trafficking laws, which would facilitate the crime. The human rights model provides that people trafficked into a state's borders are viewed as victims of a crime rather than criminal defendants. Human rights are provided for trafficked persons by the state, despite the fact that they are in and have entered the state illegally. States must implement some legal measures to ensure that trafficked persons are able to take advantage their fundamental rights. This combines the protection of national and international human rights, as the trafficked person is outside his or her home state. Fry (2009) has found in his study that human trafficking is the global phenomenon and it is a transnational crime. Further, he has tried to identify the causes which are responsible for the human trafficking at country level. Moreover, this study examine the effects of United Nation's Trafficking Protocol on human trafficking is best approached through the adoption of a program evaluation framework, beginning with the process evaluation phase at the country level.

These studies try to figure out the factors of human trafficking and point out two theoretical models such as epi-criminological and criminal and human rights models. It is operant from these studies that how human trafficking may be studied through these studies. But, these studies are not enough to explain multiple factors of human trafficking. In these studies one or two factors have been pointed out behind human trafficking while multiple factor school of criminology explains, there are so many factors are responsible for committing any crime. So, human trafficking is the result of many factors. Now, we will discuss multiple factor school of criminology to explore the factors of human trafficking.

Multiple Factor School of Criminology and Human Trafficking: Criminologists have made use of multiple factor school to define the factors of crime. The followers of this school believe that crime is the result of a combination of various factors which cannot be discussed in terms of general proposition. According to this school, there are so many factors of committing crime and it demonstrates this fact in the context of causality of crime that no scientific theory of criminal behaviour is possible *(Chaturvedi, 2007: 67)*. In the regarding of crime, Ferrie says that crime is the result of many factors. These factors are close to each other and through deep study; these factors can be revealed in the society. Those factors are social, natural and anthropological. Moreover, American criminologist William Healy explains that it is not one or two factors which turn a man delinquent but it is a combination of many factors which cumulatively influence him to criminal conduct. These factors are migration, culture conflicts, family background, political ideology, religion and crime, economic conditions, ecology of crime *(Paranjape, 2011:76)*. Further, he argues that all the factors associated with a particular crime may not have equal importance as a cause of that crime. Without collecting these factors criminal behaviour cannot be explained.

So far now, we have discussed about multiple factor school of criminology and how various factors affect in committing crime. Now, we will examine to explore the factors of human trafficking with the support of multiple factor school. In contemporary era, any social phenomenon cannot be examined on the behalf of one or two factors. Every social phenomenon is affected by a number of factors. Similarly, if we observe human trafficking by using multiple factor school of crime, outcome reveal that many factors are behind human trafficking. These factors are such as poverty, tourism, migration, religious prostitution, globalisation, corruption, illiteracy and weak law enforcement.

Poverty and Human Trafficking: Poverty influences human trafficking to a considerable extent. Now a days, economic growth has paralysed the social life. The institution of family has disintegrated to such an extent that control of parents over their children has weakened thus leaving them without surveillance. Under the circumstance, those who have lack of strong will power fall an easy prey to trafficking. The employment of women and their outdoor activities have enhanced the opportunity for sexual exploitation *(Paranjape, 2011:82)*. It has been seen that there is a close relation between poverty and human trafficking. Poor households in debt or struggling with insecure livelihood may be compelled to hand over their children into debt bondage or allow them to migrate by themselves *(Shrivastava, 2007: 70)*.

Migration and Human Trafficking: The rapid growth of industrialisation and urbanisation in recent years has led to expansion of means of communication and travel facilities. As a result, human interaction has gone beyond close relation with increased changes of migration. Migration of persons to new places where they catch easily in trafficking to see better job opportunity. Migration and human trafficking are closely linked each other. It is observed that the situations and circumstances are influencing people for migrating and these factors make them vulnerable for traffickers. Traffickers use the migrants for their own advantages, which is the worst form of human rights violation *(Sen, 2003: 184)*.

Tourism and Human Trafficking: Now-a-days, tourism is the world's largest industry which contribution is almost 11.6 per cent of the GDP and employing approximately 9.4 per cent of the labour. According to a report, 2.4 million tourists arrive in India every year, which comprises 0.4 per cent of the world's total tourist traffic. Tourism provides anonymity and opportunity for various illegal activities. The anonymity enjoyed by tourists, couple with their craving for pleasure and entertainment. In which poverty and unemployment of local people play an important role in commercial sex for the tourists (*Sen, 2003: 186)*.

Religious Prostitution and Human Trafficking: There is close relation between religious prostitution and human trafficking. It deals with the degeneration of some of the practices and how this degeneration has led to trafficking and commercial sexual exploitation *(Sen, 2003:194)*. In India, a number of women are engaged in commercial sex due to religious prostitution. Religious prostitution is known as *devadasi pratha* which is socially accepted in some parts of Indian society. Young girls from socially disadvantaged communities are given to God and they become *Devadasi* and have to be sexually available to men in the temple *(Shrivastava, 2007:67)*.

Globalisation and Human Trafficking: Globalisation has

vastly increased human trafficking last two decades. The world economy is affected by process of globalisation and this economy has played an important role in the flourishing of human trafficking. Now-a-days, human trafficking is a lucrative business that has become more rewarding for the traffickers with advent of globalisation. Globalisation affects trafficking with both push and pull factors *(Brewer, 2011:46)*. Unemployment in supply countries is a push factor that forces people to seek opportunity to improve their economic condition *(Richter and Richter, 2011: 2)*. The spread of global culture serves as a pull factors in which people expect for a better life elsewhere. International labour Organisation (2008) estimates that annual global profits generated from trafficking amount to around U.S. $ 32 billion. Moreover, other factors are also responsible for the human trafficking such as corruption, illiteracy, lack of awareness, false marriages and weak law enforcement etc.

Objectives: There are five objective of this paper. The first objective is to identify the nature, problem and area of child trafficking. The second and third objectives are to explore the factors of child trafficking and to understand human trafficking as a human rights abuse. Moreover, two other objectives are to analyse various crimes under penal code and special laws and to examine remedial process and legal provisions.

Methodology: This study is based on secondary data. Secondary data have been collected from National Crime Record Bureau. A starting point for the analysis of available data is National Crime Record Bureau that collects data on trafficking through State Crime record Bureaus and Union Territories. These data provide an indication of the level or reporting of trafficking within India. Data available through National Crime Record Bureau is collected through first information reports (FIRs), lodged in police stations. FIRs have been lodged by victims, NGOs and members of civil society.

This bureau collects trafficking data under the different sections of penal code and special laws which are related to human trafficking; which crimes are observed under Indian Penal Code, they are procuration of minor girls (section 366-A), importation of girls (section 366-B), selling of girls for prostitution (section 372) and buying of girls for prostitution (section 373 I.P.C.). Similarly, which crimes are observed under special local laws, those laws are such as Immoral Trafficking (Prevention) Act, 1956, Child Marriage Restraint Act, 1929, Child Labour

(Prohibition and Regulation) Act, 1986, Transplantation of Human Organ Act, 1994 and Bonded Labour System (Abolition) Act, 1976.

Findings

Various Crimes under Child Trafficking during 2005-2009 (Table-A)

Sr. No.	Crime Head	Year 2005	2006	2007	2008	2009
1.	Procuration of Minor Girls	145	231	253	22	237
2.	Importation of Girls	149	67	61	67	48
3.	Selling of Girls for Prostitution	50	123	69	49	57
4.	Buying of Girls for Prostitution	28	35	40	30	32
5.	ITP Act, 1956	5,908	4,541	3,568	2,659	2,474
Total		**6,402**	**5,096**	**4,087**	**3,133**	**2,851**

Rate of Crime under Child Trafficking during 2005-2009 (Table-B*)

Sr. No.	Year	Child Trafficking Cases	Rate of Crime
1.	2005	6,402	0.6
2.	2006	5,096	0.5
3.	2007	4,087	0.4
4.	2008	3,133	0.3
5.	2009	2,851	0.2

Sources: National Crime Record Bureau 2009.

Result: Registered Cases of Human trafficking: A total of 2,851 incidents of crimes under various provisions of laws relating to trafficking have been reported in the country during 2009 as compared to 3,133 during 2008 recording a decrease of 9.0 per cent during 2009. 6,402 cases relating during 2005 relating to trafficking have been reported during 2005 as compared to 5,096 and 4,087 cases reported in 2006 and 2007 respectively.

Importation of Girls (Section 366-(B) I.P.C.): A decrease of 28.3 per cent has been observed in such cases as there were 48 cases during the year 2009 as compared to 67 cases in the previous year 2008.

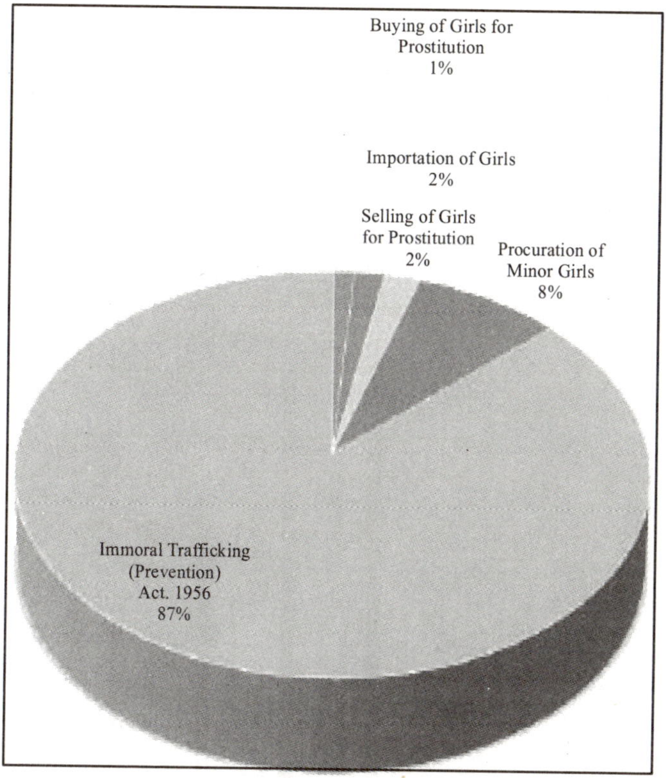

Fig. 1. Child Trafficking During 2009.

Sources: National Crime Record Bureau 2009.

Procuration of Minor Girls (Section 366-(A) I.P.C.): There were 237 cases reported in year 2009 as compared to 224 such cases in 2008.

Selling of Girls for Prostitution (Section 372 I.P.C.): There were 57 cases reported in the country during 2009 as compared to 49 such cases in 2008.

Buying of Girls for Prostitution (Section 373 I.P.C.): There were 32 cases reported in country during 2009. These cases indicate a 6.7 increase in the incidence over 2008 when 32 cases were reported in the country.

Immoral Traffic (Prevention) Act, 1956: There were 2,474 cases reported under this act which are showing decline of 6.9 during the year as compared as previous year 2008 when 2,659 cases were reported.

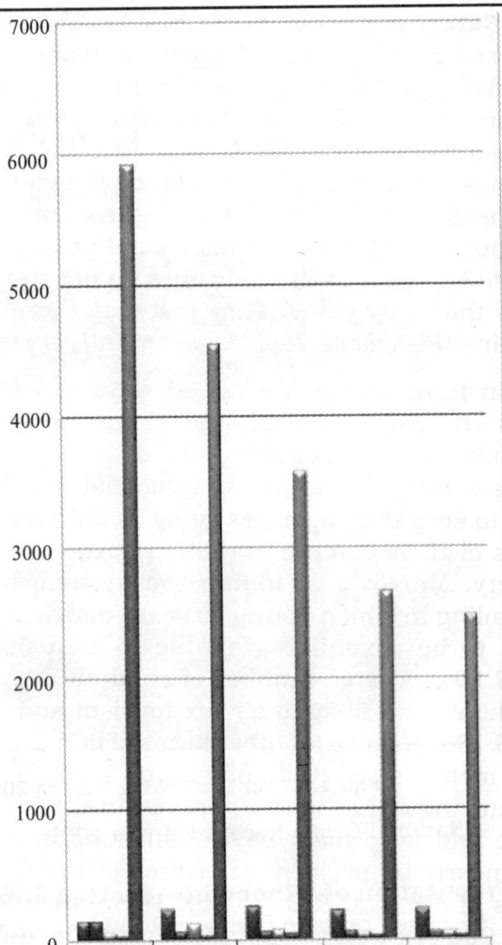

	2005	2006	2007	2008	2009
Procuration of Minor Girls	145	231	253	224	237
Importation of Girls	149	67	61	67	48
Selling of Girls for Prostitution	50	123	69	49	57
Buying of Girls for Prostitution	28	35	40	30	32
Immoral Trafficking (Prevention) Act. 1956	5,908	4,541	3,560	2,659	2,474

Fig. 2. Child Trafficking: Various Crime During 2005-2009.

Sources: National Crime Record Bureau 2009.

Discussion

Nature and Problem of Child Trafficking: Child trafficking is based on distinctions of gender, place and age. Trafficked girls from rural areas are used by urban people as street vendors or domestic servants, whereas boys are used by rural men on farms or plantations. While the younger child is not necessarily the most abused, traffickers can be drawn to apparent docility and ignorance *(Manzo, 2005:394)*. As one infamous trafficker has put it, "A little child knows nothing; older children know how to escape, but the little ones do not run away, they do not know their way home. They just stay there working, working, working (*Philomene Tegble, quoted in Frenkiel 2001*)".

In India, there are varied ways of employing trafficked children. They are exploited in industries and farming, in brothels and households, forced to work as smugglers and beggars *(Sen, 2003:159).* Commercial matchmakers need the girls to keep their agencies going. Children have to work off the loans of their parents and often spend years of their lives in slavery. Moreover in Indian society, religious prostitution is prevailing in which young girls are married to a local God and have to be sexuality available to men in the temple *(Sen, 2003:194).* A large number of children are trafficked not only for the sex trade such as sex tourism and pornography *(Sen, 2003:188)* but also for other forms of non-sex based exploitation that includes servitude of various kinds of such as domestic labour, industrial labour, agricultural labour, begging, organ trade and false marriages. Trafficking in children is on rise, and nearly 60 per cent of victims of trafficking are bellow 18 years of age (N.C.R.B., 2005). There are estimated to be over 9,00,000 sex workers in India. Approximately, 30 per cent are believed to be children. Recent reports estimate that the number of children involved in prostitution is increasing at eight per cent to 10 per cent per annum (*Shrivastava, 2007: 68*).

Area of Child Trafficking: There are the following areas where child trafficking is flourishing (*Khan, 2011:3*):

- **Labour:** There are under this bond labour, domestic labour, agriculture labour, carpet industry, garment industry and construction work
- **Illegal Activities:** There are under this begging, organ trade and drug peddling smuggling.

- **Sexual Exploitation:** There are under this forced exploitation, sex tourism, pornography, religious prostitution and false marriages.
- **Entertainment and Sports:** Child trafficking takes place in circus, dance troupes, bars and camel jockeys.

Factors of Child Trafficking: Trafficking is the most serious problem in contemporary society and which is the worst form of inhumanity. There are a number of factors behind trafficking of children. Poverty is the root cause of trafficking. Trafficking flourishes where poverty is itself a symptom of a structural problem. Here, a better life is not signaled by education and training but by the lure of wage, whereas children are more likely to emigrate to find work away from their parents. Where there is lack of political, social and economical stability, lack of access to education and information and lack of public awareness of the danger of trafficking, there is more possibility of child trafficking. Furthermore, other factors are also behind child trafficking including human trafficking such as domestic violence and disintegration of family structure, increasing demand for cheap and exploitable labourers in the construction, agricultural and industrial sectors, rising in the demand for sex workers in the highly lucrative and globalising sex industry. Besides these factors, one alarming factor is lack of effective anti-trafficking legislations and if such legislations exist, the lack of effective enforcement. So for now, we have explored various crimes under human trafficking, nature and problem, area and factors of trafficking; now we will move to examine how trafficking violates human rights and how remedial process and legislative provisions are attempting to control trafficking of human beings.

Human (Child) Trafficking as a Human Rights Abuse: The Constitution of India which is the highest law of the India and from which all laws emanate, guarantees equality as a human rights and prohibits trafficking of human beings. Article 23(1) specifically prohibits traffic in human beings, beggar and other forms of forced labour (*Constitution of India, 2009:16*). Human rights apply to all age groups; children have the same general human rights as adults. But children are particularly vulnerable and so they also have particular rights that recognise their special need for protection. Human rights are those rights which are essential for an individual as a consequence of being human. They are also necessary to create an environment in which people may develop their full potential and lead productive and creative lives in accordance with their needs and provide suitable conditions for the material and moral uplift of the human. Therefore, they must be preserved and defended if peace and prosperity are to be achieved (*Agarwal, 2010:3*).

Trafficking clearly violates the human rights to lead a life with dignity. It also violates the right to health, right to freedom from torture, violence, cruelty of person. It violates all these rights to children who have trafficked or victims of child marriages and right to education, besides, it violates the right to employment and the right of self-determination. Trafficking of children for coerced prostitution is an abuse of human rights in which children are exploited mentally and physically. It violates the right of children to liberty and safety and may even abuse their right to life. It renders children to a sequence of human rights abuses at the hands of traffickers and of those who buy their services *(Shrivastava, 2007:70).*

Remedial Process and Legal Provisions: The problem of trafficking may be controlled through following remedial process and legal provisions:

- **Anti-Human Trafficking Unit:** It is a collective unit of anti trafficking which focuses on different dimensions of human trafficking. Its goal is to trafficking and traffickers and trace trafficked victims. This unit also combines other agencies of law enforcement such as department of health, social welfare, labour, women and child, criminal justice administration and non-governmental organisation. Anti-Human Trafficking should be set up by police administration especially in the care of SP/DSP. Such units will be the best mechanism in the given situation to prevent and combat trafficking (*Nair, 2007: 58*).
- **Psycho-Sociological Interfere:** People who involve in trafficking, they are exploited mentally and socially by which they are weak emotionally. When such persons are traced, social-psychologists are present because mental and social conditions of victims are often neglected by police and other after-care agencies during tracing (*Nair, 2007: 38*).

- **Victim Welfare Programme:** Often society does not pay attention more on trafficked victims for their welfare, reform, protection and rights. Therefore, government should start such programme including NGOs and local communities *(Dixit and Dixit, 2007:9)*.

- **Advisory Committee:** Advisory committee may play an important role in anti-trafficking programmes and activities. Therefore, all state governments should organise advisory committee including NGOs, members of civil society and human rights activists and police *(Dixit and Dixit, 2007:9)*. Moreover, positive attitude of society, role of family, sensitisation and vocational education, role of media and rehabilitation programmes may also play an important role in remedial process.

Legal Provisions: Government of India and State Governments have implemented effective legal provisions to control human trafficking time to time, which are following:

Article 23 and 24 of Constitution: Guarantees right against exploitation, prohibits traffic in human beings and forced labour and makes their practice punishable under law. Article 24 prohibits employment of children below 14 years of age in factories, mines and other hazardous employment. **Indian Penal Code, 1860:** There are many provisions related to trafficking in I.P.C. (*Nair, 2007: 6*), significant among them are:

- **Section 366A:** Procuration of a minor girl below 18 years of age from one part of the country to another is punishable.

- **Section 366B:** Importation of a girl below 21 years of age is punishable.

- **Section 372:** Selling of Girls for Prostitution is punishable.

- **Section 373:** Buying of Girls for Prostitution is punishable.

- **Section 374:** Provides punishment for compelling any person to labour against his will.

Immoral Traffic (Prevention) Act, 1956: The objective of this act is to abolish traffic in women and girls for the purpose of prostitution as an organised means of living. Many offences have been specified under this act such as procuring, including or taking persons for prostitution, detaining a person in premises where prostitution is carried on, soliciting for prostitution, living on the earning of prostitution, seduction of a person in custody and keeping a brothel or allowing premises to be used as a brothel (*Nair, 2007: 7*). Similarly, Child Labour (Prohibition and Regulation) Act, 1986, Information Technology Act, 2000, Juvenile Justice (Care and Protection of Children) Act, 2000, Karnataka *Devadasi* (Prohibition of dedication) Act, 1982, Andhra Pradesh *Devadasi* (Prohibiting Dedication) Act, 1989 and Goa Children's Act, 2003 have been implemented to prevent trafficking and protection of women and children.

Moreover, many international organisations have implemented effective laws to control child trafficking and to promote welfare of children, these provisions are following:

- The Convention on the Rights of the Children, 1989.
- The Optional Protocol to the Convention on the Rights of the Child on the Sale of Children, Child Prostitution and Child Pornography, 2000.
- The Convention on the Elimination of All forms of Discrimination against Women, (CEDAW) 1979.
- Declaration on Social and Legal Principles Relating to the Protection and Welfare of Children, With Special Reference to Foster Placement and Adoption Nationally and Internationally, December, 3, 1986.
- SAARC Convention on Regional Arrangement for the Promotion of Child Welfare, 2002.

Conclusion

Trafficking in human beings, especially in children, is a worst form of human rights violation in contemporary society. It violates the right to health and health care, liberty and security of person, and the right to freedom from torture, violence, cruelty or degrading treatment. This study provides an analytical framework of various factors and areas which are responsible for child trafficking in India. It has been examined through this study that there are so many factors of human trafficking but study has emphasised on poverty, lack of opportunity and impoverishment. These are such factors which are making victim to people easily due to trafficking. In this paper an attempt has been made to explore the nature, problem of trafficking, factors and area of trafficking and how trafficking of human beings affects human rights. The study has shown that cases of human trafficking have decreased significantly. It implies that remedial process and legal provisions in this regard are playing an important role.

References

Agarwal, H.O., 2010, *Human Rights*, Central law Publications, Allahabad, pp. 2-3.

Bhamathi, B., 2011, *Evolving Strategies to Tackle Human Trafficking*, All India Police Science Congress, Dehradun, pp.1-19.

Brewer, Devin, 2011, *Globalisation and Human Trafficking*, Accessed on 5-11-2011,

Chaturvedi, Muralidhar, 2007, *Criminology and Penology*, Allahabad Law Agency Publications, Allahabad, pp. 67-68.

Constitution of India, 2009, Kanoon Prakashak, opp. Gurudwara, Anand Cinema, Jodhpur, p. 16.

Crime in India, 2009, National Crime Record Bureau, New Delhi, pp. 99-103.

Dixit, Arun Kumar and Sona Dixit, 2007, *Mahilaon aur Bachcho ki Taskari,* Kurukshetra, New Delhi, Vol. 54, pp. 9-11.

Esquibel, Monica, 2005, *Human Trafficking: A Violation of Human Rights, A Universal Issue*, Florida State University: pp. 20-26.

Fry, Lincoln J., 2009, *what was the Significance of Countries Ratifying the UN Protocol against Human Trafficking? A Research Note*, International Journal of Criminal Justice Sciences, Vol. 4(2) pp.118-130.

Khan, Intezar, 2011, *Child Trafficking in India: A Concern*, Dept. of Social Work, Jamia Milia Islamia University, New Delhi, pp.1-14.

Lutya, Thozama Mandisa, 2009, *Epi-Criminological Responses to Human Trafficking of Young Womenand Girls for Involuntary Prostitution in South Africa*, Journal of Scandinavian Studies in Criminology and Crime Prevention, Routledge Publication, Vol. 10, pp. 59-78.

Manzo, Kate, 2005, *Exploiting West Africa's Children: Trafficking, Slavery and Uneven Development,* Area journal, Wiley Blackwell Publisher, 37(4), pp. 393-401.

Nair, P.M., 2007, *Trafficking Women and Children for Sexual Exploitation*, UNIFEM, New Delhi, pp. 6-7.

Paranjape, N.V., 2011, *Criminology and Penology with Victimology*, Central Law Publications, Allahabad, pp. 76-81.

P.P.I., 2010, *Human Trafficking in India*, Accessed on 01-10-2011, http://www.policyproposalsforindia.com/article.php?article_id=203&languageid=1.

Recommended Principles and Guidelines on Human Rights and Human Trafficking, 2010, United Nations Press, New York and Geneva: pp. 3, 52.

Richter, William L. and Linda K. Richter, 2011, *Human Trafficking, Globalisation, and Ethics*, Accessed on 5-11-2-011, http://www.google.co.in/#hl=en&sugexp=kjrmc&cp=27&gs_id=4u&xhr=t&q=globalisation+an d+human+trafficking&pf=p&sclient=psyab&rlz=1C2

Root Causes of Human Trafficking, Accessed on 02-10-2011, http://www.caritas.org/activities/women_migration/caritas_migration_trafficking_and_women.html?cnt=431

Sen, Sankar, 2003, *A Report on Trafficking in Women and Children in India*, National Human Rights Commission, New Delhi, pp. 42,159,188,194-202.

Sharma, Renu, 2007, *Trafficking in Women and Children in India: A Situational Analysis in Maharashtra*, International Journal of Criminal Justice Sciences, Vol. 2(2) pp. 85-100.

Shrivastava, Deepti, 2007, *Child Trafficking: A Human Rights Abuse*, The Indian Police Journal, B.P.R.D., Vol. LIV No.1, pp. 65-74.

Sutherland, E.H. and D.R. Cressey, 2011, *Principles of Criminology*, Surjeet Publications, New Delhi, pp. 3-4.

Yuko, Elizabeth Ivana, 2009, *Theories, Practices and Promises: Human Trafficking Laws and Policies in Destination States of the Council of Europe*, Dublin City University: pp. 22, 23, 29.

Walker, T.K. Logan Robert and Gretchen Hunt, 2009, *Understanding Human Trafficking in the United States*, Journal of Trauma Violence & Abuse, Sage Publications, Vol.10 (1), pp. 3-30.

15 From Victimhood to Agency: An Alternative Theoretical Construction of Women in Crime

Moitrayee Sanyal

Introduction

The issue of female criminality has assumed a complex nature in contemporary Indian society. Although a numerical minority, women constitute a significant proportion of the offending population in India. However, there is an acute paucity of scholarship in the area of female criminality in Indian sociology. In comparison with relatively significant documentation on different aspects of male crime and delinquency, the amount of work carried out in the area of women and crime is extremely inadequate in India. It has been argued that the number of female offenders is so small that there is no subject matter to justify research. As per the NCRB report of 2011, there are 1,382 functioning jails in India having a total capacity to house 3, 32,782 prisoners. As of the same date, there were 3,72,926 inmates in jails across India. Males at 3, 56,902 make up 95.7 per cent of prisoners while females at 16,024 represent 4.3 per cent. Deviance of women is therefore a non-problem to both social scientists and society in general.

Deviant actions by women, particularly violent offenses are seen as signs of abnormality. Early criminological discourses in the west have constantly attempted to pathologise and medicalise deviance in women. This is mainly because 'crime' is constructed as act of aggression by men that reinforce stereotypes of masculinity. By constructing masculinity in terms of dominance, aggression and agency, criminological theories have tried to normalise and naturalise men's deviant behaviour. By contrast, femininity is typified in terms of passivity, docility and lack of agency. Thus the deviant woman emerges as an aberrant category, displaying signs of abnormality and difference (Braidotti, 1997). From the lawmakers to the police to the judiciary and correctional officers, the category 'crime' has been

Table 1. Prison Population in West Bengal as on 01.12.12

Sr. No.	Correctional Home	Condemned		Convict		UTP		Others		Released Prisoners		Children	
		M	F	M	F	M	F	M	F	M	F	M	F
(1)	(2)	(3)	(4)	(5)	(6)	(7)	(8)	(9)	(10)	(11)	(12)	(13)	(14)
1.	Presidency CH	1	0	706	0	1396	0	9	0	5	0	0	0
2.	Howrah DCH	0	0	42	0	516	0	0	0	0	0	0	0
3.	Hooghly DCH	0	0	15	0	298	29	0	0	0	0	1	3
4.	Alipore WCH	0	0	0	92	0	185	0	0	0	4	10	17
5.	Serampore SCH	0	0	0	0	156	10	0	0	0	0	0	0
6.	Chandannagar SCH	0	0	0	0	99	4	0	0	0	0	0	0
7.	Arambag SCH	0	0	2	0	64	3	0	0	0	0	0	0
8.	Uluberia SCH	0	0	2	0	138	0	0	0	0	0	0	0
9.	Alipore CCH	5	0	636	0	1158	0	0	0	1	0	0	0
10.	Burdwan DCH	0	0	34	5	207	24	0	0	0	0	2	5
11.	Asansol Spl CH	0	0	8	2	210	9	0	0	0	0	0	1
12.	Durgapur SCH	0	0	5	0	124	0	0	0	0	0	0	0
13.	Kalna SCH	0	0	0	0	69	1	0	0	0	0	0	0
14.	Katwa SCH	0	0	0	0	107	0	0	0	0	0	0	0
15.	D/Harbour SCH	0	0	5	0	208	15	0	0	0	0	2	0
16.	Dum Dum CCH	0	0	865	59	1743	174	0	0	112	44	27	25
17.	Krishnanagar DCH	0	0	75	7	587	61	0	0	0	0	2	2

(Contd...)

(Contd...)

(1)	(2)	(3)	(4)	(5)	(6)	(7)	(8)	(9)	(10)	(11)	(12)	(13)	(14)
18.	Ranaghat SCH	0	0	2	0	156	0	0	0	0	0	0	0
19.	Kalyani SCH	0	0	0	0	82	0	0	0	0	0	0	0
20.	Bongaon SCH	0	0	3	2	315	34	0	0	0	0	2	1
21.	Basirhat SCH	0	0	0	0	296	0	0	0	0	0	0	0
22.	Barrackpre SCH	0	0	2	0	230	5	2	0	0	0	0	0
23.	Tehatta SCH	0	0	0	0	115	0	0	0	0	0	0	0
24.	Midnapore CCH	0	0	699	10	384	18	4	2	0	0	1	1
25.	Bankura DCH	0	0	13	2	220	17	0	0	0	0	2	1
26.	Purulia DCH	0	0	26	0	207	0	0	0	0	0	0	0
27.	Purulia WCH	0	0	0	46	0	21	0	0	0	0	1	5
28.	Tamluk SCH	0	0	1	0	86	4	0	0	0	0	0	0
29.	Contai SCH	0	0	0	0	91	9	0	0	0	0	1	0
30.	Haldia SCH	0	0	4	0	85	4	0	0	0	0	1	0
31.	Ghatal SCH	0	0	1	0	32	15	0	0	0	0	1	2
32.	Jhargram SCH	0	0	1	0	106	5	0	0	0	0	0	0
33.	Bishnupur SCH	0	0	4	0	59	2	0	0	0	0	0	0
34.	Raghunathpur SCH	0	0	1	0	40	0	0	0	0	0	0	0
35.	Berhampore CCH	0	0	1128	78	862	38	0	0	134	13	19	15
36.	Suri DCH	0	0	146	13	164	9	0	0	0	0	1	0
37.	Malda DCH	0	0	88	5	546	26	2	0	0	0	2	0
38.	Balurghat DCH	0	0	228	6	291	25	0	1	0	0	3	2

(Contd...)

(Contd...)

(1)	(2)	(3)	(4)	(5)	(6)	(7)	(8)	(9)	(10)	(11)	(12)	(13)	(14)
39.	Lalgola OACH	0	0	91	0	0	0	0	0	0	0	0	0
40.	Bolpur SCH	0	0	0	0	68	4	0	0	0	0	0	0
41.	Rampurhat SCH	0	0	1	0	71	3	0	0	0	0	0	0
42.	Kandi SCH	0	0	0	0	108	4	0	0	0	0	0	0
43.	Jangipur SCH	0	0	0	0	173	3	0	0	0	0	0	0
44.	Lalbagh SCH	0	0	13	0	316	18	0	0	0	0	1	0
45.	Jalpaiguri CCH	0	0	476	18	566	39	0	0	17	0	2	1
46.	Darjeeling DCH	0	0	4	0	83	6	0	0	0	0	0	0
47.	Coochbehar DCH	0	0	161	24	110	21	0	0	22	0	22	13
48.	Raiganj DCH	0	0	99	2	183	10	0	0	8	0	3	2
49.	Siliguri Spl CH	0	0	29	6	225	15	0	0	0	0	0	0
50.	Alipurduar Spl CH	0	0	38	2	397	28	0	0	0	0	4	2
51.	Kalimpong SCH	0	0	1	0	27	1	0	0	0	0	0	0
52.	Kurseong SCH	0	0	0	0	27	5	0	0	0	0	0	0
53.	Mathabhanga SCH	0	0	0	0	30	4	0	0	0	0	0	0
54.	Mekhligunj SCH	0	0	0	0	17	2	0	0	0	0	0	0
55.	Tufangunj SCH	0	0	0	0	31	2	0	0	0	0	0	0
56.	Dinhata SCH	0	0	4	0	49	4	0	0	0	0	0	0
57.	Islampore SCH	0	0	11	0	185	6	0	0	0	0	0	1
	Total	6	0	5670	379	14113	922	17	3	299	61	110	99

Source: West Bengal Correctional Services, 2012.

constructed predominantly within the male domain, by the male. This has led to a systematic concealment of women as a subject matter of criminology not just in academia but also in the actual treatment of women in courts and penal institutions.

Contemporary trends in feminist research have mainly focused on victimisation of women in constructing an image of women offenders responding to abusive situations as helpless victims of crime. By this logic, the act of the crime by a woman is viewed as her response to economic dependence, poverty, sexual and physical abuse, i.e., conditions emanating from and rooted in the patriarchal structure of society. By emphasising the links between victimisation and offending in the life cycle of the female offenders, feminist theories have largely ignored the role of women's agency in crime. This theoretical inadequacy in understanding women as rational, purposeful and motivated agents of crime has led to the portrayal of women as demotivated and dehumanised perpetrators of crime. Thus, there is a tendency within traditional criminological as well as feminist discourses to adopt a binary approach and essentialise women's use of violence. Women are portrayed either as hapless victims or as cruel and unthinking perpetrators of crime, i.e., the mad or the bad woman. There has been little effort to understand experience and agency of female offenders in terms of the pathways they travel and the patriarchal power relations they negotiate in their everyday lives, both before and after their arrest and conviction.

The purpose of the present study is to argue for a theoretical framework that accounts for experience and agency of women offenders, advocating punishment for violation of collective rights, without demonising representations of women who commit crime. In doing so, I have attempted to chart the trajectory of theoretical development from early pre-feminist criminological literature to contemporary feminist development in the west. Efforts have also been made to understand historical conception of female crime in colonial India that had strong underpinning of women's rational choice in crime, as opposed to the largely descriptive socio-economic account of female offenders in contemporary Indian literature that focused mainly on their victim status in interpreting their crime.

Early Theoretical Perspectives of Female Criminality

The subject of women and crime suffered from criminological

neglect until the late 20th century. Much of early criminological theorising was informed by the legacy of positivism. Positivism's major attribute is its insistence on the unity of scientific methods in order to arrive at a universal explanation of crime and a solution to the problem of crime (Walkate, 2001). The male-centric bias in criminology can therefore be explained in terms of its linkages with the 19th century conception of science that encouraged criminology to view women and men in particular ways. Women were naturally positioned in the domestic sphere as the property of their fathers and husbands who occupied the public sphere and the very essence of a woman was linked to her biological role of reproduction and motherhood.

In the early days of criminology, theoretical debate was dictated from a predominantly biological perspective. Attempts were made to establish a link between the physiological characteristics of an individual and their propensity to commit crime. The most significant early studies of female criminality are the works of Lombroso and Ferrero (1895). In 'The Female Offender' (1895), Lombroso and Ferrero explain the concept of atavism that constructs the female criminal as an abnormal type. Lombroso and Ferrero (1895) drew a distinction between the occasional female criminal and the born female criminal.[1] The occasional female criminal was characterised as biologically and behaviourally normal but lacking in moral strength. By contrast, the born female criminal was described as muscular and strong, with thick hair and a virile face. A born criminal was overtly sexual, completely lacking qualities associated with the feminine, such as maternal and religious feelings. The prostitute was for example perceived to be anthropologically and morally more male than female. Emerging medical discourses reinforced principles of masculinity in explaining the etiology of female crime (Davies and Rhodes-Little 1993; Frigon, 1995).

The works of Thomas (1923) are indicative of the development of a liberal tradition in criminology. It carries over from Lombroso's work belief that deviance is pathology, but it is a socially induced pathology, rather than a biological abnormality. Thomas argued that women are likely to become more 'unadjusted' when social sanctions are removed. Thus, the source of female criminality, which he believed to be mainly sexual, lay in the breakdown of the traditional restraints on women.

Pollak's study of female criminality, 'The Criminality of Women' (1950), reveals the developing influence of sociology, psychology and psychoanalysis on criminology. Pollack's analysis focused on the 'masked' character of female criminality whereby women worked as mastermind behind criminal organisations in instigating rather than perpetrating crime. In fact, the relation between criminality and mental sickness is the commonest explanation of female crime. Hysteria and lunacy are cited as the real reasons for crime proneness in women, thereby denying motive, meaning and agency to the criminal actions women undertake.

Cowie, Cowie and Slater's study, 'Delinquency in Girls', (1968), has remained very close to the positivist tradition of Lombroso. Although, they have rejected the concept of atavism, there are significant features in their analysis, which bear strong resemblance to Lombroso and Ferrero's approach. They have retained the view that criminality is a sign of pathology, thereby relegating social and environmental factors to insignificance. This biologically deterministic theory of female criminality traced the source of crime to the physiology of women. Thus, the female criminal was in need of treatment, while the existing social conditions could be largely ignored.

The explanation of female criminality in terms of social differentiation of gender roles represents one of the first real attempts to analyse female crime in factors other than biological or psychological. Role theorists have examined the significance of factors such as differential socialisation, differential opportunity structures and differential social reaction to explain female crime and deviance. These theorists argue that women are socialised into passive roles of compliance. Even where they commit crime, the pattern of crime appears to reflect their gender-role socialisation. For example, in cases of homicide, women have been found to kill with a weapon, which is usually a domestic tool. According to Hoffman-Bustamante (1973), women have most often played secondary and supportive roles in the commission of crime, as accomplices of men.

Tracing the continuance of sexist assumption from Lombroso (1895) to Pollak (1950) and beyond, Smart (1976), examined how assumptions of abnormality of female offenders came to dominate both theory and criminal justice policy. Thus, women were ignored, marginalised or distorted, both in their deviancy and in their conformity. Eileen Leonard summarised mainstream criminological theory by stating:

> "Theories that are frequently hailed as explanations of human behaviour are, in fact, discussions of male behaviour and male criminality. We cannot simply apply these theories to women, nor can we modify them with a brief addition or subtraction here and there" (1982:181)

This exposure of mainstream criminology as the criminology of men marked the starting point of feminists' attempt to find alternative modes of conceptualising deviance, conformity, punishment and control.

Development of Feminist Criminology

Feminist perspectives gained momentum during the 1960's and became a major force in criminology and legal studies in the 1980's. The early feminist critique of mainstream criminology has focused on two main themes of neglect: first, women account for a very small proportion of all known offenders, thus little attention has been given to them in criminological research; second, even when women were recognised, they were depicted in terms of stereotypes based on their supposed biological and psychological nature.

Theoretical explanations for the growing incidence of female crime in the late 1960's and early 1970's was put forward by Adler and Simon, who argued that women offenders were changing their patterns of offending to more 'masculine' styles, becoming more aggressive and violent. This change was attributed to the growth of modern women's movement, popularly known as the 'liberation hypotheses' (Adler, 1975).[2] However, this account of female crime was considered unsatisfactory, because empirical finding showed that women who offended were not empowered as a result of women's movement. On the other hand, the direct beneficiaries of women's movement were not involved in crimes. The 'liberation hypothesis' reiterated male criminality as the norm against which female crime was measured and interpreted.

Understanding the Role of Gender as a Key Variable that Shapes the Victimisation to Offending Links in the Life Cycle of Offending Women

Contemporary research in the area of female crime has

indicated the centrality of gender in explaining the differences in the nature and causes of female and male crime. Gender is understood not as a natural fact, but as a complex historical and cultural product related to but not simply derived from biological sex difference and reproductive capacities. (Gelsthorpe, 2002). The organisation of gender in terms of patriarchal social control, sexual and reproductive role of women and their moral and relational concerns contrive to limit their access to criminal opportunity and motivations for crime. The recognition of gender as a powerful variable shaping female crime has established the theoretical foundation of exploring links between victimisation and criminal offending in women. Most studies documenting the victimisation-to-offending cycle of female offenders in the west use data collected from adult women to trace their childhood and other life experiences to examine how these experiences might be related to their subsequent criminal activity. Research on women's pathways into crime, for instance, recognised that gender has a significant role in shaping criminality.[3] Women and men enter the criminal justice system via different pathways. Among women, the most common pathway to crime that produce and sustain female criminality, are histories of physical and sexual abuse, mental illness tied to early life experiences, substance abuse and addiction, economic and social marginality, homelessness and dysfunctional relationship.

Women are often primary care-takers of the children at the time of arrest and have separate and distinctive mental and physical needs. Their involvement in crime is often economically motivated, driven by their dependent status, poverty and substance abuse. Research indicates that female participation in crime is highest for those crimes that are most consistent with traditional gender roles and norms and for which females have greater opportunity. Studies on gender differences in delinquent offences indicate that girls are more likely to commit what the justice system calls 'status offense' (prostitution, truancy or running away) than boys who commit offences of far serious and aggressive nature. Risk-taking preferences and styles in women differ from those of men. While men take risks in order to build status or gain competitive advantage, women take risks to protect loved ones or to sustain relationship (Steffensmeier and Allan, 1995).

Women engage in serious property crimes, as accomplices of their male super ordinates (Steffensmeier and Allan, 1995). Female violence is also shaped by the organisation of gender. Research indicates that female violence is less likely to be directed at a stranger, and female motivation for murder continue to be driven by relational concerns. Victims of women are likely to be either a male intimate or a child. Furthermore, violent women are likely to commit their offences within the home, and they frequently cite self-defence or depression as causal factors of their crime (Dobash et al. 1992).

The organisation of gender also shapes gender difference in substance abuse. The importance of relational concerns is reflected in the fact that women are often introduced to drugs by husbands or boyfriends. (Dept. of Health and Human Services, 1984, Cited in Schwartz and Steffensmeier, 2008:66). The relational aspects of addiction, for example become clear in the case of women offenders who cite pain of personal relationship as the cause of addiction and self-medication.

In the context of family and relationship, causes and patterns of crime vary considerably in terms of gender. Research indicates that it is disconnection and violation rather than growth-fostering relationships that characterise the childhood experiences of most women in the criminal justice system. Widom (1999) has shown in her work that experiences of neglect and abuse in childhood influence entry into criminal activity. Abused girls are twice as likely to be arrested as juveniles and adult offenders. In another study Rivera and Widom (1990) found that abused and neglected boys were less likely to become violent, but abused and neglected girls showed a greater tendency for increased risk of arrest for a violent crime while still a juvenile.

Belknap and Holsinger (2008) found that among incarcerated delinquents, 59 per cent of girls and 18 per cent of boys reported histories of sexual abuse and victimisation. The study further reported that almost a quarter of the girls and one-tenth of the boys reported sexual abuse by a family member. Over half of the girls and 14 per cent of the boys reported sexual abuse by non-family member, and 46 per cent of girls and 14 per cent of boys reported that sexual abuse was repeated over time. Thus, it is evident from the study that sexual abuse of delinquent youth is clearly gendered, with girls reporting significantly more violation than boys.

Research also documents the increased risks of offending that woman in battered relationship face. Richie (1996) has used the concept of gender entrapment to explain how some women are forced into crime by their culturally expected gender role, the violence in their intimate relationship and their social position in the larger society. Such women may be coerced to commit crime, such as selling drugs, robbing or prostituting, by their abusive partner.

In another study, Gaarder and Belknap (2002) conducted intensive interviews with girls in a juvenile justice system. They found that the lives of these girls were fraught with abuse and trauma, while they were stoically processed and convicted as offenders in the criminal justice system. Further, when these girls reported their victimisation to the school officials or to the police, their complaints were not taken seriously.

In a study conducted by Arnold in 1995 with 50 African American women serving sentences in a city jail, it was found that these girls were victims of both sexual and class abuse. Thus to be young, Black, poor and female is to be in a high-risk category for victimisation and stigmatisation on many levels. Arnold (1990) has argued that women involved in crime are structurally dislocated from three primary institutions of socialisation: 1. the family, 2. the educational system, 3. the occupational system. Patriarchal power relations manifest in the norms of marriage and family and place of work, create gendered environs, thereby pushing women into crime, through victimisation, role entrapment, economic marginality and survival needs.

Another study linking victimisation with offending was conducted by Gilfus (1992) with women in a north-eastern facility. She conducted intensive interviews with twenty incarcerated women and analysed their life histories to understand their 'routes of entry and immersion into street crimes'. This study showed that all women had life histories of street crimes such as prostitution, shoplifting, and fraud or drug law violation. Most of these women had grown up with severe childhood abuse and continued to experience violence in their relationship with intimate partners. Their survival skills included running away from home, using drugs and prostitution. These women were economically disadvantaged and reported severe educational neglect. Teachers were verbally and physically abusive and educational authorities were indifferent to their obvious abuse at home. Additionally, Black women reported racial violence they experienced as children, at schools. Many of these women reported revictimisation in their lives on the street, including rape, assault and attempted murder. The care-taking role of women in the families, combined with their lack of education and marketable skills for employment generated conditions that necessitated their involvement in economic crime. Thus, women in this study considered their illegal activities to be a form of work, which was undertaken primarily for economic necessity.

A study conducted by Mimi H. Silbert and Ayla M. Pines in 1981 with 200 former and current female prostitutes in San Francisco Bay area exposed the victimisation-to-offending cycle of females. In this study, 60 per cent of the sample reported being sexually abused before the age of 16, by an average of 2 sexual abusers each. Two-thirds of the sexual abuse victims were abused by father or father figures and only 10 per cent of the victims were abused by strangers. The sexual abuse was almost always followed by running away from home, which led to prostitution and other street work.

Meda-Chesney Lind and Noelie Rodriguez (1983) also found instances of child sexual abuse and multiple victimisations in the lives of incarcerated women, establishing beyond doubt the link between childhood victimisation and adult offending. A study focusing on women convicted of killing children found that these women had very violent pasts, including extreme sexual and non-sexual victimisations (Crimmins et al., 1997). Documenting high levels of victimisation in general among imprisoned women, Lake (1993) found that abuse by an intimate male partner was the most prevalent form of victimisation. Dembo and his colleagues (1992) noted in their analysis of male and female detainees that a background of family problems and experiences of sexual and physical abuse were related to delinquent behaviour and substance abuse.

Daly (1998) developed a typology for differentiating the ways in which women's lives lead up to a pattern of illegal activity. This framework is important because it pinpointed the key gender-related influences on crime, such as childhood abuse, victimisation by an intimate partner, and the central role of relationship with men.

- *Street women*—had been severely abused in childhood, lived on the streets and were brought to court for crimes related to supporting their drug habits, such as selling drugs, prostitution and stealing.
- Like street women, *harmed and harming women* were abused as children, but they responded with anger, often acting out in a violent manner. For some, the use of drugs and alcohol contributed to violent behaviour.
- *Battered women* typically had little or no criminal record, and they had harmed or killed men, who had violently attacked them or threatened to do so.
- *Drug-connected women* used or sold drugs as a result of relationship with a male intimate, children or their mothers, and also had a limited criminal record.
- *Economically motivated women* committed crimes to cope with poverty or out of greed.

Recognition of the distinctive life stories and experiences of female offenders generates greater empathy and sensitivity in their treatment in the criminal justice system. For the women, the pathways to crime are diverse and different from those of male offenders.

Women's low share of recorded criminality has important consequences for those women who do offend. Women who do offend are seen to have transgressed not only social norms, but gender norms as well. Thus, a concern over the anomalous position of deviant women leads to excessive zeal in their treatment in custody and more medicalised intervention. Women suffer especially from stigma associated with deviance. According to Condry, relatives of serious offenders are shamed and stigmatised and this stigma has its roots in ideas about familial blame and contamination (Cited in Heidensohn and Gelsthorpe, 2007: 400).

Construction of Female Criminality in Colonial India

The notion oı crime underwent drastic changes during the colonial period in India. The British administrative set up with its emphasis on the establishment of a uniform civil code and regularisation of justice through law courts redefined many colonial social practices and customs as 'crime'. The policy of the British Government to extend colonial laws upon subjects led to the erosion of traditional legal systems such as caste courts and village councils. These impersonal laws applied uniformly throughout India, showed deep disregard and lack of understanding of the traditional institutions and practices. Combined with this was the impact of rapid economic changes that included industrialisation and urbanisation of the pre-industrial colony.[4] This was an era of new types of crimes, some of which were driven by poverty and underdevelopment and some of which were driven by colonial ruler's desire to impose Western morality upon the subjects. In keeping with the standards of European morality, many traditional Indian customs and practices were redefined as 'crime', thereby leading to the emergence of the new Indian criminal. In these changing circumstances, women's actions revealed their resistance to medieval patriarchy as well as intrusion of an alien state power (Anagol, 2002).

In this context, crime acquired a broad dimension, ranging from street crimes such as pick-pocketing and burglary to white-collar crimes such as embezzlement and forgery. Of these, there were certain types of criminally defined acts for which women alone were held responsible. These included prostitution, foeticide and infanticide.

Criminality was identified as a masculine trait and female law breakers were stereotyped as delinquents of a special type. Thus, crimes committed by women caused moral panic and social outrage because such acts went against the essential nature of women, which was assumed to be passive, nurturing and maternal. Sumanta Banerjee wrote in '*Victims and Villains: The Construction of Female Criminality in Colonial Calcutta*':

> "Contemporary Bengali chapbooks as well as memoirs left by police officers abound with descriptions of such women, who are invariably painted as dark-skinned, huge and muscular, always chewing *paan* and smoking *bidis,* spewing abuses and behaving like boorish male hoodlums.[5] Yet, if one reads between the lines of these highly misogynistic accounts, one can occasionally discover the complex forms of social oppression and economic exploitation that led these women to break the law. Lawbreaking was often the only rational option available to women who suffered from discriminatory gender relations and an exploitative class system in Calcutta." (2008:29)

Historical accounts of diverse types of women criminals in 19th century Calcutta, for instance, shatter many stereotypical notions of crime's interrelation with femininity. There are well documented instances of men and women, who have carried out with equal agency the role of a murderer or a fraud. In the police records of Calcutta for instance, prostitutes constituted the bulk of female criminals (Banerjee, 2008). Historical records set in colonial Bengal further point out to the existence of women who worked as accomplices of their male counterparts in manufacturing and circulating counterfeit coins. There were also women from some Bengali households who consciously became a part of the Calcutta underworld in order to achieve their personal goals (Banerjee, 2008).

In 1864, the Calcutta High Court passed a judgement on ten year old Aimona who was accused of killing her nineteen year old husband with a chopper while he was asleep. The provocation for the murder was thought to be the beating that she got from her husband for some act of mischief. The young girl was charged with murder. Instead of according the death sentence to her, the benevolent Raj considered her age and announced transportation of life for her (Weekly Reporter, Vol. 1, 1864, cited in Banerjee, 2008).

In his memoirs, police detective Priyanath Mukhopadhyay narrated another incident where he investigated a case involving a housewife who killed her seven year old son who had found her entertaining her lover during her husband's absence (Mukhopadhyay, 2004).

Mention may be made of Sushila, the mistress of a well-known barrister of Calcutta, who later became an active member of the Calcutta underworld; or Trailokya, a prostitute and a serial killer, who committed heinous murder in cold blood in her struggle for survival (2008:30). Women of colonial Calcutta were also associated with the hotel business in Calcutta. Priyanath Mukhopadhyay in his '*Darogar Daphtar*' wrote that around 1710, the earliest among such entrepreneurs was Demingo Ash, who ran a hotel and a liquor selling shop. He also wrote about Muslim women owners of coffee shops and hotels in some parts of central Calcutta, who were notorious for peddling drugs mixed in coffee or *paan* (cited in Banerjee, 2008).

Padma Anagol has argued in her essay "*The Emergence of*

the Female Criminal in India: Infanticide and Survival Under the Raj" (2002), that crimes committed by women need to be understood in the context of changing gender relation and their interaction with wider social and political structures in colonial India. Female crime was often the result of a limited range of strategies for survival, available to subordinated groups in oppressive situations.

One of the most important variants of the female criminal was the infanticidal woman, who engaged in the killing of her newborn. The infanticidal woman emerged in the 19th century after the passing of the Infanticide Act in 1870 that aimed at curtailing the heinous practice by imposing death penalty or transportation for life.[6] The act of infanticide bore link to the Hindu norms of prohibition of widow re-marriage. The fear of social sanctions very often led young widows to kill their illegitimate newborn. The prosecution and trial of infanticidal women generated a compelling body of negative knowledge about Indian female sexuality. The woman who committed infanticide was perceived as lustful, depraved, perverted and wholly lacking in maternal instincts. While there was complete silence on the role of the men who were equally involved in the reproductive process, it was a woman's chastity rather than infanticide itself that became the central point in the discussion.

Reiterating their administrative stance, Justice West wrote:

> "...the accused must have known when she indulged her lust, or yielded to the indulgence of the lust of someone else, that these dire consequences might follow; and what was the value, either morally, or from any point of view of sensibility which was sufficient to make a woman destroy her own offspring, but which was not sufficient to guard her against the indulgence of her lust" (cited in Anagol, 2002:79).

Another variant of the female criminal was the Indian prostitute. In pre-colonial times, the prostitutes had a definite social location on the margins of the patriarchal social order. Although considered to be a '*patita*', meaning someone who had morally fallen from a respectable position in society, a prostitute was considered to be a functional necessity for satisfying the sexual appetite of men.

Sumanta Banerjee has argued in his essay that the dynamics of crime and women in colonial Calcutta should be analysed in the context of several official policies of the colonial rulers that determined the social attitudes of the time. During the nineteenth century economic policies, the British created a sharp divide between the rulers and the ruled, thereby affecting the fate of the poor classes in the colony. It became easy to criminalise the poor as the 'dangerous classes', who either aggressively demanded better wages or surreptitiously violated the laws of the state for their survival. These people were looked upon by the establishment as a threat to social stability. The colonial rulers associated poverty with crime which they candidly expressed through their various policies of administration. *The Times* while describing the miserable living conditions of the poor working class in White-chapel in inner London wrote:

> "We have long ago learned that organic refuse breeds pestilence.............Can we doubt that neglected human refuse as inevitably breeds crime, that crime reproduces itself like germs in an infected atmosphere, and becomes at each successive cultivation more deadly, more beastial, and more absolutely unrestrained" (cited in Banerjee, 2008:44).

The criminalisation of the poor also affected the fate of the women, especially from the poor classes. Women were not only subject to medieval patriarchal control, they also experienced poverty and loss of identity in the context of the transitional economies of the colonial times. Historically, many of these women were drawn into the ranks of prostitutes, who found employment opportunities in the emerging urban centres of colonial India. From the beginning, the prostitutes and their workplace became a part of the criminal underworld. The need for protection from unwanted men led them to depend on local gangsters and professional criminals. They remained equally vulnerable to police repression in the colonial administrative set up. Thus, these women negotiated the two spheres of violence in their day to day lives, one dominated by the colonial administration and the other, by the indigenous underworld. Under these circumstances, the prostitutes became both victims and agents of violence.

These conditions combined with the peculiar perception that the colonial rulers developed about the oriental woman further aggravated the deteriorating status of women in the colonial times. The typical construction of the oriental women as an enchantress, by the Western traveller of the seventeenth and eighteenth century, made the Indian woman a suspect from the very beginning of the colonial rule. In an early nineteenth century guide book, Captain Thomas Williamson warned the British soldiers who set feet in Calcutta for the first time:

> "Totally ignorant of the language, and without any guide, it is by no means surprising that so many impositions are practiced on our countrymen as soon as they arrived in India...................Add the allurements held out by the sable beauties, who will contrive means to retail their charms so long as they think money is to be had." He further cautioned the Englishmen about the 'fatal consequences' of their association with such women as, "never failing first to drain the purse, and, in a few days or weeks, the constitution also" (cited in Banerjee, 2008:45).

The colonial policy towards the Indian prostitutes reflected the contemporary European mindset and a patriarchal bias with regard to the etiology of sexual diseases. As one English medical doctor, explaining the increased virulence of syphilis in the port towns of England in the 1880s said:

> "The fact is, that the slight irritation caused in the female by the early stage of venereal (disease) rather excites than dulls the sexual appetite. As would naturally be expected from so many women with excited sexual appetites being suddenly allowed to disseminate disease, there was a large increase of syphilis among the men" (cited in Banerjee, 2008:45).[7]

The prostitutes were blamed for the spread of venereal diseases among the British troops and the Contagious Diseases Act criminalised the profession of prostitution forever (2008:38).

The female criminal of the nineteenth century India was constructed out of the binary of the chaste and virtuous woman as opposed to the unchaste and impure. This representation absolved men of their responsibility for parenthood outside marriage and also successfully diverted attention away from the abject material living conditions of women in India.

An important outcome of the process of urbanisation in the nineteenth century Calcutta was the rise of juvenile crimes. The juvenile delinquents were children of migrant workers who grew up on the streets without much parental supervision.

Historical records point out to most of the children being trained in the art of pick-pocketing and begging on the streets. The girls were more vulnerable to physical exploitation and often ended up in police custody as 'juvenile criminals'. Some of these girls were listed in police records as child prostitutes and many others operated as active accomplices of thieves and cocaine and opium smugglers.

Thus, the construction of female criminality in the nineteenth century Bengal, as well as elsewhere, was the product of a variety of factors that included colonial distrust of the subject race, upper class apprehensions of the misgivings of the lower classes and traditional patriarchal norms that oppressed women.

Nature and Causes of Female Crime in India

Although the recorded incidents of crime committed by women in India remain low in comparative terms, there is a need to understand the pattern of female offending in terms of the various pathway factors that create a gendered context for the commission of crime. Suvarna Cherukuri (2008) has argued that in order to gain a critical insight into the phenomenon of female crime, there is a need to adopt an intersectional perspective that focuses on cross-cutting factors such as caste, class and gender. The importance of caste and class lies with regard to the fact that in India, women belonging to the lower caste groups are also socio-economically backward and highly exploited. According to N.K. Sohoni (1974), arrest and conviction occur in the case of mostly those who are socio-economically marginalised in society. His understanding was based on analyses of data relating to the socio-economic background of female offenders.

Apart from caste and class, it is also relevant to understand the dynamics of power relations that women negotiate within the family structure, that very often lead them from one form of control to another. Significantly, both the family and the prison constitute institutionalised domains of patriarchal power that, women, criminal or otherwise experience. Ahuja (1969) in his study of female offenders in India has considered maladjustment in the family as the most important cause behind female crime. This is also because the relational concerns of women are greater than men, as women are socialised into the roles of care-givers from the beginning. Several other studies conducted by M. Bilmoria Rani (1977) and Shankardass (2000) also point out to the role of family marriage, lack of education and poor economic status as factors responsible for crimes committed by women.

According to Devasia and Devasia (1989), socially constructed gender roles mould women into passive and submissive victims of patriarchal violence within the family. In the vast majority of these cases, victimised women take recourse to violence as survival strategy, leading to the involvement of women in homicide.

According to S.K. Ghosh (1993), the processes of rapid industrialisation and urbanisation have led to over-crowding in the cities and the growth of slums. Under the changing economic situations, poverty and scarcity of resources have become important factors for women's crime. This is especially true if one considers a woman's role as a care-giver to the young and old in her family. In a similar study conducted by Smriti Bhosle (2009) with 90 undertrial female prisoners in Mumbai, it was seen that the women were young, married, illiterate and generally belonged to low socio-economic status groups in their region. Young age, combined with their dependent status very often created conditions leading to maladjustment, stress and conflict in the family.

In the recent times, police data show an increase in the incidence of spousal violence and homicide in different parts of the country. According to social psychologists, jealousy and sexual passion are often the main motives for murders involving intimate relations. In its January 2012 issue, '*India Today*' magazine reported on '*The New Art of Domestic Murder*', drawing attention to the range of atrocities committed by very close kin, within the set up of the extended family. Social psychologist Ashish Nandy in the same report has argued that these instances indicate serious stress and thinning out of relationship in the family (*Indian Today*, January, 2012). In other incidents of premeditated murder committed by women, the case that gripped the nation's imagination was the Neeraj Grover murder by Kannada actress Maria Susairaj and her fiancé, former naval officer Emile Jerome.

Understanding Agency in Crime: Shattering the Essentialist Myth

With reference to the above theoretical overview in the area of female criminality in India and the West, it is easy to notice the relative lack of attempt to understand agency and experience of the female offenders in mainstream as well as feminist discourses of crime. Mainstream criminological discourses have constructed crime within an essentialist framework underpinned by fixed dualism of masculine and feminine. Essentialism in this sense can include a belief that things have a fixed and natural set of characteristics that science can discover. Such natural essence is therefore prior to existence. Essentialism thus frames categories of people as man/woman, heterosexual/ homosexual in terms of intrinsically fixed and natural traits. Such an essentialist framework tends to homogenise the realities of female offenders, interpreting it as one. According to Naylor, there are six archetypes that are deployed to explain women's aberrance that reinforce the essentialist framework. These include Madonna/whore; sexual passion/love; reproduction and madness; the evil monster/witch; the criminal woman as not-woman and the female as devious and manipulative (Naylor 1993; Scutt 1993; Frigon 1995). Mainstream criminological discourses have used frameworks of sexuality, madness, domesticity, social control of the family and economic dependency to examine women's offending behaviour. These pathological and familial discourses in mainstream research have given rise to the categories of the 'mad' or 'bad' women, the unfit mother and the fallen woman. So, while for men, 'crime' is viewed as 'normal' legal contravention of rules to be dealt within the legal/punishment paradigm, for women, crime is symptomatic of pathology, demanding treatment.

Feminist criminology's refusal to pathologies, women's deviance has led to the inevitable reconstruction of women's experiences into discourses acceptable to the law courts and penal institutions. In the process, the label of an aberrant woman is replaced by the label of the helpless victim with low self-esteem. Thus, in emphasising upon the victim status of women offenders in theoretical conceptions of crime, much of feminist criminology has reinforced traditional essentialism in terms of portraying women as abused and passive recipients of crime. This feminist trope of victimology has worked in favour of women offenders in law courts and police custody that have granted them lenient sentences.

Understanding victimisation of women, specifically male violence, is no doubt necessary to break away from the paternalistic treatment/welfare model for women offenders towards a new paradigm of restorative justice based on gender responsive strategies of rehabilitation and care. However, this theoretical framework that places women in a position of passivity and submission in interpreting their 'acting out' as a response to earlier crime simply precludes the possibility of constructing women as agentic, purposeful and motivated actors in the commission of crime.

Agency in this sense can be understood as exercise of rational choice brought about by a clear sense of purpose in committing the crime. Rational choice as a paradigm has long since been dominant in economics, but in the recent decades, it has become widely used in other disciplines. Rational choice theory is based on assumptions of self-interested and motivated actors as exercising rational choice in order to maximise their goals. The central element of rational choice theory is the calculation of cost-benefit analysis in carrying out both deviant and conforming behaviour. The starting point of rational choice perspective in crime is that crime is chosen for its benefits. Rational choice theory asserts that if the benefits of crime are high and the costs low, crime will occur. However, if the benefits of crime are lower than the costs, crime will not occur (Serdar Kenan Gul, 2009). Piquero and Hickman (2002) argued that while traditional criminology viewed criminals driven by their conditioning and environment, more recent economics based theories portray them as rational decision makers who base their decisions to commit crimes on an analysis of the risk of the venture compared with the expected profits.

In examining questions of subjectivity and agency (or the lack of it), I have borrowed from Butler (1993) for whom subjectivity is a fundamentally performative and denaturalised concept referring not to a stable, autonomous entity, but to an array of constructions.[8] Subjectivities are produced by discourses and constrained by it. Subject constitution is dependent upon performance, which entails enactment of scripts pertaining to particular subjectivities within particular discourses. The dominant discourse of hetero-patriarchy operating within the institutions of monogamous marriage and nuclear family prepare women in a certain way for enactment of scripts pertaining to wifehood and motherhood. Such discourse delimits and deauthorises the subject positions created by women through transgression of societal expectations and gender-norms.

Morrissey (2003) argued, for instance, that the image of a battered woman promoted an understanding of passivity that pathologised them. Thus, battered women who kill are denied agency, suggesting that the act of killing is really determined by another's act of battery. The notion of a battered woman creates a false dichotomy between victimisation and agency. All battered women are portrayed as victims lacking agency. There inner strength and resilience as survivors is completely ignored. Morrissey (2003) argued:

> "Battered women who kill their abusers occupy an especially anomalous position within Western hetero-patriarchal cultures.[9] In the first instance, their killings are particularly traumatic for the dominant discourses of heteropatriarchy because they challenge one of its major institutions, exposing the family as a site of violence and fear rather than perpetuating a myth of safety and care. Second, the women are themselves deeply perplexing, viewed as both victims and perpetrators, as culpable yet blameless. In short, they inhabit a paradox, where extreme victimisation leads finally lethally effective retaliation" (67).

Morrissey (2003) further argued that the label 'mad' that is applied to women who kill relies on the discourse of irrationality that removes agency and responsibility for the commission of the crime. On the other hand, the label 'bad' represents a mythically evil murderous woman, who is inhuman and thus non-agentic in the act of crime. Their representation as merciless killers or victimised women/children clearly shows how mainstream legal discourses exclude women from its construction of rational subjectivity in terms of the unified figure of the 'reasonable' legal subject, who is always a man.

Apart from the 'mad' or 'bad' labels, both of which emphasise irrationality and lack of human agency there is a third narrative which has arisen with the advent of feminist interventions in legal discourse. Morrissey refers to this representation of the 'abused child' subjectivity as the 'impotent victim' model. "It indicates the coalescence of two major theses in feminist theorising, victimology and feminine difference, and has produced a subject whose victimhood and powerlessness are the hallmarks of her difference from men" (65). Thus, by denying the possibility of female agency in crime, mainstream theories also deny women the full right to be human. In contrast to the reasonable legal subject, who is independent, rational and responsible and almost always male, women are not accorded full subjectivity because they are seen as deficient in reason.[10] Indeed as Carol Smart stated that law is actually a gendering strategy in itself, producing gendered subjectivities to which individuals are tied (Smart, 1998:26).

Belinda Morrissey (2003), explained that female agency in the act of crime is denied through three techniques: vilification or monsterisation, mythification and victimism. Vilification/ monsterisation works by insisting upon the evil nature of the offender, thus denying her of human agency. Morrissey explained "the murderess is considered to have acted, but not as a human woman" (25). Vilification is followed by mythification, which works in a similar manner to relate women who kill to mythic characters. The woman is not just monsterised "but transformed into the living embodiment of mythic evil through her relation to figures traditionally interpreted this way" (25). Kristeva points out that the feminine is often aligned with the abject, the criminal.[11] The potential for feminine evil is always ever present (1982:64-65). Female abjection relates to the very permeability of female bodies. It is through sexual and reproductive processes that female anatomy blurs the line of distinction between self and others, clean and unclean. Morrissey explained: "The woman's vagina is penetrable and engulfing, her menstrual blood is a primary abject pollutant, while her capacity to give birth raises the subject's terror of encompassment and subsequent loss of self. Finally, the baby's early dependence on the mother gives her enormous power, and the fear this evokes, combined with the abject nature of the female body, has been narrated repeatedly in myths and legends of evil and dangerous women throughout history" (Morrissey, 2003:2). Women who killed reiterated their typically feminine evil potential that lay in contrast to the benevolent qualities of the good mother. Such women provided rude reminders of the destructive power of femininity which at times is more potent than feminine creativity. Thus, the process of mythification worked to distance the female offender from her immediate social context and render unreal and mythical the act of violence perpetrated by her. Finally, representations of the murderess as victim functions to deny her "responsibility, culpability, agency, and often her rationality", in an attempt to secure sympathetic legal treatment for her (Morrissey, 2003:25). In emphasising victimhood of women offenders, agency and autonomy are often denied.

In the recent years, more and more domestic violence theorists have rejected the image of a helpless battered woman lacking agency. They argue that in our everyday discourse, agency and victimisation are constituted in terms of binaries, i.e., they are known by each other's absence. Thus, if one is a victim one can in no way be an agent. Hooks (1989) and Collins (1998) argued that oppressed people cannot afford to feel powerless. Collins stressed that battered black women must acknowledge and deal with their victimisation without being paralysed by it. Thus, what becomes clear is the agency that women as victims exercise in resisting and countering the violence in their everyday lives. Abraham (2000), in her study of South Asian battered women found that contrary to stereotypical images of passivity, the South Asian women used many creative strategies to challenge their abuser's power and control. These included a wide range of tactics such as silence, avoidance, confrontation, hiding, talking back, hitting, and challenging the abuser's fiscal control. These finding as well as finding from other studies on battered women suggest that battered women are not passive in the face of abuse, but they do fight back within the institutional structures that constrain them. Mahuya Bandyopadhyay (2010), in her study of women inmates in a correctional institution of Kolkata for instance observed that inmates employed various modes of resistance through subversive practices that enabled them to redefine their interactional space within the prison. These strategies ranged from hunger strikes, body piercing, tattooing, use of illicit drugs to non cooperation with correctional staff and maintenance of complete silence. The notion of 'agency' is of vital importance as it works to reconstitute the 'criminal' identities of women. Thus, the very women who were once constituted as 'wives' by the dominant discourses of patriarchy now come to acquire a new definition of their personhood and self.

Conclusion

In constructing women offenders as agentic and motivated actors therefore, one needs to understand the lived experiences of women placed at particular intersections of patriarchy and class. In theoretical terms, it becomes necessary to recognise the fact that women offenders do not form a uniform group, a homogenous category. Thus, any attempt to define agency of women offenders must also take into account their different social locations in terms of class, age, sexuality, ethnicity and religion, as well as the different modes of resistance they employ to negotiate class and/or patriarchy both within and outside the criminal justice system. It is through the life stories of the inmates that a narrative connection, at the experiential realm can be established, between their lives, before and after incarceration. This exercise becomes crucial in the constitution of the 'self'. According to Seyla Benhabib the self is 'both the teller of tales and that about whom tales are told' (1992:198). In this sense, the self consists of multiple narrations, which are integrated into a coherent self-identity, a 'meaningful life-history' (1992:198). It is in this context that the narratives of inmates and the narratives told about them can enable the researcher to understand the multiple and overlapping dimensions of 'self' that are produced in the act of telling and retelling the stories.

Thus, there is a need to create a new paradigm for understanding female criminality by delinking the essential paradox between femininity and crime. Masculinity can no longer serve as an adequate theoretical standard against which deviance of women can be measured. Crime must be viewed as a 'normal' act of deviance, which any rational self-interested actor is capable of committing. Seen from this perspective, the prostitute, the drug peddling woman or the woman who murders her battering spouse can be understood as agentic actors in carrying out specific acts of resistance specific to her experience and social location. By recognisng a woman's capacity to exercise free will in executing independent decisions, criminological discourses must thereby recognise her right to be full human.

Notes

1. Atavism refers to a situation where an individual member of a species could be identified as a throwback to an earlier genetic period. The concept of atavism established the foundations of biologically deterministic theories of crime.

2. The issue was first raised by Adler and Simon, who argued that female crime rates had been rising more rapidly in the late 1960's and early 1970's. They also asserted that women offenders were changing their pattern of offending to more 'masculine' styles, becoming more aggressive and violent. This change was attributed to the growth of modern women's movement, popularly known as the 'liberation hypotheses'.

3. The 'pathways perspective' incorporates a whole-life perspective in the study of crime causation. The pathways research has used extensive interviews with women to uncover the life events that place women and girls at risk of criminal offending. See Gender Responsive Strategies: Research, Practice, and Guiding Principles for Women Offenders; by Barbara Bloom, Barbara Owen and Stephanie Covington; published the National Institute of Corrections; July 2003.

4. Rapid economic changes due to colonial expansion brought about a decline in the indigenous industrial base. It led to widespread impoverishment and famines throughout India.

5. *Paan* refers to betel leaf and *bidi* is an indigenous form of tobacco.

6. Infanticide was perceived differently from female infanticide. With female infanticide, responsibility was assigned to the leaders of the group, but for infanticide, blame was fixed exclusively on the woman.

7. Some historical accounts reveal that Portuguese sailors who had come to Bengal had infected the native women with venereal disease, thus giving rise to the term '*phiringee rog*' which literally means foreign disease.

8. Seyla Benhabib is critical of Butler's theory of performative subjectivities on the grounds that it cannot account for human capacity for self-determination and change. See 'Subjectivity, Historiography, and Politics', in S. Benhabib, J. Butler, D. Cornell and N. Fraser's *Feminist Contentions: A Philosophical Exchange*, New York: Rouledge, 1995.

9. This is a concept that links naturalised heterosexuality with intersecting frameworks of power and oppression represented by race, nation and patriarchy. This concept has been used in this study to demonstrate the ways in which norms of heterosexuality and patriarchy mutually reinforce each other.

10. In '*The Man of Reason*' (1986), Genevieve Lloyd studied theories of the reasonable subject expounded by various Western philosophers dating from Aristotle to Sartre,

and argued that despite variations in individual theorists, the characteristics of the typical subject is equated with those considered intrinsic to male identity.

11. In the '*Powers of Horror*' (1982), Kristeva refers to the term abject as human reaction to a threatened breakdown in meaning caused by the loss of distinction between subject and object or between the self and other. The corpse especially exemplifies Kristeva's concept since it literalises the breakdown of the distinction between subject and object that is crucial for the establishment of identity and for our entrance into the symbolic order.

References

Abraham M. 2000, *Fighting Back: Abused Women's Strategies of Resistance.* In M. Abraham (Ed.), *Speaking the Unspeakable: Marital Violence among South Asian Immigrants in the United States,* New Brunswick, NJ: Rutgers University Press. pp. 132-153.

Adler Freda. 1975, *Sisters in Crime: The Rise of the New Female Criminal,* New York: McGraw-Hill.

Ahuja Ram. 1969, *Female Offenders in India,* Meerut: Meenakshi Prakashan.

Anagol Padma. 2002, *The Emergence of the Female Criminal in India: Infanticide and Survival under the Raj,* in *History Workshop Journal,* No. 53, pp. 73-93.

Arnold R.A. 1990, *Women of Colour: Processes of Victimisation and Criminalisation of Black Women. Social Justice,* 17(3), pp. 153-166.

Arnold R.A. 1995, *The Processes of Victimisation and Criminalisation of Black Women.* In B.R. Price and N. Sokoloff (Eds.), *The Criminal Justice System and Women.* New York: Mc Graw-Hill.

Bandyopadhyay Mahuya. 2010, *Everyday Life in a Prison: Confinement, Surveillance, Resistance,* New Delhi, Orient Blackswan Private Limited.

Banerjee Sumanta. 2008, *Victims and Villains: The Construction of Female Criminality in Colonial Calcutta,* in Kalpana Kannabiran and Ranbir Singh (eds.): *Challenging The Rules of Law: Colonialism, Criminology and Human Rights in India,* New Delhi: Sage.

Braidotti R. 1997, *Mothers, Monsters and Machines.* In K. Conboy and N. Medina and S. Stanbury (Eds.), *Writing on the Body: Female*

Embodiment and Feminist Theory. New York: Columbia University Press.

Belknap Joanne and Holsinger Kristi. 2008, '*An Overview of Delinquent Girls: How Theory and Practice Have failed and the Need for Innovative Changes*', in Ruth T. Zaplin (eds.): *Female Offenders: Critical Perspectives and Effective Interventions*, Massachusetts: Jones and Bartlett Publishers.

Benhabib S. 1992, *Situating the Self*. Cambridge, Polity Press.

Bhosle Smriti. 2009, *Female Crime in India: Theoretical Perspectives of Crime*. New Delhi: Kalpaz Publications.

Braidotti R. 1997, *Mothers, Monsters and Machines*, In K. Conboy, N. Medina and S. Stanbury (Eds.), *Writing on the Body: Female Embodiment and Feminist Theory*. New York: Columbia University Press.

Cherukuri Suvarna. 2008, *Women in Prison: An Insight into Captivity and Crime*. New Delhi: Cambridge University Press.

Collins, P.H. 1998, *The Tie that Binds: Race, Gender and U.S Violence. Ethnic and Racial Studies, 21*, pp. 917-938.

Cowie J., Cowie V. and Slater E. 1968, *Delinquency in Girls*, London: Heinemann.

Crimmins S., Langley S., Brownstein H.H., and Spunt B.J. 1997, *Convicted Women Who have Killed Children. Journal of Interpersonal Violence*, 12, pp. 207-228.

Daly Kathleen. 1998, *Women's Pathways to Felony Court*. In Kathleen Daly and Lisa Maher (Eds.), *Criminology at the Crossroads: Feminist Reading in Crime and Justice*, Oxford: Oxford University Press.

Davies S. and Rhodes-Little A. 1993, History, Sexuality and Power: Deconstructing the 'Lesbian Vampire Case'. *Australian cultural history*, 12, 14-28.

Dembo R., Williams L., Wothke W., Schmeidler J., and Brown C.H. 1992, *The Role of Family Factors, Physical Abuse, and Sexual Victimisation Experiences in High-risk Youths' Alcohol and other Drug use and Delinquency: A Longitudinal Model*. Violence and Victims, 7(3), pp. 245-266.

Devasia R. and Devasia V.V. 1989, *Female Criminals and Female Victims*, Nagpur: Dattsons.

Dobash R.P, Dobash E.E, Wilson M, and Daly M. 1992, *The Myth of Sexual Symmetry in Marital Violence. Social Problems*, 39, 71-91.

Frigon S. 1995, *A Genealogy of Women's Madness*, In R.E Dobash,

R.P Dobash and L. Noaks (Eds.), *Gender and Crime.* Cardiff: University of Wales Press.

Heidensohn F. and Gelsthorpe L. 2007, *Gender and Crime, in Maguire,* Mike, Morgan, Rod and Reiner, Robert (ed.) *The Oxford handbook of Criminology*, Fourth Edition, Oxford: Oxford University Press.

Gaarder E. and Belknap J. 2002, *Tenuous Borders: Girls Transferred to Adult Court. Criminology*, 40, 481-517.

Gelsthorpe L. 2002, *Gender and Crime*, in Maguire, Mike, Morgan, Rod and Reiner, Robert (ed.) *The Oxford handbook of Criminology*, Third Edition, Oxford: Oxford University Press.

Ghosh S.K. 1993, *Women and Crime*, New Delhi: Ashish Publishing House.

Gilfus Mary E. 1992, From Victims to Survivors to Offenders: Women's Routes of Entry and Immersion into Street Crime in Women and Criminal Justice 4 (1), pp. 63-89.

Gul S.K. 2009, *An Evaluation of the Rational Choice Theory in Criminology*. In, *GAU J. Soc. and Appl. Sci.*, 4(8), pp. 36-44.

Hoffman-Bustamante D. 1973, *The Nature of Female Criminality*, in *Issues in Criminology*, Vol. 8, No. 2.

Kristeva, J. (1982), *Powers of Horror: An Essay on Abjection.* New York: Columbia University Press.

Lake E.S. 1993, *An Exploration of the Violent Victim Experiences of Female Offenders*, Violence and Victims, 8(1), 41-51.

Leonard E. 1982: *Women, Crime and Society: a Critique of Criminology Theory*, New York: Longman.

Chesney-Lind M. and Rodriguez N. 1983, *Women Under Lock and Key. Prison Journal*, 63, pp. 47-65.

Lombroso C. and Ferrero W. 1895. *The Female Offender,* London: T. Fischer Unwin.

Morrissey Belinda. 2003. *When Women Kill: Questions of Agency and Subjectivity.* New York: Routledge.

Mukhopadhyay Priyanath. 2004. *Darogar Daptar*, Vol. 1, 2. Kolkata: Punashcha

Naylor B. 1993. *Sentencing Female Offenders in the Magistrate's Court: Preliminary Report on a Pilot Study*. Paper presented at the Women and the Law, Canberra.

Piquero A. R, and Hickman M. 2002. The Rational Choice Implications of Control Balance Theory. In *Rational Choice and Criminal Behaviour*, (Eds.) by Piquero, Alex R. and Tibbetts, Stephen G. New York: Routledge.

Pollak Otto. 1950: *The Criminality of Women*, Philadelphia: University of Pennsylvania Press.

Rani M.B 1977: A Report of Female Criminality in India, in *Yojana*, April 15.

Richie B. 1996: *Compelled to Crime: The Gender Entrapment of Black Battered Women*, New York: Routledge.

Rivera B. and Widom C.S. 1990. Childhood Victimisation and Violent Offending. *Violence and Victims*, 5(1), pp. 19-35.

Schwartz, Jennifer and Steffensmeier, Darrell. 2008, *The Nature of Female Offending: Patterns and Explanation,* in Ruth T. Zaplin (Eds.): *Female Offenders: Critical Perspectives and Effective Interventions,* Massachusetts: Jones and Bartlett Publishers.

Scutt J. 1993. *The Incredible Woman: A Recurring Character in Criminal Law*. In P.W Easteal (Ed.), *Women and the Law Conference Proceedings*. Canberra: Australian Institute of Criminology.

Shankardass R.D 2000, *Women, Crime and Jail Justice*, in R.D Shankardass (ed.) *Punishment and the Prison: Indian and International Perspectives*, New Delhi: Sage Publications.

Silbert M.H & Pines A.M. 1981, *Sexual Child Abuse as an Antecedent to Prostitution. Child Abuse and Neglect*, 5, 407-411.

Smart Carol 1976: *Women, Crime and Criminology: A Feminist Critique*, London: Routledge and Kegan Paul.

Smart Carol 1995: *Law, Crime and Sexuality*, London: Sage Publications.

Smart Carol 1998. The Woman of Legal Discourse. In Daly K. and Maher L. (ed.) *Criminology at the Crossroads: Feminist Readings in Crime and Justice*. New York: Oxford University Press, pp. 21-36.

Sohoni, N.K 1974: Women Prisoners, in *The Indian Journal of Social Work*, 35 (2), July, pp. 137-148.

Steffensmeier D. and Allan E. 1995. Gender, Age, and Crime. In J. Sheley (Ed.), *Handbook of contemporary criminology*. New York: Wadsworth.

Thomas W.I. 1967. *The Unadjusted Girl*. New York: Harper and Row.

Walklate Sandra. 2001. *Gender, Crime and Criminal Justice*. Devon: Willan Publishing.

Widom, S. Cathy. 1999 *'Childhood Victimisation and the Derailment of Girls and Women to the Criminal Justice System'*. Conference on *Criminal Justice Research and Evaluation: Enhancing Policy and*

Practice through Research, Vol. 3. Organised by The national Institute of Justice, Office of Justice Programmes.

Reports

NCRB, *Crime in India*, 2011: Ministry of Home Affairs, Publication.

West Bengal Correctional Services, 2012.

India Today, January 2012 Issue.

16 Institutional Services for Delinquent Children

Jharana Swain

Introduction

The aim of institution for delinquents is the alleviation of symptoms and neuronal modification of those forces, factors or conditions, which produced the delinquent act. In an institutional set up, there will be an opportunity to be treated, trained and brought up in an atmosphere to which one is auctioned since infancy. The climate, food, language and customs differ from state to state. The child should as far as practicable, be allowed to grow in a familiar atmosphere. If a child remains in a surrounding with almost all factors dissimilar to those of his own, there is every possibility that his spontaneous growth may be stunted and his psychological development may also be defective.

Correctional institutions for juveniles are often known as training or reform schools. When originally developed, juvenile institutions were patterned after adult prisons. Over the years, however, the major characteristic that has set them apart from adult institutions has been their increased emphasis on education and occupational training. Unfortunately, juvenile institutions after all fall short of the book set for them by other agencies of the juvenile justice system. As a result, they are used only as a last resort where all other methods of handling have been exhausted or when the juvenile is too dangerous to remain at large in the community.

Juveniles may be placed in severe residential institutions for a number of reasons. They may be committed to a training school as a result of a juvenile states offence (Truancy, curfew violation, or consuming alcohol) an offence for which an adult is liable for prosecution on a parent's request for help in controlling a child. Commitment may also result from factors unrelated to the delinquent of the youth children who are neglected, dependent or in need of supervision have been temporarily housed in these institutions in some jurisdiction until other arrangements can be made for their care.

State-managed training schools, forestry camps, and other residential institutions for juvenile receive adjudicated young stars referred by the juvenile counts, those awaiting court action or probation violators. Although, some youngsters remain in the institutions for only a short time, it is designed for extended care and treatment in a secure, restricted setting. The training school has the responsibility of trying to change the behaviour, attitude and values of its inmates so that they will not get into trouble after release from the institutions.[1]

All social institutions whether family, marriage, job, club, union or association have well defined roles for their members. This is true of correctional institutions as well. As we shall see, living up to what is expected of us, or role fulfillment, is an important part of the process of institutionalisation.

The institutionalisation process within correctional institutions works exactly as it does in outside society. Behaviour, social response, or roles are learned through modelling, reinforcement, punishment, and social pressure.

History of Juvenile Justice System and Institutionalisation of Children in India

Human child is a product of social environment and every child has a right to family. Family is a primary social group, where the child seeks love and affection and the fulfillment of his basics needs. If, in case, he is deprived of family life, it affects his growth and development. Children who cannot remain in their biological family are required to have alternative arrangement. The Government of India resolution on National Policy for children adopted in 1974 reads as follows:

> ".... It shall be the policy of the state to provide adequate service to children, both before and after the birth throughout the period of growth, to ensure their full physical, mental and social development. The state shall progressively increase the scope of such services so that within a reasonable time, all children in the country enjoy optimum conditions for their standard growth."

The institutional care for children becomes inevitable in a country like ours. More than 50 per cent of the population lives below poverty line. Under these circumstances, among every hundred children who enter the school, less than half complete class five and 27 per cent complete class eight. These children are forced to accept jobs at an early age to supplement their family income. Though the earning of these children balances the inequlibrium between demand and supply, the children have been deprived of their rights towards education, recreation, health care etc. Recent statistics, according to 'FUTURE', a publication of 'UNICEF' reveals that 40 per cent of children are malnourished, 50 per cent suffer from anaemia and about 40,000 children turn blind every year due to vitamin deficiency. In addition to these factors, the child labour constitutes about six per cent of the labour force of the country and every working child in the World is an Indian and India accounts for one-third of child workers in Asia. So, the problem of street and working children is also in the increase and they have been exploited and abused. In the circumstances, the institutional treatment of children is the only means for their betterment. Majorities of the children are from the poor socio-economic parents. According to a recent survey on the child labour in Madras, a "Study conducted by the Year of Child Development Trust", 55.7 percent are living in huts and 79.5 per cent lead their life on the pavement of the cities. These factors mainly contribute to the legion of juvenile delinquency and it could be controlled if the institutional treatment of children is carefully planned and implemented.[2]

The concern of Indian for care and development of children goes back to time immemorial. India had an in-built mechanism of providing care for children through joint family system kinship and other social institutions. In ancient and mediaeval period voluntary and community efforts provided main sustenance to child welfare services. There were some enlightened rulers who also in a limited way, promoted child welfare activities under their patronage. During the British rule, voluntary effort rather than state endeavour was the main provider of child welfare services.

Apprentice Act XIX of 1950, marks the beginning of the Juvenile Justice machinery. This Act empowered magistrate to commit children between 10 years to 18 years as apprentice to employers and provided to control the relations between the employers and the apprentices. These were the children who had been convicted of vagrancy or the commission of any petty offence.

Indian Penal Code (1860) has recognised separate status of children. It seems to presume that children below seven years cannot have criminal intent and hence cannot be held responsible or accountable for their actions. Section 82 of IPC (1860) presumes innocence of children below seven years of age and bars them from being convicted of any offence. According to the section 83, a child between seven years and twelve years may be convicted of an offence only, if he has attained sufficient maturity of understanding to judge the nature and consequences of his conduct on that occasion.

- In 1897, the Reformatory Schools Act was passed which provided for the establishment for Reformatory Schools where youthful offenders upto the age of 18 years could be detained. Boys over 14 years could be released on license if suitable employment was found for them.
- The code of criminal procedure enacted in 1898 provides for specialised treatment of juvenile offenders (Sec. 29). Section 399 provides for commitments of juvenile offenders upto 15 years to Reformatory Schools. Section 562 provides for probation of good conduct to offenders upto 21 years of age.
- The Indian Jail Committee (1919-20) appointed by the Government of India under British Rule brought out a detailed report of its observation and recommendations. It emphasised that the child offender should be given different treatment from that of the adult. It held that imprisonment of child offenders should be prohibited. It recommended the provision of Remand Homes, Children's Courts and Certified Schools, which approximate to ordinary schools. It stressed the importance of pre-sentence inquiry into the child's social background as well as his physical and mental health. It advocated the child's release on probation of good conduct with or without the supervision of a probation officer. The committee suggested provision of supervision after release. Maintaining statistics of after-results was also considered important as a feedback for policy consideration.

- The recommendations of the Indian Jails Committee (1919-20) were followed by the legislative action in some of the states. Madras, Bengal and Bombay enacted their children acts in 1920, 1922 and 1924 respectively. After independence, the subject of welfare was placed in the State-list and Uttar Pradesh (1951), Hyderabad (1951) and Saurashtra (1954) passed their Children Acts accordingly. The Central Children Act, which is meant for the Union Territories, was enacted in 1960. It is also supposed to serve as a Model Act for other States.

There seems to be a difference in the spirit of the Acts enacted before and after independence. This is evident from the stated aim of the Madras (1920), Bengal (1922), Bombay (1924) Children Acts, which state "An Act to make further provision for the custody, trial and punishment of youthful offenders and for the protection of children and young persons." The more recent Acts are not more elaborate in expressing their own aim but have also categorically avoided the word "punishment" which seems contradictory to the philosophy of giving informal and non criminal treatment to the offender child. The stated aim of the more recent Acts is to provide care, protection, maintenance, welfare, training, education and rehabilitation of neglected or delinquent children and for the trial of delinquent children. Section 28 of Madras Children Act (1920) and section 27 of Bombay Children Act (1929) included sentencing a child for about 14 years to imprisonment, as one of the alternatives for dealing with delinquents. Madras Children Act (1920) sanctioned whipping and Bombay Children Act (1924) caning as a punishment to be used against offender children. The Bombay Children Act (1924) added a sentence of caning in default of payment of fine, if the court is satisfied that the offender is able to pay the fine.

The post-independence Acts do not contain such grossly punitive measures. The power to send delinquent children to prison is still maintained by the recent Acts, but the matter has to be reported to the Administrator for further orders.

Presently, Government of Orissa has enacted the Children Act, which is known as Orissa Children Act, 1982, just after 33rd year of the Republic of India. This act so enacted is a step to provide care, protection, maintenance, welfare, training, education and rehabilitation to neglected or delinquent children and for the trial of delinquent children in the State of Orissa. Chapter I, Sec 2(b) of the Act defines 'child' as a boy, who has not attained the age of 16 years or a girl, who has not attained the age of 18 years.

All the states, except Meghalaya, have enacted Children Acts. It should be noted, however, that more than 60 years after the first children act was enacted, three States and three Union Territories have not enforced the Children Act as yet. Out of the total 418 districts are covered by the children Acts.

- It envisages special approach towards prevention and treatment of juvenile delinquency in keeping with the developmental needs of children.
- It established norms and standards for administration of juvenile justice in terms of investigation, care, treatment and rehabilitation.
- It lays down appropriate linkages and co-ordination between the formal system of juvenile justice and voluntary organisations. It specifically defines the roles and responsibilities of both.

While progress has been made in implementing the various provision of the legislation, qualitative improvement in the existing services has been rather slow in coming. Juvenile Courts and Welfare Boards are still to be set up in many states. Separate handling of delinquent and other children is not ensured and the involvement of voluntary organisations at all stages of implementing the Act is meagre.

Scheme for the Prevention and Control of Juvenile Social Maladjustment

With a view to providing some financial support for upgrading and strengthening existing infrastructure for effective implementation of the provisions of Act, the Ministry of Welfare formulated a scheme for the prevention and control of juvenile social maladjustment in the year 1986-87. The financial assistance available under this scheme is for upgradation of infrastructures in both governmental and non-governmental sectors. It is a centrally-sponsored scheme in which the expenditure is shared by the Central and State Government on 50:50 bases. However, when the scheme is implemented through the involvement of voluntary organisations, they have to bear

10 per cent of the expenditure and the remaining 90 per cent is shared equally between the Central Government and the State Governments. During the year 1991-92, a sum of Rs 446 lakh was released to the State and the UT Administrations under this scheme. A provision of Rs 500 lakh was made under this scheme for the year 1992-93.

It is hoped that with the vigorous implementation of the various provisions of the Act, a new era in the administration of juvenile justice will usher in and the care, treatment and development of children apprehended under Juvenile Justice Act would take place in the letter and spirit of the provisions contained in the National Policy for Children.

Objective, Philosophy and Scope of Institutionalisation of Delinquent Children

The observation varies regarding the short stay institutions that are intended for keeping Juveniles during the period of trial or inquiry. Hence during the period of their stay in the institution, the juvenile is expected to be observed analysed and tested. Soon after the placement is over the juvenile is placed in juvenile home or special home as the case may be, where the real institutional services for the juvenile start.

The prime function of a juvenile treatment institution is to re-educate and train the child to become a responsible well-adjusted citizen. It should be the prime objective of juvenile institution to re-educate and trend the child to become responsible well-adjusted citizen. It should essentially be treatment facility with an integrated professional service, wherein the disciplines of education, case work, group work, psychology, psychiatric medicine, vocational rehabilitation, religion, all play an important role. Through such an integrated treatment programme, the child is expected to learn self-discipline, to accept more responsibilities and act and react in a more socially acceptable manner.

Delinquent Children

Delinquent is a phenomenon of anti-social behaviour, where the child comes in conflict with law. These children were dealt with until recently within the framework of Children's Acts. These Acts dealt with three categories of children namely the delinquent, uncontrollable and neglected. The delinquent children would be taken by the police and produced before a juvenile court magistrate or other magistrates authorised to the Child Welfare Board by the parents and guardians and neglected children would be handled by the police, the probation officer and the superintendent of an Observation Home or a Remand Home. Such children are however, to be produced before the Child Welfare Board or the Juvenile Court within twenty-four hours. Apart from the above, other types of children covered under the Children's Act include children of leper parents, children of beggars, girls in mortal danger and children of unsound mind, whose parents are not able to look after them properly.

Magnitude of the Problem

There is lack of data on the incidence and magnitude of the problems of juvenile delinquency. According to a report published on crime in India, 1.79,962 juveniles were apprehended for crimes under Indian Penal Code (IPC) and local and special laws in India in the year 1987. In 1988 and onwards, as per new definition of juvenile 16-18 age group consists of only girls and 18-21 age group is not considered juveniles at all. As per new definition 30, 816 (Boys 25,629 + Girls 5,547) juveniles were apprehended during the year 1990 for the crime under IPC and local and special laws in India. This includes 16, 836 children apprehended under IPC alone. Available statistics indicate that in all, there were 609 institutions under the Juvenile Justice Act in 1991-92. Out of these 269 were Observation Homes, 249 Juvenile Homes, 40 Special Homes, and 51 After Care Institutions. The total capacity of these institutions was 43,965.

Juvenile Justice Act

Enactment of the Juvenile Justice Act, 1986 by the Parliament for the entire country is a landmark in the history of juvenile justice system in India. The Act apart from rectifying the inadequacies of Children's Act provides a comprehensive scheme for the care; protecting, treatment, and development are rehabilitation of neglected and delinquent juveniles. With the enactment of Juvenile Justice Act, 1986 all Children's Acts applicable in different parts of the country have been repealed. The new Act has come into force throughout the country except the State of Jammu and Kashmir from 2 October 1987. The Juvenile Justice Act provides a uniform legal framework for

Juvenile justice in the country so as to ensure that no child under any circumstances is put in jail or police lock-up.

National Policy for Children

During the 1951-74, India had gathered considerable experience in the planning of child welfare programmes. The experience indicated that there was a need to formulate a National policy for children, which could provide direction to national efforts in the organisation of child welfare programmes. Accordingly, on August 27th, 1974, in the 27th year of its Independence, India adopted a Resolution of National Policy for Children. The Resolution recognises children as the nation's supremely important asset and declares that the Government should take over the responsibility for their 'nature and solicitude'. The Resolution also emphasises that "Children's programmes should find a prominent part in our national plans for the development of human resources." It further emphasis that "within a reasonable time all children in the country enjoy optimum conditions for their balanced growth." The policy also recognises the role of voluntary organisations in child welfare. Adoption of policy also recognises the role of voluntary organisation in child welfare. Adoption of policy had led to setting up a National Children's chairmanship of Prime Minister for effective co-ordination of child welfare programme.

The United Nations Convention on the Rights of the Child

The momentous resolution on the National Policy for Children in 1974 was adopted in the backdrop of United Nations General Assembly Declaration of the Rights of the Child in 1959 to which India is party. The observance of 1979, as the International year of the child also gave impetus to the programmes of child development. A National Plan of Action to observe the In International year of Child was prepared. In the Indian context, the main theme for International Year of child was 'Reaching the Deprived Children'. Further, on the model of National plan of Action, many State Governments in India as also non-governmental organisations formulated their own plans of action with specific programmes and activities to be taken up during the year in their respective areas. Thereafter, there has been large-scale expansion in child welfare and development programmes in subsequent years.

The UN Convention on the Rights of the Child was adopted

by the General Assembly of the United Nations in November 1989. The Convention has been acceded to by India. The World Declaration on the Survival, Protection and Development of Children in 1990 indicates the challenges and the tasks and stresses and the need for political action at the highest level for the well – being of children. A plan of Action to serve guidelines for Governments has been prepared for implementation of the 1990 Declaration. As a follow up of the promises made by the global fraternity at the World Summit for Children, this plan of Action sets out quantifiable targets of India's Charter of Action for Women and Children.

The National Plan of Action as a commitment to child represents India's response to the unprecedented opportunities, which the decade of nineties has ushered in both through technology as well as a global ambience for redeeming India's age-old pledges. This plan of Action identified quantifiable targets in terms of major as well as supporting spectral goals representing the needs and aspirations of almost 300 million children of India in the sphere of health, nutrition, education and related aspects of social support.

Constitutional and Statutory Frame Work of Juvenile Justice System

Post-independence period ushered in a new era in the field of child welfare. The efforts in this field were inspired by various provisions in our Constitution regarding the need for ensuring welfare of children, safeguarding their interests and protection of their rights. In fact, the Constitution of India provides a frame world within which the Constitutional vision of the rights of the Indian child can be given a concrete shape. The Constitution if India postulates the goal of a Welfare State and envisages child welfare activities as an organised part of National development. Articles 24, 39 and 45 have a bearing on the well being of children. These enjoin on the State of ensure that children are prohibited from employment in any hazardous employment; that the tender age of children is not abused; that the childhood ad youth are protected against exploitation and against moral and material abandonment; and the provision for free and compulsory education of all children are made until they complete the age of fourteen years.

Efforts in Five-Year Plan

With the adoption of the Constitution of India in 1950 and

establishment of the Planning Commission in 1951, India embarked upon the path of planned economic and social development with the ultimate goal of establishing a socialist society. The aim of any effort for economic and social development is the welfare of the family. Since, the child is most precious asset in the family, the strategy of planned national development also focuses on the young child. The first five-year Plan document (1951-56) observed that considering the number involved, the needs of children should receive much greater consideration than commonly given to them. The First Five-Year Plan proposed to ensure childcare through services in social welfare, health and education. However, the main thrust in the first Five-Year Plan was to build up a strong child welfare movement in India through voluntary efforts and the role of Government was by and large confined to providing guidance or technical training to child care functionaries engaged in implementation of child welfare schemes and assisting voluntary agencies with financial resources. The second Five-Year Plan (1956-61) continued to place the emphasis on voluntary agencies for introducing new schemes for the welfare of children with financial assistance from Government. During the Third Plan (1961-66), while emphasising the importance of child welfare programmes, the concentration effort was on organising child welfare services in a more co-ordinate and sustained manner.

Child welfare extended over the spheres of social welfare, education and health and community development. In fact, a new milestone was reached in the third Five-Year Plan when the resources of a number of Central Ministries were mobilised to achieve the maximum results in promotion of child welfare services in an integrated manner. The Fourth Plan (1969-74) drew attention to the problem of neglected and destitute children who had not received due attention hitherto. The Plan also pointed certain drawbacks out in the planning of child welfare programs such as lack of statistical data, absence of counseling and advisory services and the need for better management and supervision of child welfare programs.

In terms of purpose, philosophy and programme orientation, all these institutions are deemed or non-pent correctional centres aiming at their formation of the delinquent and non-delinquent juveniles. In theory, these institutions have a setting blended with control, protection, treatment and rehabilitation, which the child may not have led to his deviant behaviour. In conformity with the current thinking, the main objective of these institutions is treatment, not custody. In order to fulfill their objective, these institutions provide a continuum of professional services including those of case workers, psychologists, psychiatrists, teachers, vocational instructors, etc.

The commitment of delinquent and non-delinquent children of juvenile correctional institutions is used for variety of reasons, for some, committed to institution is a protective umbrella, because there is no responsible adult who is willing to care for them. For others, institutional commitment is a method of punishment so as to teach such children a lesson, shake them up and thereby set them straight. Institutionalisation, in their case, is rooted in the belief that delinquent children, even though different from adult offenders must be held responsible for their action, and their crimes should not go unpunished. The only difference that could be made is that child offenders should be committed to special institutions and is sheltered from adult abusers and influences.

These varied rationales for the institutional commitment of delinquent and non-delinquent children have remained unquestioned, presumably under the belief that such children need the benevolent custody of a state agency established for their conscientious care, constructive discipline and general up-lift. The underlying notion, harden, i.e., that a good dose of institution could only work to the child's best interest. This interest advocacy years the Juvenile Justice administration towards the goal of correcting the juvenile rather than punishing him. In pursuance of this goal, the Juvenile institutionalisation in a controlled environment is not regarded or an equivalent to imprisonment or a sentence. On the contrary, institutionalisation is considered or positive steps towards making the child unlearn his negative values and learn other positive ones in the interest of his rehabilitation in the community. Towards this end, juvenile correctional institutions make certain arrangements for education, counseling, guidance, treatment, training and rehabilitation of both the delinquent and non-delinquent children.

The professed purpose of institutions under the children Acts is to provide for a protective and rehabilitative umbrella, to children in conflict with law, or also for these found in institutions of social maladjustment and vulnerability to crime. The more vocalised purpose of using the institutional apparatus of delinquency control are to provide for the care, protection, maintenance, welfare, training, education and rehabilitation of delinquent children, or also for those living in situations of social marginality. The Institutions are mainly intended to act as reform-adorer, where the delinquent and the distressed children could be trained and prepared for a productive future.

While in theory, the purpose of these institutions is to serve as correctional centre with the minimum of custody and more of care, in actually, however, institution bear little resemblance to what their original founders imagined them to be. Many of the institution fact looks like mini prisons where preoccupation with custody, security and discipline seems large. In this scheme of things, institutions seem to cage on confined children so that they could do no harm to the community. The institutions carry out their artificial manatee into environs, where confinement, corporal punishment and subjugation to official ruler are omnipresent. Building of juvenile's self emerge and encouraging him to learn to accept society's value can hardly be accomplished in this atmosphere. Here arise the question of wide disparity between the treatment ideal and the institutional practices. While the institution have been given a progressive non-stigmatic name; training schools, industrial schools, reform-adorer with an avoided purpose of breaking from any connotation at penal institution, these tempting labels have not changed their essentially persecutory penal character.

Although, the rational for the setting up these institutions sounds noble, the reality, however, is a euphoria. The benign philosophy at committing children to institution for purposes of their treatment and training has been defeated through institutionalised. Operational practices that stem from the maxim spare the rod and spoil the child. The actual operational philosophy wedded to custodial and security concerns in all set against any meaningful behavioural change, and they're by to delinquency control. The resources in these institutions are mainly channelled into custody administration and housekeeping. In the final analysis, most such institutions function in ways, which are at cross-purposes with their official aims.

Features, Functions and Role of Institutional Service for Delinquent Children

During the period of placement in Juvenile homes and special homes the Juvenile are to be imparted academic, food, shelter, clothing as well as pre-vocational and vocational training. Several elements, that presents children from developing in a healthy way both physically and emotionally tends to bring about a pattern of emotional disturbances. The majority of children in Juvenile homes and special homes have already been disturbed emotionally and physically when they were at the clutches of their employer or during their association with anti socials and criminals. The abnormal family relationship, social disorganisation or derangement, individual mental and emotional pathology and organic conditions of brain conditions of the body have already damaged the physical and emotional factors of the juveniles, they should feel confident in the way of treatment in the institutions.

The juvenile should be natural and relax in the institution. The juvenile should feel at home. The educational and pre-vocational training for juvenile are to be imparted with the optimum aim of serving his economical needs when he goes out. The treatment of juvenile should not be a routine on ways and means for the emotional and psychological needs are to be found out and set right.

Function and Role

Before we discuss the facilities of institutional system, it is necessary to know the minimum standards of these institutions. At first in every institution, there must be commonly accepted norms, which the services must observe, towards its fulfillment. An essential pre-requisite for developing minimum standard in children's institutions should be to create conditions as class to a healthy home atmosphere as possible. To ensure this, number in each unit must be small so that each child receives individual attention and emotional security essential for rehabilitation. The standard in these institutions have to be worked out keeping in view of our economic standard, cultural background, current practices and existing level of services such as health, education and welfare programs. Along with the minimum standard of these institutions, it is necessary to know the intake and capacity of these institutions.

Every institution should have a definite intake policy, various types and age group, having dangerous disease children should not be mixed up. Normally there should not be more than 50 children in an institution and less than 20 children, which would be uneconomical.

Feeding

Every prisoner in the Juvenile Jail shall be given in the ordinary diets, for children below 15 years recommended allowances should be given 2,000 calories and for above 15 years 2,800 calories. The standard menu should be prepared in consultation with experts. Timing of food supply, quantity of food supply, item of food, satisfaction of children, and supervision at the time of distribution and involvement of children in food preparation, non-partiality attitude at the time of food distribution, should be taken care of.

Food is the very basis of life and sustenance. The quality of life is meaningless without health, which has direct linkage with diet. Unless the children get the minimum food of service, tomorrow there will be no future to enjoy.

Housing or Shelter

A shelter facility is as important as the food to the children of the Juvenile Delinquent due to their area of minimal choice affected and influenced for bad work. Due to poor income and occupation, they suffer poor shelter/housing. Many of the Juvenile Delinquents are homeless or more have a hut in slum.

In institutionalisation system, the minimum requirement of space for residential purpose should be 50/60 sq. per inmate. Bed should be three feet apart in living room and six feet apart in sick room. House plan should be prepared a hall with sliding partition could be made use of in one room not more than six children should be housed. Each child should have a mattress, a bedside locker or almira. At least a lavatory, a bathroom urinal and a washbasin each for every 10 children, playground 2000 sq. yards land for 50 inmates in addition to playground in the community should be used. One common room for recreation with indoors play equipment. One separate room with one cot and other accessories for nourishing. Single storey building should be preferred, if multistoreys the portion for small children should not be more than double storeys. The upper storeys can be used for older children or for older children or for residential accommodation for staff. For proper security, a big wall with security guard should be provided.

Clothing

Poverty never allowed these children to wear clean and good cloth rather soiled and dirty, holes and patched cloth. The use of detergent is rare. Many children frequently naked protection for feet is become comfort for them. Due to poor position of minimum clothing, it becomes inadequate for proper protection of body in all the seasons.

In Institutionalisation, system provide children clothing and bedding is must, at least two set of dress in every year with a set of bedding foot week in a month, one com a cake of toilet soap, ¾ kg of working soap and to use once of hair oil, one towards a common mirror in every residential room should be provided.

Medical Services

Health is one of the basic human needs and access to health service is undesirable right of everyone. Conversely protection from illness is an incontrovertible prerogative of everyone. Urban area and related pollution affects the poorest most severely. Sewage water, solid waste disposed, acceptable housing and transportation have been particularly deficient in marginal area. The existing infrastructure services are entirely inadequate. These factors affect the well being of people in slums and most of all constitute a very important factor or co-factor in disease. The main victims of the hazards of poor sanitation are generally the children.

Institutionalise medical facilities should have a first-aid kid at least two members of staff should be trained to give first aid. Every member of staff should be trained in health education and developing proper health habits among inmates. Medical check-up at the time of admission, proper maintenance of medical records for each child. Exist, whenever necessary referral services should be proved.

Education

In general among delinquent education is a poor attainment. Poverty is the main cause of their illiteracy. Due to poor economic condition, they were compelled to enter into the labour market to supplement their family income. It is also felt that poor educational attainment is not due to the lack of intelligence but may be due to lack of opportunity. Although free education is provided to scheduled caste and scheduled tribes, even then, the delinquent had a very low level expectation and aspirations regarding their future which in turn is due to lack of encouragement and unawareness of their parents that they play true.

Institutional arrangement should make the learning interesting and should understand each and every child personally according to its strength and weakness. Both the formal and non-formal education should be imparted to encourage the student for this better educational interest. Library with various types of books, freedom to choose any sort of books to children, library, counseling, education having some practical utility should be given emphasis among the children.

Vocational Training

Adequate vocational training programmes leading to economic rehabilitation of the inmates is necessary. Vocations to be selected should be determined mainly on the basis of aptitude and interest of inmates and employment opportunities available in the society. In most of the institutions Juvenile convicts are imparted vocational training in blacksmithy, carpentry, tailoring and gardening by skilled institutes out of it some in-tutors are full-time and others are part-time in nature.

Basically, the delinquent's concentrate is on two full time courses like carpentry and smithy. Most of the boys and all the girls seem to be interested in tailoring. Specialised instructor gives instruction, how to use foot and hand, how to use knife and cult and piece of cloth. Besides this cloth measurement and cutting of cloth is also instructed.

Besides this gardening is routine work of every delinquent. Every day two-hour (morning and evening) gardening work done by the inmates in the Juvenile home primes. These inmates were supervised by the warden, i.e., land distribution to each children, seed use pattern, transplanting tree, pour water to the tree, use of fertiliser and other necessary things about gardening.

Hobbies

It develops children's creative abilities; it engaged children doing good things rather bad work. Poverty never allowed these children to maintain develops their hobbies. In an institutionalised sector, children should be given some facilities to develop their hobbies, e.g., drawing, painting, clay modelling, cardboard and paper work, kitchen gardening etc. Hobbies not only help for creative development but also facilitate the children to make themselves busy rather Borden the mix with or think about the antisocial activities.

Recreation

Recreation is essential for a person. The child must get free time for recreation depending upon opportunities and means for recreation, the child relaxes his body and mind and becomes creative. Among these children, the level of fulfillment of the recreating need is very unsatisfactory.

In an institutional set-up, minimum one hour in a day's programme should be devoted to games and other group recreation on a planned basis according to the needs of each group.

Psychological and Follow-up Services

Psychological counselling with needs satisfaction counts as a prime human satisfaction. A starving man is not concerned with social approval or status; he is pre-occupied with obtaining food. If he is really hungry, he does not even wonder where tomorrows meal is coming from (safety need)—only today's meal count. But once he is assured of eating today that is of his psychological need satisfaction for a short run he can be in worry about the future and ask whether his psychological needs will always be met. Thus he moves on safety needs. The poor in society will be mostly concerned with psychological and safety needs. Psychological needs refer to human psychology and subsistence minimum. The main psychological needs may be categorised—food, nutrition, clothing, shelter, health care, immunisation and sports and games.

Besides these, in institution set-up casework, group work, motivation and related counselling services should be arranged according to the problem of the children and its remedial measures. The related agencies working in this field should be made use of in the time child is in the institution or child is released from the institution. It is the duty of the institution to see its social contact, its rehabilitation and its future aim satisfaction etc. After the child is released outside an institution, family contacts through visits, correspondence, parents', meetings, after-care and rehabilitation services in collaboration with other agencies should be made.

Above all, institutional facilities should give importance in its staff and record maintenance. In an institutionalised set up experienced and trained staffs that have children's institution with strength of more than 50 children should have the services of experience, qualified supervisors, assisted by matrons and house parents. Separate and adequate staff for kitchen, sanitation, watch and ward should be provided. The ratio between inmates and staff 1:20 Office staff should be excluded from this calculation. The ratio should be considered according to the age group of children.

Every institution should maintain proper records and registers about the children's admission. The record should include admission register, individual detail case history record, circumstance that led to admission, periodic progress, health record, follow-up and rehabilitation record etc.

Minimum standard was talked about during the day of institutional models of social welfare. It has been found that residential facilities are the times costlier than preventative measures and results from different methods of care show that children brought up in homes made least satisfactory showing. It has been reported that children in the overcrowd houses are twice as aggressive as in others. Models of welfare will affect the budgetary pattern and maintenance of minimum standards therein. The minimum standard will be governed by goals that institution sets for its remedial to development. It is not fixed or static. They could at best serve as a norm for a period of time only to be upgraded, improved later when they have been achieved. Central and State Governments have accentuated problems of minimum standard because of the variation in policy in grant-in-aid. Organisations have to raise resources to maintain better standard. In one agency, two norms are followed for the group of children. Concern for distribution of time on services is least expressed by voluntary organisations. Lack of qualified staff to keep service and specific needs, specific records or undertake studies in these areas in order to improve standard of services.

To know the minimum standard of institutionalised set-up, a periodical analysis, use of modern method and technique for supervision, proper utilisation and attitude of grant-in-aid policy and Government, trained staff, and planning of resources should be taken care off.

Rehabilitation

During the period of placement in juvenile homes and special homes the juvenile are to be imparted academic as well as pre-vocational and vocational training.

Every element that presents children from developing in a healthy way—both physically and emotionally tends to bring about a pattern of emotional disturbance. The majority of children in juvenile homes and special homes have already been disturbed emotionally and physically when they were at the clutches of their employer or during their association with anti-socials and criminals. The abnormal family relationship, social disorganisation or derangement, individual mental and emotional pathology and organic conditions of brain, conditions of the body have already damaged the physical and emotional factors of the juvenile; they should feel confident in the way of treatment in the institutions.

The juvenile should be natural and relax in the institution. The juvenile should feel at home. The educational and pre-vocational training for juvenile are to be imparted with the serving of his optimum economical needs when he goes out. The treatment of Juvenile should not be a routine one—ways and means for the emotional and psychological needs are to be found out and set right.

In order to achieve social, economic and psychological/ emotional rehabilitation, the following points should be kept in mind.

While growing up, even normal child with normal home conditions, experiences some psychological problems. This is because, while growing up, the child has to face new situation at home, at school and in community. As a result, there is the possibility of temporary personality problems.

In comparison, the psychological problems among the destitute delinquent children are more, as they do not experience the security of home, love and acceptance of their parents/

guardians often delinquent children are distributed without adequate reason suddenly leading to fights among children. Other problems are excessive fear, inferiority complex, anxiety, low frustration, tolerance, home sexuality, lying, preferring etc.

While discussing rehabilitation of children through educational development in an institutional set up, it is seen that these children are having low scholastic performance, because in childhood, before entering this institution, some of them have suffered emotional stress, some must not have gone to school, some might have run away from school or faced failure in school examination. As a result, they could not get opportunity to develop the talents to build their character. While taking their problems, each child should be studied and treated individually.

Education is vital for social make up of the child. It helps the child to acquire knowledge, broaden outlook towards life, freedom of movement and expression of thought develops and contacts in outside develops a sense of responsibility and discipline, develops co-operative and collaborative sprit, develops skill of housekeeping, budgeting, accounting etc., but due to various reasons, children lacks in showing their interest in studies. So to bring or develop the interest among the children, it is necessary to understand the child individually, division of children according their IQ level and interest for studies, concept of library and children is likely books should be introduced. Arrangement of essay/debate competition should be encouraged, picnic and educational excursions, and lastly to make children realise about the advantages of education.

The other way of rehabilitation of children is vocational training. In the present institutionalised set-up, the given training programmed should be updated, often training is imparted to keep children busy rather its long-term effectiveness. Untrained and inexperienced instructors with frustrated programmes and often institution choose training, which required minimum raw materials and inexpressible equipments. Training is seems to be less employment-oriented rather wastage of time and energy. Due to lack of proper training and unfinished work it is very difficult to market the prepared material by the children. As a result, children fell frustrated and take up any job unrelated to the training received. This leads to wastage of resources.

For the delinquent children through their backward in scholastic activities, vocational training is quicker means of developing talents and faculties in comparison to formal education. It provides child an assurance that he is a worthwhile member of the society to which he has to adjust. He develops fresh outlook about his capability of supporting himself and later on, his family through honest means. Vocational training is insurance for the child against future or employment and consequent social-economic insecurity in comparison to those who go for formal education and seek white colour jobs. There is less employment and economic security. Knowledge on vocational training is gathered not by memory, but by doing himself. He may make mistake, corrects them and learn the tasks he has to perform. What he acquires thus as knowledge becomes a part of his personality; with this knowledge his capacity to work develops. In the process of vocational training, the child learns to work in co-operation with the teachers, classmates and the institution. It is the sure remedy for many of the social ills, shortcoming and problems of personality development. Young persons and teenagers, who are aggressive and tough, need some physical hard work to get rid of their aggressive instinct and temper tantrums. Experience has shown that aggressive and angry boys have enjoyed being trained in tin-smithy, carpentry, working on lathes etc. This provides them an outlet for their extreme energy, anger or resentment. In this process, child learns to develop, co-ordinate, the efforts of—hand, mind and body.

Thus, vocational training is the foundation on which all educational and rehabilitative programmes must be based on productive work frees a child from inferiority complex. His feeling of self-reliance inculcates a sense of responsibility and systematic functioning.

Rehabilitation of girls in an institutionlised set-up should force on home management, cooking, first-aid, home nursing, child rearing, house decoration etc., socialise training by different groups, people and train how to talk, how to behave, how to wish etc. These girls should be equip with recognise professional training. If possible, the selection of life partners must be in professionals, government employees, as there are less chance of misbehaviour, breakdown of marriage, steady income etc. The girls in an institution have lot of difficulty, as social stigma; most of the destitute do not have their antecedents and family history. In case of emergency, there is nobody from near family members to support. Wrong notions that most of the institutionalised children face—behavioural problems, do not adjust with others.

For successful rehabilitation, role of programme personnel caseworker counsellor, probation officer etc., are very important. When a child is admitted to institutions or observation home, thorough inquiry should be made about his family, if need to financial or material support or employment may be provided to family members.

In order to fulfill their role satisfactorily, the programme personnel should be well versed with the sociological and psychological aspect of juvenile delinquents and destitute as well as broad understanding of human nature. They should have warm, friendly and human approach; frequent interviews with the child and also observation of his behaviour will throw light on the problems faced by the child. The discussion with the child should be taken in informal and friendly manner and the child should feel that the worker is trying to help him out of his difficulties. Attitudes of the worker towards the child should inspire confidence, so that the child talks to him freely and expresses himself clearly.

Visits to child's home will bring out the social and economic background of the child, its home and family circumstances, information about neighbourhood, influence of friends and associate and various other clues will reveal clues and pattern of child behaviour and the problems faced by the child. In short, worker should have genuine interest in the welfare of child.

Even after the child is reinstated in the community through adoption, marriage, or employment, programme, personnel should keep constant touch with the child in order not to allow the child to relapse. For adoption, adoptive parents are given guidance and counselling before giving child on adoption and even after the child is adopted.

Just after rehabilitation we cannot ignore the child though rehabilitation includes both care and after-care, so after-care services organised to facilitate completion of process or rehabilitation. After-care is provided to a person, who has been admitted to an institution for some treatment.

To sum-up, for successful rehabilitation positive attitude

of social worker and close family members/relatives are very necessary. They should be in constant contact with child, share experiences; does guidance and counselling like friend, philosopher and guide.

Problems and Prospects of Institutional Services for Delinquent Children

The professed purpose of institutions under the children Acts is to provide for a protective and rehabilitative umbrella to children in conflict with law, as also for those found in situations of social maladjustment vulnerability to crime. The more vocalised purpose of using the institutional apparatus of delinquency control are to provide for the care, protection, maintenance, welfare, training education and rehabilitation of delinquent children, as also for those marginally living institution. The institutions are mainly intended to act as reformatories where the delinquent and the distressed children could be trained and prepared for a productive future.

Like prisons, juvenile correctional institutions in India are bad evil led with multifarious problems and difficulties. The central ones of these arises from inadequate fiscal appropriation, lack of infrastructure facilities and potentials for the inmates treatment and training development of poorly selected, untrained and unspecialised staff lacking in personnel warmth, sensitivity and ability to handle children humanely and skilfully and finally and virtual absence of any aftercare programme for the inmates discharged from these institutions. Many of these problems have been discussed and debated in several official documents, but their redressed resolution has not yet been forthcoming. The officials are several statuses and union territories where children Acts are poorly implemented cover up the institutional deficiencies by a usual executes of money shortage.

The report of all India committee on jail reforms, commented on the unavailability of this argument. "If for lack of funds are welfare of children is neglected, the nation can hardly justify its claim of being a welfare state: The reports frowned upon the practice of excluding the expansion of the work under children Acts and other schemes of child welfare from the purview of the five-year plan expenditure, and thereby starring the child welfare from the preview of the five year plan expenditure, by putting it under non-plan sector allocations. After more distressing revolution made in the committee. Report is that many of the concerned child welfare departments in several states and union territories which usually complain of money shortage have, over the years, been unable to spend fully the funds allocated for the purpose. In such a shocking scenario, the committee observed; these facts show that there is no anxiety on the part of several state governments for the development and expansion of welfare services for children in distress and difficulty. In its reflective mood, the report further observed that the real reason for the lack of funds is the lack of sensitivity in the State Governments and Union territories about the urgency of the problems of children need of care and protection. The report said that had the concerned.

Facilities/Standards of Institution

The children Acts are the backbone of the Juvenile Justice System. These have been enacted with a view to divorce the Juvenile group from the adult group and give separate treatment of children. The philosophy behind this seems to be that for the ordinary healthy child, criminality is mainly the product of unfavourable environment and that he is entitled to a fresh chance under better surrounding. Full recognition of laws of property comes gradually and offences against property are largely due to lack of suitable training and bad upbringing childhood and youth are the stages when habits have not become fixed and prospects of reformation are most hopeful. Chances are that proper training will be successful. But such training cannot be given in prisons. Imprisonment will only bring the fear of prison, which is one of the determinants of crime. Moreover, state has a responsibility towards children, which must be exercised through giving opportunity for reformation at an early age rather than letting him become an adult criminal. This also seems to serve the self-interest of the society.

In keeping view of this all, the child Acts in India have provided for establishment and maintenance of observation/ Juvenile homes for temporary reception of children during the tendency of any inquiry regarding them under the Act, 1982 deals with said programme. The Administrator can also recognise other institution, which is fit for temporary reception of children during the pungency of inquiry as an observation home.

The primary objectives of the observation home are to keep child in a place of safety and provide him with the basic necessities. He is given clothes, bedding, proper learning arts, crafts and music etc. The main aim behind this is not to provide him with skills in a trade, but to give him a positive attitude with learning and provide him with a sense of achievement at least in one area. Facilities for recreation are also present.

One of the important functions of the observation homes is to closely observe and diagnose the child. Apart from medical examination, psychological tests are also conducted. Detailed interviews with the probation officers and also great help probation officer play a vital role in carrying out the functions of an observation Home.

As per the Juvenile Justice Act, the state shall prepare diet scale for juvenile in consultation with nutrition experts so that the diet becomes balanced, nutritious and varied. Special diet may be provided on national days and festivals.

As per the observation of the reservation in the said institution, the diet provided is not sufficient as the staff said the financial provision does not allow them to provide minimum standard because whatever money is permissible it has not revised in the present rate of the materials; secondly on time flow of fund is also creating problem for the institution, people to run residential institution with four time food supplement. To get grocery from the local shopkeeper is also a problem because of heavy advance credit.

The majority inmates of these institutions are very much against of the food provided, because as most of the children are habituated with taking rice and due to financial crunch at night they are getting *chapati* which they do not like and that is also insufficient. Repetition food items, partiality in providing same food again and again brings displeasure in the inmates.

Issue of the Clothing, Bedding and Other Articles

Each juvenile shall be provided with clothing and bedding including customary under-garments, towels, jersey for winter, school uniform for juvenile attending outside schools, mattress, bed-sheet, blanket, pillow, chapel or shoes, etc., utensils as required and tooth powder, soap, oil, comb, etc.

The researcher observation shows though clothes are provided them regularly, but dresses are very untidy, unclean may be because of improper guidance and lack of supplement of soaps, training for stitching the damage of one.

Sanitation and Hygiene

According to Juvenile Justice Act 1986, each institution shall have the following facilities, namely sufficient and treated drinking water, sufficient water for bathing and washing clothes, maintenance cleanliness on the premises and for flushing latrines. Proper drainage system, arrangements for disposal of garbage, protecting from mosquito, sufficient number of bath rooms in the proportion of at least one bath room for ten children, sufficient number of urinals, sufficient number of washing places, arrangement for getting the entire premises and building of the institution thoroughly cleaned at least once a day, cleanliness in the kitchen, fly-proof kitchen, arrangements for boiling clothes once a week, arrangement for washing clothes every day, sunning of bedding and clothing twice a week and scrofulous cleanliness in the hospitals.

As per observation of the research except some drinking water facilities, proper drainage system, cleanness of premises of the institution other prescribe, functions of juvenile home is totally nil. This is due to lack of awareness of caretaker, lack of staff to guide the children, sweeper to clean latrine etc., and materials like bleaching powder, phenols, detergent, mosquito oil etc. Old building with lots of damages, lack of proper maintenance, stinking atmosphere, it is doubtful, how far help these children get for their psychosocial behaviour.

Accommodation

Juvenile Justice System has provision for standard accommodation namely Dormitory, 40 square feet per child. Classroom sufficient accommodation, workshop sufficient workspace and playground with sufficient playground area should be provided in each institution according to the total number of juveniles in the institution. The dormitory classrooms and workshops shall have sufficient cross-ventilation and sufficient light.

As per observation of the Juvenile homes studied in Orissa though it has a spacious premises building but lacks from proper arrangements, it gives a impression of the jail atmosphere, no separate room is provided for classroom, workshop facilities is totally nil.

Medical Care

Each institution shall be provided necessary medical staff and ensure that regular facilities are available for the medical treatment of inmates, arrangements are made for the immunisation coverage and a system is envelope for the removal of serious causes to the nearest civil hospital or treatment centres, immediate action in accordance with the previous section 48 of the Act, shall be taken in respect of the juvenile who is suffering from leprosy is of unsound mind or is addicted to a drug. Each juvenile admitted in an observation home as far as possible within forty eight hours after his admission to the observation home as far as possible within forty eight hours after his admission to the observation home and also in the case of a juvenile known to be a awaiting removal to a juvenile home or special home, within a similar period before such removal and further at any other time or times that may be considered necessary by the medical officer or the superintendent.

An inmate known or suspected to be suffering from an infectious disease shall forthwith be removed to a Government hospital and if this is not practicable shall be isolated from other inmates. If any infectious disease breaks out in an institution and subsequently admitted, juvenile shall so far as practicable be kept separate from those who are known or suspectable to be suffering from the infectious disease.

No surgical treatment shall be carried out on an inmate without previous consent of his parent or guardian unless either the parent or guardian cannot be found or the condition of the inmate is such that any delay in the opinion of the medical officer would involve unnecessary suffering or injury to the health of the inmate. A health check up on each juvenile in the institution shall be maintained on the basis of his quarterly medical check-up.

The studied institutions have a good medical response; caretaker and staffs are very regular in taking care of the inmates though comparatively these children needs less medical attention. Minor illness, cold and cough, wound are seem to be more, which required personnel attention and some first-aid medicine for children to be healthy and sound.

Other Institutional Programmes/Facilities

Each institution shall provide for physical exercise and recreational facilities. The recreational facilities may include the provision of radio, television, library, music games (indoor and outdoor) etc., with the trained staff available for the purpose.

Each institution shall organise activities and programmes for the socio-cultural uplift of the inmates, such as cultural meets, parent inmate's staff meetings, community contacts, visits to outside institutions, excursions, etc.

Casework services shall be provided in all institutions to deal with the individual problems of inmates. The services of psychologist or psychiatrist shall also be availed of—preferably by establishing linkage with child guidance clinics, counselling and guidance centres, psychiatric departments or similar agencies in the community or by appointment on part-time or full-time basis as per requirement.

The education programme shall be developed as an integral part of the educational routine. Emphasising on the academic health, social, moral and ethical aspects, educational programme shall be organised on the pattern recognised by the education department of the state Government including non-formal adult education techniques. The inmates shall be organised under the supervision of trained staff.

A diversified programme of vocational training shall be organised in all juvenile and special homes with special reference to employment opportunities available in the community, so as to facilitate their rehabilitation. The course shall be designed on the lines approved by the technical departments of the State Government. The trained vocational instructor shall be appointed for the purpose. Vocational training facilities in the community shall also be availed for inmates on selective basis by providing linkage with welfare institutions, placement agencies and industrial and other production units.

A well rounded programme of pre-release planning and follow up of cases discharge from juvenile and special homes shall be organised in all institutions as far as practicable in close collaboration with voluntary welfare organisation.

Above all, these facilities provided by the Juvenile Justice Act, as the aim of the research in how far these facilities are provided to the inmates in juvenile home; so after a long discussion observation and interview with the inmates it came to notice that except the provision of television to each institution other facilities like—radio, library, music games, sometimes some institution provided carrom and football etc., which are very lasting and profaning, never allows the institution in charge to supply it again after a short break by which children suffer boredom, busy in quarreling, destroying etc.

Inmates of these institutions especially girl inmates participated in mass prayer and other inmates also organised Ganesh Puja, Independence Day celebration etc. Parent inmates-staff meeting concept is not there, sometimes the staffs of these institutions visit other institution inside and outside the state to attend seminar, training, workshops and visits and excursion is a dream to these inmates.

Observation and reference of individual case file show casework services provided to these institutions are very poor, there may be lack of trainees personal and social workers as per the Juvenile Justice Act provision. Though, the staffs in charge of social workers having 10 to more years experience but they lack from technical and professional attitude to deal with problematic children like Juvenile delinquents.

Education provided to these inmates is good, teachers are sincere, taking interest to teach students good stories, and teaching by those who are poor in education but no special attention is provided to them, education is totally non-formal type which most of the students are dissatisfied and interested for formal education which is not provided by these institutions. It should be mentioned that most of the inmates are good students due to circumstances they have been in these institutions, so special provision should be made to give some educating facilities to good students by which they will not use their good intelligence in any other bad work.

Provision for vocational training to the inmates is poor, except tailoring provision for girl. Vocational training has a great role in this sort of institution to make the inmates busy, physically and mentally, which give them a way to choose their career in future rather engaged in anti-social activities. But due to lots of difficulties, these institutions are not able to continue maintain vocation training among the inmates after 15 to 20 years of their working in this field.

Intake Procedure

As per the Juvenile Justice Act, the State Government as far as possible may set up separate observation homes for neglected and delinquent juveniles. Separate homes may be established for juveniles below and above the age of 12 years. In any case, boys above 12 years shall be lodged in separate homes.

Each institution shall have a reception unit under the charge of a case worker for admission of few arrivals. Newly admitted juveniles may in suitable cases be kept in the reception unit for 10 days initially. Where necessary, the superintendent may suitably extend this period to facilitate a detailed study of the juvenile. The juvenile suspected to be suffering from contagious diseases; mental ailments, addiction, etc., shall immediately be segregated in specially earmarked dormitories or wards.

Some procedure should be followed in respect of the newly admitted juveniles like, receiving and search in the receiving unit, hair-cut, unless prohibited by religion, issue of soap and disinfectant 10 disaffection and storing of juvenile's personnel effects, bathing issue of disinfected clothes, bedding and other outfit and equipments, housing, medical examination and treatment where necessary, attending to immediate and urgent needs of the juvenile like letters, interviews, family matters, personnel problems etc. and verification by the officer-in-charge of order of the competent authority, identification marks, register entries, cash property etc.

Each institution shall follow a schedule of orientation talk for the newly admitted juveniles covering the following aspects, namely interpretation of rules and regulations, framed under the Act, health, sanitation, hygiene, institutional discipline and standards of behaviour, respect for elder, teachers, self-improvement opportunities and responsibilities and obligations.

An overall study of the juvenile admitted to an institution shall be undertaken on the basis of their social history, behavioural pattern and attitudes towards others. Information regarding their socio-cultural and economic background shall be collected through all possible and available sources including home, parents or guardians' employer, schools, friends and community contacts. The educational level and vocational aptitude shall be assessed on the basic of tests and interviews conducted by the teachers, the workshops, supervision and other technical staff. For this purpose, appropriate linkage shall also be established with outside specialist and community-based welfare agencies.

All inmates in the reception unit shall be given work like, self-help in maintaining inmates which should be displayed and should provide among other aspects for regulated disciplined life, physical exercise, educational classes, vocational training, organised recreational games, moral education, group activities prayer and community signing.

For Sunday and holidays, the daily routine shall include; washing of clothing and bedding, library reading, recreational programmes, games, sports, radio, television and recorded music, properly planned excursions, social activities should be taken care off.

Record Maintenance

The case file of each inmate shall be maintained in a juvenile home or special home, containing the following information namely; commitment papers, count documents and other relevant papers, probation officer report, information from previous institution, initial interview material, information from family members, relative, friends and miscellaneous information, sources of further information, observation reports from stall members in charge of admission programmes, reports from medical officer, questing, aptitude testing, educational tests, social history summary and analysis by officer-in-charge of the reception unit, initial classification sheet instruction regarding terminal and treatment programmes and about special precaution to be taken, leave and other privileges reports from various sections, review sheet, M.C. report (in case of girls) pro-release progrmmes, final progress report, release on license, final discharge, follow-up reports, central index number and remark by the concerned authorities.

After Facilities

The State Government may provide a comprehensive scheme of aftercare with following objectives, namely to extend help, counselling, support and protection to all released juveniles whenever necessary to help a released juvenile to overcome his mental, social and economic difficulties. To impress upon the juveniles, the need to adjust his habits, attitudes, approaches and value schemes on a rational appreciation of social responsibilities and obligations and also of requirements of community living. To help the juvenile to make smooth adjustment to his post-release environment, to encourage the juvenile in making satisfactory readjustment with his family, neighbourhood and community should assist. The juvenile in functioning as a self-dependent and self-reliant socially useful citizen, to assist in the process of the juvenile physical, mental, vocational, and economic social and attitudinal post-release re-adjustment and ultimate rehabilitation and to complete in all respects, the process of the juvenile final re-adjustment resettlement and rehabilitation, all things should be taken care of.

The State Government should establish and maintain as many after-care homes as may be necessary for the reception of the Juvenile discharged from the juvenile homes and special homes for the purpose of enabling them to lead an honest, industrious and useful life. Where the State Government is of the opinion that any institution other than an institution establish under sub rule (2) is fit for the reception of the juvenile to absent there from the juvenile homes and special homes he may recognise such institution as an after-care home of the purpose of the Act. Every after-care home to which a Juvenile is sent under these rules shall not only provide the Juvenile with accommodation, maintenance and educational and vocational guidance but also provide him with facilities for the development of his character and abilities to ensure all round development of his personality as well as opportunities to enable him to reintegrate to the community as law abiding citizen and shall perform such other functions may be prescribed from time to time. Before a juvenile is discharged from a juvenile home of special home, as the case may be, and is sent to an after-care home, the probation officer or the case workers shall prepare and submit a report regarding the necessity and nature of after-care assistance required by the juvenile the period of such after-care and this supervision thereof. The superintendent of the after-care home in which the juvenile is placed shall submit periodically a detailed progress report on the juvenile to the chief inspector till the juvenile reintegrated into the community. The internal management functions and responsibilities of the after-care home and the standards and nature of services to be maintained by it shall regulated by the instruction as issued from time to time by the State Government.

Duties of the Superintendent

The general duties, functions and responsibilities of the superintendent as the head of the institution is to provide homely atmosphere of love and affection, care and welfare to juvenile, planning, implementing and co-coordinating all institutional activities programmes and operations, maintaining minimum standards at the institution, classification of juvenile, training and treatment programmes and correctional activities, supervision over juvenile discipline and morale, preparation of budget and controller financial matters, supervision over office administration, monthly office inspection, daily inspection and round of the institution and inspecting and testing food prepared for juveniles.

Duties of the Probation Officer

On receipt of information from the officer-in-charge of a police station under clause (b) of section 19 or on the order from the juveniles welfare board, the probation officer shall inquire into the antecedent's family history of the juveniles and such other material circumstances as may be necessary and submit a preliminary report in form IX to the competent authority as early as may be. Every probation officer shall carry out all directions given to him by the competent authority and the chief inspector and shall perform the following duties namely he shall make inquiries regarding the home and school condition, conduct, character and health of juvenile under his supervision. He shall attend regularly the court of the competent authority and submit report, he shall maintain daily case files and such registers and may be prescribed from time to time, he shall visit regularly the count of the competent authority and submit reports. He shall maintain daily case files and such registers as may be prescribed from time to time, he shall visit regularly juveniles kept under his supervision and also the places of employment or school attended by such juveniles and submit for monthly reports in form X regularly. He shall accompany the juveniles whenever possible form the count of a competent authority to observation home, to juveniles home special home or fit person, he shall bring the juveniles before the competent authority immediately who have not been of good behaviour during the period of supervision. He shall follow up juveniles after their release from the institutions and extending help and guidance to them and he follow up establish linkage with voluntary workers and organisations to facilitate rehabilitation and social reintegration of juveniles and to ensure the necessary follow up. Finally, probation shall not employ a juvenile under his supervision for his own private purposes or take any private services from him.

Duties of Case Workers

The general duties, functions and responsibilities of case workers shall be as like, making social study of the juvenile through personal interview and from their family, social agencies and other sources, clarifying problems of the juvenile and dealing with his/her difficulties in institutional like participating in the orientation classification and reclassification programmes, establishing co-operation and understanding between the juvenile and the administration, assisting the juvenile to develop contacts with his family, participating in the pre-release programme and helping the juvenile to establish contacts which can provide emotional and said support to juvenile after their release.

Duties of Care-Taker

The general duties-functions and responsibilities of care-taker shall be as follows namely, handling juveniles with love and affection, taking proper care and welfare of juveniles, maintaining disciple in institution, maintenance of sanitation and hygiene, implementing daily outline in an effective manner looking after the security and safety arrangement of the institution and escorting juveniles whenever they go out of the institution.

Besides this, job chart for taken shall be worked out by the chief inspector, which shall be strictly adhered to in all institutions.

A care-taker shall be liable for departmental action for willing or negligently permitting an inmate to escape, giving or attempting to give an inmate for taking out or attempting to take out from the institution, any article, not allowed by the superintendent and wilful disobedience, neglect of any rules, regulations or orders.

Training of the Personal

The state Government shall provide persons for training of each category of staff in keeping with their statutory responsibilities and specific job requirements. The training programme shall include, training of newly recruited staff, refresher training courses for every staff members at least once in every five years, staff conference, seminars, workshops etc. at various levels of the personal set up.

Funding and Finance

The State Government may create a fund under such name as it thinks fit for the welfare and rehabilitation of the juvenile dealt with under this Act. There shall be credited to the fund such voluntary donations, contribution or subscriptions as may be made by any individual or organisation. The fund created under sub-section (1) shall be administered by such officers or authority in such manner and for such purpose as may be prescribed.

Under the scheme, neglected and delinquent juveniles are maintained and corrected in the observation Home, special Home and Juvenile Home. The maintenance cost is borne by the state Government and Central Government in the ratio of 79:21 respectively. During the year 1994-95, the State Government share was Rs 5.64 lakh and the Central Government share was Rs 1.56 lakh. In the meantime, the new observation Homes have been recognised which will become functioned during current year through non-government organisations. The strength of the neglected juveniles has been proposed to be increased from 150 to 300 during the current year.

A total sum of Rs 8, 94,600 has been received from Government of India for maintenance of neglected and delinquent juveniles from 1988-99 to 1993-95 out of this amount of Rs 2,37,167 has been spent during 1989-93 towards the Central share, learning a balance of Rs 6,57,433. Due to inadequate number of juveniles available in the existing observation Home and special home, the above balance among could not be utilised, the State Government can utilise this un-spent amount during the year 1995-96 as new observation Home will become functional. So, a sum of Rs 6.58 lakh will be required towards the maintenance of juveniles during the year 1995-96 towards the matching state share.

Role of Parents and Guardians

The parents and near relations of the inmates shall be allowed to visit an inmate once a month or in special cases more frequently if the superintendent so permits. The superintendent shall fix the visiting hours. The receipt of letter by the inmates of the institution shall be restricted and they shall have freedom to write as many letters as they shall like at all reasonable times. However, the institutions shall ensure that where parent-guardians or relatives are known at least the inmates write one letter every week for which the postage be provided.

The superintendent may peruse any letter written by or to an inmate and may for any reasons inmate's health, mortality or well-being that he consider sufficient to refuse deliver or issue the letter and may destroy the same after recording his reason in a book maintained for the purpose.

Analysis on Impact and Effectiveness of Institutional Services for Delinquent Children

In the present context, institution is a solution to give a break to the juvenile delinquents against their delinquent activities. Existing institutions are helping delinquent children with their minimum resources; still the researcher was interested to know from the voice of inmates of juvenile homes and their care-taker, about the existing facilities and their reaction.

Questions like periods of their stay, their first impression and reaction to this institution, means of arrival, person who accompanied them, parental visit, positive charge, nature of their abuse, delinquency in the institution, correctional major taken by the institution, health problem, reaction police, staff, institutional facilities etc.

After the child is declared as a delinquent, he is punished under cognisable crime under Indian Penal Code, such as murder, kidnapping, dacoit, robbery, house breaking, cattle theft, cheating.

An attempt was made to collect about the admission to this institution. Majority (25 per cent) said they have taken admission in the end of the year 1996. Around 22 per cent said they have taken admission in the year 1997 and their case is still pending in the court. In the year 1998, 24 per cent, in the year 1999 around nine per cent and last but not the least, in the year 2000 around 20 per cent came to this institution. This table shows that children are waiting for their case finalisation that ever case is finalised they left this institution.

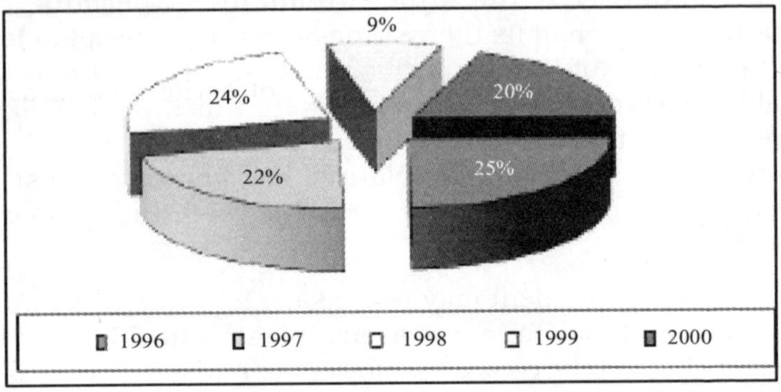

Fig. 1. Distribution of respondents according to their year of admission to these institutions.

Table 1. Respondents' First Impression in the Institution

Impression	*No. of respondents*	*Percentage*
Good	64	25.6
Bad	29	11.6
No Reaction	157	62.8
Total	**250**	**100.00**

Children after caught by the police, public, or any other person became very much frightened and when they heard about the court and jail they became more nervous and some of them patience to see the matter.

When a question was asked to these children about their first impression when they were taken to this institution, more than one-fourth (25.6 per cent) of the respondents said the institution to be good. These respondents feel that the institution does not aim at giving them harsh punishment rather will provide good treatment. Around 12 per cent said that they felt bad because the place of their living was a prison and especially their friend circle once aware of would underestimate them. However, more than three-fifth (62.8 per cent) expressed no reaction.

Table 2. Respondents means of arrival in the institution.

Medium	*No. of respondents*	*Percentage*
By Public Bus	29	11.6
By Police Jeep	56	22.4
By Cycle	16	6.4
By Walk	15	6.0
Any Other	134	53.6
Total	**250**	**100.00**

Delinquent children arrive the institution through public, police, local NGO's or social workers. When we are discussing about the means of their arrival to the institution response varies from child to child.

Twelve per cent of the respondents said that police through public buses took them to the juvenile institution. Police jeep only help 56 (22.4 per cent) to collect children to the institution. Sometimes police pick-up children by cycle said by 16 (6.4 per cent). Nearby Juveniles taken up by police by means of walk said (15.6 per cent). The majority of children, i.e., 134 (53.6 per cent) said they taken up by public, social activities and local NGO's through their convenience.

The above graph reveals that the police is more active to send the juvenile delinquent to the juvenile home because when public hand over the child delinquents to them it is their responsibility afterwards to send them to the juvenile home. It should be mentioned that police brings 76 per cent of children

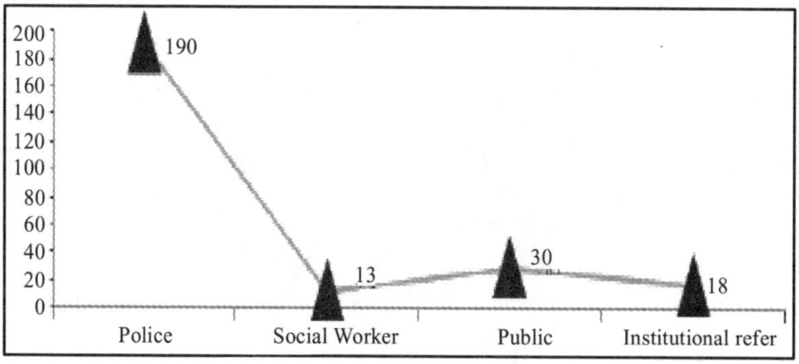

Fig 2. Distribution of Juvenile Delinquents by Means of Intake (Also Brought).

to juvenile home. Sometimes, social workers/activists (4.8 per cent) help bringing the neglected and delinquent Juvenile to the Juvenile home. Public also help to bring the juvenile to the juvenile home (12 per cent). Last but not the least, Institutional referrals (7.2 per cent) like some NGOs help in bringing the juveniles to the juvenile home.

Table 3. Respondents According to Their Period of Imprisonment

Period	*Number*	*Percentage*
1 Years or less than it	130	52.0
2 to 3 Years	61	24.4
More than 3 years	59	23.6
Total	**250**	**100.0**

After conviction, the delinquent child is kept in the juvenile home/probation home or special home for finalisation of case, observation, trial, waiting for bail etc. In the process of all sort or official procedure the child have to spend his valuable time in the prisons. Some spend more than three years (23.6 per cent) because either they do not have anybody to take them from the jail due to economic crises or they have to stay because they do not know their home address. 24.4 per cent said they are in this institution from last two to three years. Majority (52 per cent) said they are admitted into the institution in less than one year back and they hope they will be released early.

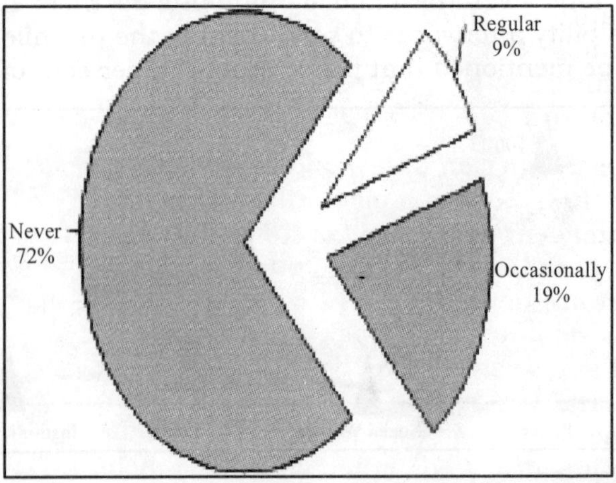

Fig. 3. Distribution of Juvenile delinquents by parental visits.

Parental visits to the juvenile observation/special home seem to very poor. This may be the cause of negligence, lack of manpower in case of (only mother is the guardian), due to lack of money etc. As per the graph above, majority of the survey respondents (73 per cent) said that the parents never visit their children. While a small proportion (eight per cent) of the respondents said that their parents visit them regularly, around one-fifth (19 per cent) that their parents visited them occasionally.

Table 4. Juvenile Delinquents by Types of Positive Changes

Sr. No.	*Changes*	*Number*	*Percentage*
1.	Disciplined	24	9.6
2.	Leadership	8	3.2
3.	Leave up bad habits	48	19.2
4.	Interested for learning	65	26.0
5.	Further Education	85	34.0
6.	Interested for self-dependent	20	8.0
	Total	**250**	**100.0**

After Juvenile delinquents' admission in the institutional set-up, some of them changed their behaviour due to fear of police, due to counselling by the teacher and care-taker, by a good environment etc. Almost all the children said they got some feedback to change themselves and some also reflected in their personality by showing respect to the senior, disciplined behaviour; leave the bad habits, interested for further education and in future to look after their old parents out of their good means of earning.

After admission of juvenile delinquent in an institutional set-up, the children came across various types of staff like superintendent as the head of the institution, care-taker, case worker, cook/ home guards, and also their co-inmates. These children are deviant in nature. In the juvenile home, senior inmates dominate the weak inmates and sometimes fight/ quarrel among themselves, put pin, blade etc., in the body of others. The observation and interview showed 10 per cent of them faced physical torture and cruelty inflicted on them by their co-inmates. While suffering from psychological harassment by cooks/home guards was reported by 14 per cent of the respondents, 7.2 per cent of the respondents reported the same

Table 5. Juvenile delinquents by Nature and agents for abused

Nature/Agents for Abused	*Superin-tendent*	*Care Taker*	*Cook and home Guard*	*Co-inmates*	*Total*
Physical torture/cruelty	—	—	—	25) (10.0 %	25 (10.0 %
Psychological harassment	—	—	35 (14.0%)	18 (7.2 %)	53 (21.2 %)
Physical labour	8 (3.2 %)	20 (8.0%)	12 (4.8 %)	5 (2.0 %)	45 (18.0 %)
Not abused	—	—	—	—	127 (50.8 %)

(N=250)

inflicted on them by their comates. Sufferings due to physical labour resulted from being inflicted on them by superintendent (3.2 per cent), by care-taker (8 per cent), by cook/home guards (4.8 per cent) and by co-inmates (2 per cent). They said they did gardening, clearing the ground, digging whole for plantation etc. Almost half of the respondents reported not being abused in any form in this institutional set-up.

Table 6. Juvenile delinquent by Nature of delinquent noticed during the period of staying in the institutional set-up

Delinquency	*Number*	*Percentage*
Bad habits (consumed intoxicants and beverage)	18	7.2
Behavioural Problem	45	18.0
Run away	3	1.2
Fighting	35	14.0
Exploits co-inmates	25	10.0
Normal	124	49.6
Total	**250**	**100.00**

During the staying period of the juvenile delinquent in institution set-up, the children showed different type of delinquent behaviour like bad habit of consuming intoxicants (7.2 per cent), some behavioural problem (18 per cent), run away

(1.2 per cent), fighting (14 per cent), exploiting their co-inmates (10 per cent). Almost half of the children respondents (49.6 per cent) showed normal behaviour.

Table 7. Distribution of Delinquency Noticed among the Inmates by Correctional Measures Taken up by the Institution

Measures Taken	*Number*	*Percentage*
Case to case counselling	125	50.0
Peer counselling	28	11.9
Group counselling	18	7.2
Punishment	9	3.6
Threatened	6	2.4
No measures taken	64	25.6
Total	**250**	**100.00**

After the admission of the juvenile delinquents in the institutional set-up, measures have been taken to modify their behaviour through different kind of counselling techniques, motivation and punishment. Various techniques being used are Group counselling (7.2 per cent), peer counselling (11.9 per cent), punishment (3.6 per cent), threatening (2.4 per cent). No measures were taken in 25.6 per cent of the cases primarily these cases being the new entrants into the institutional setup. Majority (50 per cent) of the inmates were counseled in individually (case-to-case counselling).

Table 8. Juvenile Delinquents by Type of Relationship with Staff

Type of Relationship	*Number*	*Percentage*
Very good	11	4.4
Good	28	11.2
Poor	123	49.2
Indifferent	88	35.2
Total	**250**	**100.00**

In the Institutional set up, staff and inmates are the only sources of interaction and it depends a lot on the understanding and temperament of both. Only 4.4 per cent of the inmates said they have a good relationship with the staff, 11.2 per cent said their relationship is good and majority (49.2 per cent) said they have poor relationship with their staff, because they have less exposure and they do not know much about the staffs.More than one third (35.2 per cent) were indifferent to the question because they had just come to this institutional set-up.

Table 9. Classification of Respondents according to their health problem

Major Health Problem	*No. of respondents*	*Percentage*
Mental	1	0.4
Physical	14	5.6
Psychological	36	14.4
Minor illness	199	79.6
Total	**250**	**100.0**

The children kept in observation and special home suffer less from health problem. Most of them being teenaged are less affected with pollution and other hazards. Majority of children (79.6 per cent) suffer from minor health problem like decentry, mums, cold, headache, ear infection, skin disease etc. Next to it is the psychological problem of the children. Suffering from psychological problems like minor depression, frustration, and irritation and fearless was reported by 14 per cent of the respondents. Hardly 5.6 per cent children suffer from minor physical problems like polio affected, visual and audio problem, crippled, etc. Only one child (0.4 per cent) suffered mental illness.

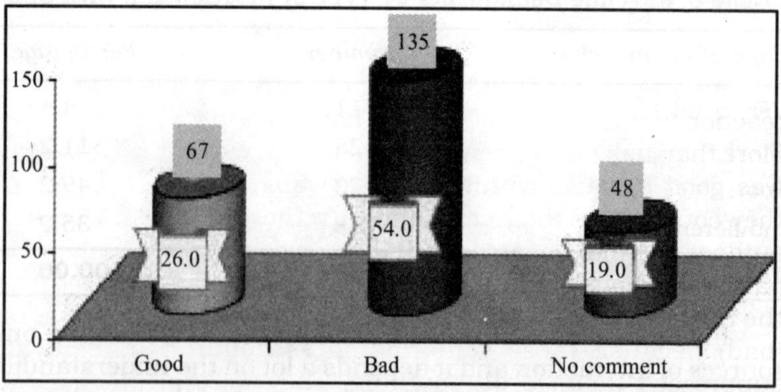

Fig. 4. Respondents according to Their Reaction about Police.

Juvenile delinquent has more or less exposure with police, as it seems necessary to ask them question about their reaction towards police. More than one-fourth (26 per cent) of the respondents from the juvenile home said they do not have any objection or allegation about police, because police never ill-treated them, abused them, scolded them. This may be due to the fact that the children did not do any bigger crime and they have very less exposure about police. More than half (54 per cent) said they have very bad impression about police, because police feels that by giving threat anybody can accept/submit their crime even if they did involve in said crime.

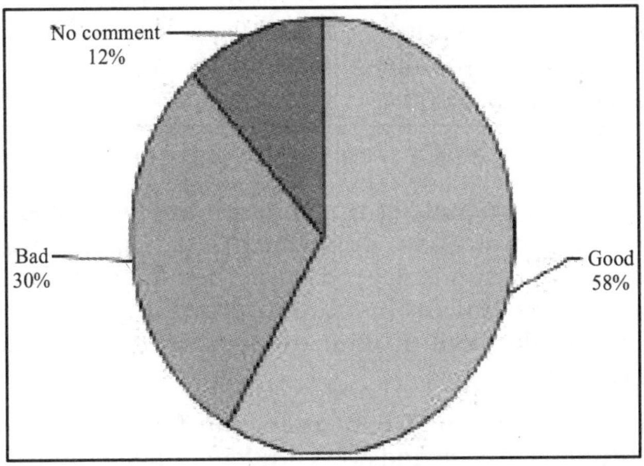

Fig. 5. Respondents according to Their Reaction about the Institution Staff.

An attempt was made during the survey to know about the reaction of the inmates of juvenile homes about their co-inmates. More than half (58 per cent) said their term with other co-inmates was good because within the four walls of the juvenile home they could share their emotions with these children. They play outdoor and indoor games with them, when they remember their parents or homes the co-inmates console them. 30 per cent of the respondents said their term with the co-inmates is not good (bad) because these senior inmates dominated them and suppressed them to do anything. They were also sometimes beaten and threatened by the senior co-inmates to do wrong things like tell in favour of them and work for them. 12 per cent did not express any opinion about their inmates may be due to the fear of their being exposed by the researcher and they had just taken admission and they do not have sufficient exposure about it.

Table 10. Respondents according to Their Opinion about Institutional Facilities

Institutional Facilities	*Respondents Opinion*			*Total Percentage*
	Good	*Bad*	*No Comment*	
Education	59 (23.6)	23 (9.2)	168 (67.2)	100.00
Health	139 (55.6)	37 (14.8)	74 (29.6)	100.00
Nutrition	87 (34.8)	105 (42.0)	58 (23.2)	100.00
Leisure activities	62 (24.8)	152 (60.8)	36 (14.4)	100.00
Vocational training	32 (12.8)	170 (68.0)	48 (19.2)	100.00

Row% *(N = 250)*

In an institutional set-up, children are facilitated various types of care, protection, supplement etc. But it varies from institution to institution depending on their financial assistance. Mostly in a government institution provision is given for five components like health, education, nutrition, vocation and rehabilitation.

In the present study, education (non-formal) is provided by the institutions to each and every student. Among these children, some have left education long back, some are fed-up due to the torture of education system and hence not at all interested to continue it again and some have just left due to being apprehended by legal system. Though teaching all these children having different mentality is a difficult task still almost one-fourth (23.6 per cent) said this institutional education pattern is good, because they have good teachers and they get more time in this institution to read. Only nine per cent of the respondents said the present education pattern is not good (bad), because their expectation is something high and they wanted formal education pattern. It seems that most of the good students at the time of class 8th and 9th left education and they wanted to complete class 10th and this jail situation never permitted them to go outside and read in the institutional set-up. Majority (67.2 per cent) never reacted, when they were asked whether they liked or disliked the educational facilities provided to them in this institution.

As regards the question asked to the children in the juvenile institutions regarding health facilities they get, majority (55.6 per cent) of the children said that whatever health facilities is provided to them is good, because they were getting health facilities at their time of need. A small proportion (14.8 per cent) said the health facility provided was bad. According to them, barring some minimum first-aid, and common medicine provision, these institutions were delaying in providing medical facilities. More than one-fourth (29.6 per cent) did not give their opinion about the health facilities, because neither they asked for health facilities nor did they know what sort of health facilities this institutions provided. A majority of these respondents not giving any comment were very new to this institution.

Regarding nutrition facilities, more than one-third (34.8 per cent) said they are happy about whatever food is provided by this institution because they either never used to get proper food outside the institution or had to struggle a lot to get their daily food. Majority (42 per cent) were not happy about the food provided to them because food was not adequate, food was not properly distributed. Also, most of them were not habituated to taking chapatti. More than one-fifth (23.2 per cent) did not give their comment may be out of their fear towards their teacher, or the researcher itself or they just did not want to say anything.

In the juvenile home, children hardly get chance to spend their leisure time primarily because of non-availability of proper sports materials, teachers interest to spend time with these children. However, only one-fourth (24.8 per cent) said they are happy with whatever sports material provided to them to spend their leisure time (like foot ball, gardening, carom etc.). Majority (60.8 per cent) said they are not happy with the prevailing leisure/ recreational facilities or freedom provided to them by the staff. A small proportion (14.4 per cent) did not give their opinion about their leisure time.

Vocational training is the real work by the juvenile home to train the children for their better future by giving them various types of vocational training like tailoring, catering, mansion work, welding, gardening etc. During the study, it was apparent that the institutions have very limited facilities for vocational trainings like tailoring, chalk making, gardening etc. Even the institutions do not have proper adequate funding facilities nor do they have technical persons to train the children. Only 12.8

per cent of the respondents said they are happy with the vocational training provided to them and if possible they will continue this preparation after release. Majority of the respondents (68 per cent) said that whatever-vocational training is provided were not of any use to them. Around one-fifth (19.2 per cent) did not say anything about the vocational training provided to them.

Summary

As one of the objectives of the study is to assess the effectiveness of Institutional services and Juvenile Justice system in order to provide care, protection, treatment, development and rehabilitation of delinquent juveniles, with this backdrop, efforts have been made to analyse the multi-dimensional aspects of institutional system for which primary data have been collected through observation, group discussion with staff as well as the inmates of the institutions, verified and analyzed reports of institutions and Government Department.

In the preceding sections, both, primary and secondary data were analysed through tabular, graphical forms administering qualitative techniques. The major folks of the analysis are; standards of institutions, staffing pattern and staff developments, functional folk analysis, intake system, supervision and monitoring, facilities and services; finance, impacts and problems etc., comparing with provisions as per Juvenile Justice system and implementing system in the study institutions.

Institutional life never gives a family atmosphere, in poor families love and affection counts much rather than money, prestige and nutritive food of rich families. Well-trained and motivated housemothers, supervisors or social workers can never be good substitutes for real parents. The children grow within the four walls of the institution where all staff members are well-wishers of the children. As such, sometimes they find difficulty when faced with odd situation outside.

Departments were earnestly seized with the passing problem of child welfare in general and of delinquent children in particular. The planning departments in the states and union territories would have made larger allocations for the expansion and development of child welfare services in the plan sector. If they had done this, it would not have been difficult for them to convince the central commission about the necessity of expenditure in the institutional and non-institutional services for the delinquent and non-delinquent children on a priority basis. Still more surprising is the fact that even in the planning commission, the urgent necessity of setting up a wide network of developmental services for children does not seem to have been fully appreciated as yet. A direct consequence of this indifference is that several thousands of children are being forced to live dehumanised in institutional settings.

Notes

1. (Juvenile delinquency in perspective—B.S. Griffin and C.T. Griffin Harper and Row Publishers).
2. Background reading material for Juvenile Justice Act functionaries sponsored by Directorate of Social Defence, Madras.

References

Spencer Milham, Roger Bullock : Locking up children (secure provision within the cataloguing in publication data

Statistics on children in India (91-694) : NIPCCD, New Delhi

The student of worlds children 1981-82 James P. Grant Exeactive Director : UNICEF

Uday Sakher (1984) : *Exceptional Children,* Stearling Publishing Pvt. Ltd.

UNICEF, (1994) : *The Child and the Law,* Indian country office New Delhi.

V.V. Devasia and Leelamma Devasia (1992) : *Criminology, Victimlogy and Corrections,* Ashok publishing house, New Delhi.

Vailland Cybulska, H (1975). : *The Legal Welfare of Children in a Disturbed Family Situation.* International child welfare review, volumn-27.

W.S.K. Phillips (1994) : *Street Children in India,* Rawat Publication, Jaipur-302004, India

William Feige Lman and Arnold Silverman : *Chosen Children, New* R. *Patterns of Adoptive Relationships.* PRAEGER, Publication

Index

E

J

N

W

Y